TOUCHED OUT

TOUCHED OUT

Motherhood,
Misogyny, Consent,
and Control

AMANDA MONTEI

BEACON PRESS, BOSTON

BEACON PRESS
Boston, Massachusetts
www.beacon.org

Beacon Press books
are published under the auspices of
the Unitarian Universalist Association of Congregations.

26 25 24 23   8 7 6 5 4 3 2 1

This book is printed on acid-free paper that meets the uncoated paper
ANSI/NISO specifications for permanence as revised in 1992.

Text design and composition by Kim Arney

This book contains information related to health care, psychology, parenting,
and mental health. It should not be used as medical advice. The author and the
publisher disclaim liability for any medical outcomes that may occur as
a result of applying methods discussed in this book.

Parts of this book were first published in different forms
at *Slate*, *HuffPost*, *Vox*, and *The Rumpus*.

"A Baby Is Born out of a White Owl's Forehead—1972," from MYSTERIES OF
SMALL HOUSES: POEMS by Alice Notley, copyright © 1998 by Alice Notley.
Used by permission of Penguin Books, an imprint of Penguin Publishing Group,
a division of Penguin Random House LLC. All rights reserved.

Library of Congress Cataloging-in-Publication Data is available for this title.
ISBN: 978-0-8070-1327-4; e-book: 978-0-8070-1326-7;
audiobook: 978-0-8070-1462-2

For Hannah and Elliott,
who taught me how to care

I want to shriek at
any identity
this culture gives me claw it to
pieces; has nothing to
do with me or
my baby and never will,
has never perceived a
human being.

—ALICE NOTLEY,
"A Baby Is Born from
an Owl's Forehead"

CONTENTS

TOUCHED OUT

AUTHOR'S NOTE

W OMEN RECEIVE AN undue burden when it comes to remember-
ing. This is especially true when they chose to tell stories about
violation and patriarchal control. This is a work of nonfiction. Some
names and identifying details have been changed to protect the identities of characters or to protect the author. Conversations have been
reconstructed from memory and some events have been compressed
for readability. Like all memoir, the personal recollections contained
herein have also been reshaped by time, memory, and the craft of
writing. They are no less true.

BEGINNING

SOMETIMES IMAGINE THERE is one forgotten trauma, one moment in my youth, when I started to unstitch from my center, but the beginning of a body is untraceable, even if, in America, we are always trying to start ours from scratch. For most women, the loss of self to the world of gender is slow, the grieving process denied. We fall apart, are told and sold methods for cobbling ourselves back together, we break again. We wake up one day to find our body is a patchwork, a lumpy foreign object to which we are evidently forever attached. The world has done its work, made us into something called *woman*. We are not always sure we like what we have become.

I suppose I was unsullied as a baby, but that didn't last long. When I was around six months old, my mother began putting me in my crib with a bottle of whole milk each night and shutting the door. "I held your sister for hours," she used to say, "but by the time you came along, I was way too tired for all that." My lonesome nights as a baby taught me something about the needs of children and the needs of mothers, and about working out my yearning alone, but my mother was not neglectful. She was just practical. She worked full-time outside the home, and even before she and my father divorced, the bulk of childcare and all the emotional labor of parenting fell on her. She took space where she could get it.

I had toys that offered early lessons on mothering: baby dolls with yarn for hair that I ferried about, tucked into a play crib with frayed washcloths, patted down. When my babies awoke, I shoved plastic milk bottles into hard, pursed lips. I learned what the world felt my arms and hands were for—woman as mode of conveyance, giver of sleep, and source of nourishment. Before I was in grade school, my mother hired a woman from El Salvador to keep the house clean and to care for me when my mother wasn't around, but after my parents' divorce, we could no longer afford the help. My mother took up an enduring refrain about the uneven division of labor that had characterized her unsuccessful marriage, but I interpreted these complaints as indications of my parents' personal failings, not signs of systemic issues. I didn't yet see their bodies or mine as belonging to the realms of work or gender. I certainly didn't see caring for children as a form of labor with deep power imbalances that were already shaping who I might become.

The way my parents spoke to me about my body as it grew, however, taught me where to locate my currency. My father, whom I split my time with unevenly, greeted me after school with comments about my clothing, my hair, and my changing shape, assessing my body, patting me on the head, and talking over me. I sank into the backseat of his old red Porsche—a relic of a time when my parents had been someone in Hollywood—and as we drove, he told me how the world was. My mother longed out loud to have my youth, my skinny frame, my legs, my tight young butt, but assured me that, as a mother, she knew about the world in ways I could not yet, but would someday, when I had children. If I grew angry or sad, she tamped me down. Over time, I became conscious that my body did not belong only to me. It was a tapestry to be admired or reviled, a tool to be used, a voice to be silenced, a vessel for reproduction, and a product to be primed for consumption.

Because I am now a mother, I am hesitant to place blame on my parents, who grew up in Los Angeles, for the self-consciousness and insecurity they passed down to me—a culture of appearances that over time morphed inside me from pride to self-hatred. In America, we so often blame those who raise us, especially mothers, for anything that hurts, and for whoever we become. But there are so many participants in the making of a body. Sociologist Nancy Chodorow argues in *The Reproduction of Mothering* that the "role-training" argument—which supposes that mothers, who are "pivotal actors in the sphere of social reproduction," train their children for the sexual division of labor by modeling gender roles and gender inequality—is limited. Economic and social institutions, their organization, the ideologies that legitimate them, in addition to socialization by schools, media, and families, rely on and reinforce the link between caring and women, such that "social reproduction comes to be independent of individual intention and is not caused by it." In turn, Chodorow writes, "Women's maternal role has profound effects on women's lives, on ideology about women, on the reproduction of masculinity and sexual inequality, and on the reproduction of particular forms of labor power."

On those of us marked *girl*, in other words, it is not just toy dolls or our parents that insist on our inevitable maternity. Every aspect of the world—from the culture we consume to our first sexual experiences— tells us how to be *woman*, largely indistinguishable from *mother*. As Melissa Febos writes in *Girlhood*, "Patriarchal coercion is a ghost," an immeasurable figure that looms, hovers, hardly seen, correcting, policing, molding. The afterimages of our gendered socialization haunt the body, telling us how to be, what to say, who to become. Meanwhile, we accumulate more debris everywhere we go, collecting, remapping, fitting bodies and minds into the world as we find it. We become possessed by what Febos calls that "specter" who "squeezes a yes out of my mouth when my body tells me to say no." We are compelled toward surrender, as the whole world rambles on, telling us who and what our bodies are for.

———

When the pandemic began in 2020, throwing into relief the troubling state of parenthood in America, I was a mother of two children under five. In my late twenties, after years of saying yes to men more times than I wanted, and years of waking up wondering whether I had consented to sex, I had found love, got married. However foolishly, I pictured relief from the confusion of girlhood—a time of botched development that made me heavy with longing and uncertainty, and that seemed to stretch interminably across my young adult life. I was enough of a feminist to raise an eyebrow at the idea that marrying and having children would make me whole. But if being a feminist meant just doing whatever I wanted and not feeling bad about it, or regretting it, or wondering whether I should have made a different choice, I was not that.

I had consumed plenty of narratives growing up that told the same story—the one that frames motherhood as the pinnacle of femininity. If asked to endorse this myth before I had my first child, I never would have done so. But I still felt it to be true. A year after I gave birth, however, I was overcome with guilt. I had wanted motherhood intensely, and now that I had it, I wanted to flee, to be alone, to check that my flesh and my capacity to think were still there. Eventually, I clawed my way back into the workforce and regained some sense of self outside my role as a mother. But when schools and daycares closed in March of 2020 in response to the pandemic, there I was again, stuck at home, my children scaling my chest and back, no escape in sight. While many in lockdown longed to hold and hug loved ones, my resistance to my kids' constant daily touch worsened. By then I saw the structural conditions—the lack of paid leave, the childcare crisis, mothers as America's only social safety net—that were depriving me of my autonomy, but without any outlet for rebellion, my body rejected intimacy with my children and husband almost involuntarily, just as it had in early motherhood. I was full of rage, but also desire.

What I wanted, more than anything, was to know and be myself, to feel as though I fully inhabited and *had* my body. But all the ideas about how I should act as a mother—how I should respond to my children's near-constant requests for snacks, their demands for attention, their volatile emotions, their hands down my shirt or smushing my face—felt like insects crawling on me. I found myself frequently rubbing my face, itching my scalp, trying to delouse. Other times I burst into anger, yelling at my children or my husband, demanding space or help, simply because I felt so small, like a little creature myself, shouting in the wide expanse of darkness and nothingness that had become my identity. I was screaming to be heard above the chaos and noise.

I struggled with the physicality of caring for children, but even more with my growing awareness that the lack of autonomy I felt in motherhood reiterated everything I had been urged to believe about my body since I was a girl. In motherhood, I had become haunted by a new ghost, and she was just as coercive as the apparition that haunted me as I came of age. This ghost, however, looked more like Virginia Woolf's "Angel in the House"—the sacrificial mother who sat by the drafty window, shivering as she gave up the last chicken leg because "she never had a mind or a wish of her own, but preferred to sympathize always with the minds and wishes of others." She too pressured me into agreement, urging me to say yes when everything inside me said no. She told me to be agreeable, to do the right things, to submit. And I yielded to the Angel, because that felt familiar, as did the question I found myself posing so often in early motherhood: *Did I really ask for this?*

In 2015, when I became a mother, the term "touched out" was becoming common millennial parlance for the physical overwhelm women felt often in motherhood—the kind that had mothers hiding in bathrooms, pressing hands out around them to create imaginary barriers between body and world, and stomping away from husbands and children. I learned the phrase "touched out" when my first child was an infant, when I was hunting in online motherhood forums for some recognition of the constant disorientation I felt. Two years later I would struggle with overpowering flashes of not wanting to be touched by my children and my husband, and of feeling like I had no escape, just as many around the world were waking up to the omnipresent nature of sexual violence.

The #MeToo movement brought a steady stream of testimony by women who had been harassed, violated, and assaulted. It felt like a watershed moment. But even in that climate, mothers I knew still spoke of feeling "touched out" as though it were par for the course. I began to wonder about the connection between how women were feeling in motherhood and the larger culture of assault in which we had all grown up. My aversion to my children's soft hands felt like an indication of a deep unresolvedness in my body. I wanted to rid myself of everything that had been piled on me—to peel my skin off and scrub it clean. Along with the feeling of not wanting to be touched came memories of being used, violated, and *seen* by men. When my children hit me in frustration, or when they studied me as I dressed or peed, or when they played with my body like a toy—then when I turned away from them, only to see the hungry eyes of my husband or the news of men ascending to positions of power despite having assaulted women—I had the desperate urge to finally say no, though I didn't know how, nor to whom I might say it.

Motherhood was triggering. "A man is always grabbing at my body," author Lyz Lenz wrote in her book about the rights of pregnant women, *Belabored*, quoting a mother of a three-year-old boy with another on the way. Patriarchal power has always been there—it's woven into the fabric of America's national character—but its shape and tenacity felt suddenly clearer in the years after I gave birth, especially after the 2016 election. The news was increasingly filled with male lawmakers attacking, with renewed vehemence, women's reproductive rights. At the time of writing, this feeling of being pursued remains. Male power feels like it's closing in around us, as new laws and legal battles worm their way into our bodies and reproductive lives. *Roe v. Wade* has been overturned. American conservatives are pursuing a national ban on abortion. They are coming next for our birth control, even though pregnancy has been effectively criminalized, with most abortions completely banned in at least thirteen states. "News story after news story breaks with news about a new law passed about birth control, about healthcare, about abortion," Lenz wrote in 2020. "It's an assault, a power grab."The rapid pace of breaking stories continues.

The news of institutionalized patriarchy rebooting itself for a new era of reproductive control is enough to upset the delicate spaces we share with children. But the basic tenets of rape culture also run through our cultural expectations of mothers, something I began to see more clearly just after #MeToo. Middle-class, bourgeois standards of parenting have created exponential anxieties for mothers. Today, women who become parents are expected to study and perform ideal motherhood at the cost of all else by consuming online parenting content to meet their children's needs with monkish detachment, and though they are often encouraged to take baths or hide in the shower if they need a break, the message is well received that women should expect to sacrifice their autonomy for motherhood, in addition to their physical and emotional well-being. The expectations of American parenthood are an assault all their own.

And yet, just as we normalize sexual violence against women, we also normalize the impossible standards of American parenting. The image of the haggard mom woefully failing to do it all has become so commonplace in American culture that her beaten-down body and psyche hardly even register as a matter of serious concern. While there is, no doubt, a certain degree of filth and fury inherent to the work of care, in a capitalist economy in which parenting is done in isolated nuclear family units and which still has no national parental leave policy and no state-supported system of early childhood care, the purportedly inbuilt suffering of motherhood has become a kind of existential truism.

We don't only normalize these expectations; we naturalize them as well. We have a wealth of scientific data proving that caregiving is not a biological predisposition accessible only to women and that the idea of maternal instinct is a myth created by men. But little has changed in the pressures we place on women to perform that deterministic ideal. The concept of women's natural predisposition to parenthood remains especially central to conservative rhetoric. Chelsea Conaboy writes in her 2022 essay on maternal instinct: "Belief in maternal instinct may also play a role in driving opposition to birth control and abortion, for why should women limit the number of children they have if it is in their very nature to find joy in motherhood?" These beliefs are regularly invoked in less evidently sinister but more widespread discourses as well, such as in "science writing, parenting advice and common conversation." Women's struggles with meeting such expectations are generally understood as either an individual wellness problem or a natural defect (or cause for pharmaceutical treatment), rather than as the result of the intentional, systemic exploitation of women's unpaid labor in the home.

The unreasonable expectations placed on mothers affect women without children, too. Silvia Federici, a feminist philosopher, historian, and leader in the International Wages for Housework campaign started in the 1970s, wrote that the unpaid nature of mothering and housework makes housewives of all women because "no matter where we are they can always count on more work from us." Women are expected to mother everywhere they go, to please and nurture and manage everyone's emotions free of charge, because housework has not only "been imposed on women but also transformed into a natural attribute of our female physique and personality, an internal need, an aspiration, supposedly coming from the depth of our female character." However mythological the story of women's biological instinct to care may be, as long as care work and housework remain unpaid and unrecognized as work, feminine servility remains naturalized, while cultural narratives of the hustling mother trying to do it all further normalize women's misery and lack of autonomy. And there is no way to disentangle the exploitation of women in the home from assumptions about what women owe men in the streets, in the workplace, and in bed, nor from how much women are expected to give up in meeting such demands.

Anti-abortion legislation that forces people into parenthood epitomizes this idea that anyone with a uterus should hand their bodies and lives over for motherhood, no matter the cost. In her 2019 book *Birth Strike*, organizer Jenny Brown opens with a powerful thesis: that "the effort to block birth control and abortion in the United States is neither fundamentally about religion nor about politicians pandering to a right-wing base." Rather these attacks, according to Brown, are about "the labor of bearing and rearing children: who will do it and who will pay for it." State governmental efforts to block gender-affirming health care for transgender youth, such as those seen in Florida, Missouri, and Texas, are also attempts to fix hierarchal social relations that rely on the gender binary. Bills like these strong-arm bodies into the heteronormative family, an economic institution in which women are meant to provide sexual, emotional, and reproductive labor to bolster men and male power.

These may seem like extreme political actions and attitudes. But even our most mundane cultural expectations of mothers emerge from this framework. It is assumed that women will give up their bodies, minds, and lives for the family—for marriage and motherhood—and that it is natural and normal to do so. What is asked of mothers is therefore inseparable from the wider culture of misogyny: these standards help regulate women's speech and behavior. And girlhood primes women for this systematic disempowerment and disembodiment, the kind they find should they become mothers (as they are expected to do). As philosopher Kate Manne has pointed out in her thorough study of the concept, misogyny is not simply the hatred of women or even sexist attitudes toward them; rather, it functions like a shock collar, keeping women in line when they break away from patriarchal order or don't give men what they think they are entitled to. Often this coercive form of control looks simply like the imperative to be "good," and for women, good means giving. "She will tend to be in trouble when she does not give enough," Manne writes, "or to the right people, in the right way, or in the right spirit." American motherhood, zenith of selfless yielding, built upon the shifty foundation of the "good mother," asks endlessly for submission.

In the years after I had my first child, as the wounds my body had suffered at the hands of boys and men reopened, I replayed memories of my early sexual life, saw them anew. But I also acquired new abrasions from the institution of American motherhood: fresh ideas about what I lacked and new reasons for self-denial, shame, and self-effacement, along with real financial and social losses. I found myself patrolling my own speech, the way I held my body, everything I felt. And in that period of resurrection and further violation, I came to see that a body is defined by its history, but also its ongoing capacity for movement, identification, community, and connection. I saw that a mother's body is slowly made over time, groomed from birth by the ideologies of womanhood that descend on us the moment we are born, piled on us all our lives, and calcified by the beliefs we inherit about what it means to be a mother in America. Fuck that.

#MeToo eventually morphed into a reactionary debate about cancel culture and a backlash that has doubled down on attempts to silence women who do come forward about abuse. But after testimonies of harassment, rape, and assault first flooded the public square, many young women understood that a broader shift in their lives was necessary. They saw the collars around their necks and wanted to unyoke themselves. Between 2017 and 2018, the birth rate declined sharply, though it had begun its descent a decade earlier. Journalists declared a "sex drought," with many attributing plunging desires to the internet and shifting career priorities. These often lackluster interpretations of a clear refusal to participate in an economy that promises everything and gives nothing—especially to women—defused the changing landscape of desire and consent in America, as well what certainly looked like a cultural awakening around reproduction. "Women in the United States are staging a production slowdown, a baby boycott, in response to bad conditions," Jenny Brown writes. The rebellion may not have been organized, but that didn't make it any less purposeful.

This book roots out how those of us who ended up on the other side of that baby boycott—specifically millennial mothers—found ourselves at sea in the brand of parenthood into which we stumbled, and what this confusion has to do with what we demand of women in America throughout their lives. Many parents have begun reevaluating their roles in the American family after feeling abandoned by policymakers during the pandemic, but the stories we tell about parenting and women's bodies that led to that shameless abandonment remain. This book considers long-held beliefs about women's bodies—about who and what they are for—but also the ways such beliefs shifted for women of my generation, and how they might shift further on the heels of a national parenting crisis. Millennial mothers' lives have been punctuated by national reckonings regarding sex, race, and care. Their lives have also been influenced by distinctive changes in work and the economy. They are clamoring for change.

I explore in parts of this book the personal torment created by bad policy and an exploitative economic system that relies on unpaid, underpaid, and unrecognized care work—issues that became more salient during the pandemic but that are foundational to American capitalism. But our bodies are also assailed and compelled by the social attitudes around and within us. The education we receive ural climate in which we are raised is stored in our g our relationships. The effects of gender and power on erefore, don't only come from policy or from extreme ult and control. They come from confusing, violating, unwanted sex; from loose attachments to popular culture; from concepts of love and family. They pass between us through touch, language, and screens, shaping ideas of care and intimacy—activities that should create pleasure and belonging but, for many, end up feeling like more violation.

This book is a personal history of a rather ordinary pain under patriarchy—of a woman looking for love, belonging, and fulfillment right where I was told I would find it and losing myself in the process. While my experiences are common, in writing this book I have come to see that like many women I had been conditioned to view the pain in my life as something I deserved, had coming, or for which I was destined. As a mother I have had similar thoughts: perhaps the problem was me, the way I saw or did things, my unrealistic desire for a sense of ownership over my body. But no one deserves to feel alienated from themselves, their own desire, their sense of pleasure. To think otherwise upholds not only the culture of assault in which we are still swimming but also the routine exploitation of women when they enter the institution of motherhood.

Motherhood and the culture of rape and misogyny in America are not often explored in tandem, but there is a rich feminist discourse on which I draw in this book. While I was writing it, a colleague told me they felt the subjects of assault and motherhood were like "apples and oranges"—disparate, unrelated. "What's the connection?" they said. To which I replied, "Our bodies." That response was one I was able to muster only because of the feminist and queer thinkers who have come before me, articulating how gender, politics, and economics shape our understanding of sexuality and family life, as well as our lived experiences of the body, the self, and this thing we call motherhood. Those thinkers have buoyed, held, and educated me, and I hope my analysis can provide a path toward thinking even further about these issues, which are pressing and expansive in an era of increasing reproductive control.

I do not assume, however, that mine is Everywoman's or Everyperson's story, even if the kinds of violation I have experienced, I know from speaking to many women, are widespread. This book does not presume to present a complete picture of the experiences of mothers and caregivers of all genders in America. My own story has been marked by immense privilege—by whiteness and educational opportunity, by a financial status that, though precarious, would for many feel like wealth. My generational identification as a millennial and my whiteness in some ways led me to believe I could do things differently than the women who came before me. I thought I could do motherhood right or better or more feminist somehow. It's laughable to me now, almost a decade into parenthood, even as I believe that many parents of a certain age are breaking patterns that no longer serve us. But the idea that we can each tape up the culture of misogyny on our own, alone at home, by being good—that if we parent better or harder, our children won't face the struggles we have—is another myth mothers are continually sold. Fix the home, fix how you do things, fix yourselves, ladies, and you'll get free, we are told.

We cannot do this work alone. With that in mind, in this book I have tried to disentangle gender from care work as much as possible. I do not believe the labor of raising children should fall only on women, or even only on parents. I also refuse the flat delimitation of the gender binary, which damages everyone's ability to liberate themselves from patriarchal control. I believe, however, that it is important to acknowledge how stories about American families lean on conceptions of "man" and "woman," consistently re-inscribing women as "natural," primary caregivers in America. At times in this book I refer to mothers, women, and motherhood when discussing individuals' self-identifications or when referencing parenting ideologies or studies that rely on binary, cisgender categorizations of bodies and people. When I speak of motherhood, I am referencing a set of social, emotional, and political scripts that act on our bodies, as distinct from care or the process of mothering, an embodied process of attuning oneself to others' needs and vulnerabilities.

The varied experiences of transgender, nonbinary, and queer parents is not my story to tell, nor can I speak personally to how "misogynoir" uniquely shapes the experience of Black motherhood. As many as six in ten Black women report having been subjected to coercive sexual contact by the age of sixteen. Transgender people are over four times as likely as cisgender people to experience violent victimization, including rape, sexual assault, and aggravated or simple assault. I hope this book will provide an opening for more discussion of how our language can better support the promise of centering care outside the white, heteronormative family and how sexual violence and misogyny intersect with other systems of racial and gender oppression.

Since the pandemic began, mothers and other caregivers have been sounding the alarm on the broken American care economy and the need for more collective approaches to care work. We have become more comfortable criticizing patriarchal capitalism and its reliance on the free and underpaid labor of women, especially women of color, who make up nearly half of the 1.5 million underpaid childcare workers in the United States. While I was writing this book, the response to the caregiving crisis in America alternated between primal screams, cries for help, organized demands for change, strained optimism, and the apathy and cynicism that has become characteristic of my generation, left behind as we have been by so many failed institutions and political actors. Between February 2020 and January 2021 women were pushed out of the workforce in droves, a loss of 5.4 million jobs. Claims that motherhood in America is profoundly flawed and that leaders had betrayed us became more routine. But the question of how to respond to a culture that had turned its back on us—beyond advocating for commonsense policy changes that have not yet come—remained open.

My own feelings about how to respond to the problems high-lighted by the pandemic—especially the lack of autonomy I have felt in motherhood—similarly alternated between rage, action, and ennui. I wanted this book to be angry, hopeful, depressing, cynical, mad, rousing. More than anything, though it's hard and painful, I wanted us not to look away. But I also wanted to communicate the profound creativity and possibility one experiences when caring for others. Despite how powerless I have felt as a mother, I have also found power in the intimate exchanges of care work. Black feminists like bell hooks and Audre Lorde, who in their writing affirm the humanity and sensuality of motherhood, and more recent writing by authors like Dani McClain, Mia Birdsong, and Angela Garbes, remind us that "to mother" is a verb accessible to all—and mothering, a communal political practice and a public good. This is something women of color, who have always worked and always cared for others, have known for a very long time.

In the early years of motherhood I worked at a daycare, and I witnessed on my shifts the skill and imagination inherent to care work. I also observed the patience of those who—it must be said—did it so much better than I did, many of whom continue to help raise my children and give me space to work and rest. As my children have returned to school and daycare in the wake of the pandemic, I have glimpsed, thanks to my network of care, what I longed for in lockdown: space to think, to write, to breathe, to sit in my body without interruption. Space to feel the way I never quite felt as a girl—like my body is my own. This is only possible because of the communal care systems I am privileged enough to access—systems that disproportionately exploit the labor of women of color.

As a woman in America, however, my access to physical and mental health, and to bodily autonomy, also remains—to some degree, as I have always known it—conditional and tenuous. Since the pandemic, I have become financially reliant on my husband, despite having more education than he has. When the children fall ill, because I am the parent with part-time, contingent work, I am the one who sets aside my day's plans. Because I live in California, should I find myself pregnant, I will likely have access to abortion services. But I worry every day about how my children's lives may be forever altered by sexual violence, by gun violence, by reproductive control, by anti-queer policies, by the divestment of public education and healthcare, by economic inequality, by climate disasters, and by the systems of racial and gender supremacy that separate us all. My family lives a life of relative comfort, and still it feels as though the threat of harm is all around us.

There is a popular version of the motherhood essay about choice— about the agonizing women often do over the decision whether to have a child or not. This essay is popular for the same reason it frustrates me: we want to believe that to become a parent is an individual choice, something we can enter or reject willingly. But the relationship one forms with a child, perhaps like all forms of love, is something we must choose repeatedly, and no one should be excused from the table of care. As Koa Beck writes in *White Feminism*, the parenting-choice essay makes it seem as though parenting is simply a singular personal decision, rather than a form of labor. "If motherhood is a 'choice,'" Beck writes, "then you don't necessarily frame it as work." From this view, parenthood is a question of one's unique "resources and circumstances, rendering structures either invisible or irrelevant." Ghostly, even.

Maybe I should have known better than to have a child in America, given what I learned young about being a woman in America. But I didn't ask for this. How could I, when it's all been hidden away? I didn't ask to raise my children in an era in which so many policymakers are determined to force people into this thing we call motherhood. I didn't ask for high childcare costs, failing care and education systems, or for the fear I feel as my children enter the world of binary gender roles at the potential cost to their own happiness and liberation. I didn't ask to raise children amid a climate crisis that keeps my family hiding indoors from wildfires that burn in my home state of California for months at a time. I didn't ask for so many aspects of my life—and the lives of people in my community—to be controlled by those who, it seems, do not care. I did not ask for the kind of motherhood I was handed. None of us did. And I certainly never asked for parenting in America to feel so nonconsensual.

I sometimes think about the periods of early motherhood that I spent pushing away my children. I wonder whether they will fault themselves or me. Maybe my children will see my struggles as a sign of the times. I have certainly encouraged this interpretation of events, trying to explain to them, exhaustively, that women can do more than mother, that their bodies are their own, that my body is my own, that every person needs time to themselves, that I am a person, that all parents are people, that it's complicated, that history lives in us, that history is happening right now, that it's hard, that it's hopeful, and that their world, when they are older, can be different. I am hesitant to place the burden of a better future in the hands of young people, who will inherit so many systemic failures, but the tender moments I share with my children are, for better or for worse, what keep me going when the world feels, as the poet Alice Notley put it in her essay "Women and Poetry," "late and ugly." In parenting, as in writing, we must do as Notley suggests: "we pretend anyway that we are the first ones, we open our mouths for the first time (there never was such a time), we speak with the first voice ever (there never was such a voice)—what do we say?"

At night I lie next to my second child, now four, to help him fall asleep. He looks into my eyes, kisses me squarely on the mouth, and talks about my skin, how it feels on his. "You're so warm, you're so soft, Mommy," he says, nuzzling in, sliding his palms up and down my arms, explaining his love as touch, as texture. He has no trouble naming the comfort he receives from my body, but he also knows to ask, to seek out my gaze, my agreement, before taking what he needs.

Sometimes I do still push him away—a misplaced effort to push away everything late and ugly, or a simple human request for the space all bodies need to recoup, recalibrate. Other times, I give in because I want to. As his eyes flutter into sleep, he asks if he can place a finger in the warm nook of my bellybutton. I wrap my arms around him, take in his whole body, check to see that he is comfortable and still enjoying the embrace. I let him tuck his finger there, pointing to where he came from, reminded that love is something we can only experience when we have consented completely.

PAIN

M Y WATERS BROKE a week after my due date—a cinematic beginning to motherhood, or so I thought. It would be another day until
I experienced with any regularity the deep knotting and tearing that
spread down my legs and wrapped around my back, like some violent,
unwelcome hug. The audible pop of my amniotic sac in the middle of
the night as I hovered over the toilet alone in the dark, I would soon
find, was no more the beginning of my tale of motherhood than it
was the beginning of labor. The breaking of my waters only brought
on sensations that felt like period cramps, sore and throbbing; yet I
had grown up with the image of women beleaguered by the sudden
onset of labor, their bodies made abject in film and TV, fluid splashing
about as they raced to the hospital. I had read enough about childbirth by then to know that labor rarely comes on that fast, but I still
expected the filmic experience.

Though birth stories usually begin with the onset of labor, mine
began long before, with the images of women I consumed as a girl.
Those women lived in me. I lay in bed all night waiting for my
contractions to deepen, thrown by the slowness of labor, my husband
snoring beside me. As a kid, I had watched Kirstie Alley's character,
Mollie, in *Look Who's Talking*, give birth after a typically unrealistic
sequence of a pregnant lady rushing to the hospital the moment that
she feels a contraction. Mollie's waters break in the backseat of a

cab driven by John Travolta's character, James. He plays the paternal role, even though he's a stranger, driving recklessly through Midtown traffic, offering to hold Mollie's hand, and encouraging her to do Lamaze breathing and avoid pain medication "because it's better for the kid." The need to contain the bedlam of childbirth is part of what brings Mollie and James together, unlike the women in other 1990s films such as Joan Cusack in *Nine Months*, who curses out her husband for impregnating her, making light of her own unwilling entrance into motherhood.

Mollie was also not the monstrous mother of other films before my time, like the *Alien* franchise, which turned childbirth into horror, but Mollie's labor pains did drive her mad. At the hospital, in agony, Mollie demands "drugs" while a nonchalant, magazine-reading nurse and James—who has followed Mollie into the birthing room, helped by hospital staff who push scrubs on him despite his insistence that he's "not the father"—urge Mollie to breathe. In a voice like that of *The Exorcist*'s Regan, Mollie growls, "Fuck my breathing." She feels like she's going "to split in two," but the nurse can't do anything without the doctor's consent, so James runs to find a doctor to quell Mollie's pain. After admitting she "dropped out of Lamaze," Mollie promises to take summer school classes if the doctor will make the pain stop, a girl begging for forgiveness. The doctor administers Demerol, and an interior shot of Mollie's womb shows Mollie's baby, Mikey, who has been personified as a full-term infant throughout the pregnancy, tripping out. As the "drugs" take effect, psychedelic music plays over the scene.

I gave birth just before I turned thirty, in 2015. Since I knew my knowledge of childbirth had been warped by narratives like these, when I found out I was pregnant I resolved to make sense of my body the way I had always worked as a writer and young academic studying literature: by engaging in deep research. My husband, Jon, and I had married two years before I conceived, moving from California to Buffalo, New York, so I could pursue a doctoral degree in literature, so I came first to childbirth with an academic's eye. I wanted to understand exactly how women's bodies had been so culturally and politically misinterpreted, so I could analyze and rewrite the birthing body accurately, releasing myself from the misleading stories I had been told. The wild agony of labor, as I saw it, was a masculine myth inscribed on women's bodies, a hangover of the belief that Eve had been marked by pain for pursuing her own pleasure, but also by other beliefs about the inability of women to endure childbirth without men intervening. I wanted to tell a new story, one that didn't see women's bodies as fearsome, cursed, or broken.

Composing that new story proved challenging. Western medicine—governed by masculine reason and a long history of pathologizing women in clinical settings and clinical literature—felt like my primary enemy. But my university insurance required that I participate in the system. I had gone to the gynecologist the year before I conceived, hoping to come home with some program for making myself more fertile. The appointment was at a local Buffalo hospital that had a high maternal mortality rate and served mostly residents who were low-income and of color. After we entered the exam room my gynecologist, explaining to me that I was in a teaching hospital, invited another man in a white coat into the room without asking me first. The lead doctor ushered my feet into stirrups, tapped my legs open, told me to relax. The cold air stung, but before long he had inserted the speculum. He spoke swiftly to the other man about what he was doing, both of their eyes peering into me as they scraped the uterine wall for my Pap test. After removing the speculum, the lead doctor unceremoniously thrust two gloved fingers deep inside me, pressing down on my abdomen with his other hand. The other man took his turn, then each of them took their gloves off and poked my breasts while I studied pockmarks in the ceiling. At the end of the appointment, I asked about fertility, but the men waved me off after a brief talk about diet and exercise.

When they left the room, I grumbled to myself alone, wiping lubricant from between my legs with the paper dressing gown that had barely covered me, then dressing myself, still sore. I put the whole interaction out of my mind. The incident unnerved me, but I had been having exams like these for years and was used to feeling uncertain about what had happened to me. When I visited Planned Parenthood with girlfriends as a teenager in Los Angeles, we braved our intakes alone, hearts racing when asked about sex and disease. We answered the questions in a manner that modeled purity and responsibility. Then we shut our eyes tight during the exam, willing ourselves to open our nervous, knocked knees. We each left the clinic with a brown paper bag filled with a six-month supply of birth control, a set of morning-after pills, and a ream of condoms, stuffing the bags deep into the bottom of our low-hanging JanSports, which patted our backs on the long walk back to my working mother's empty apartment, as though in approval of what we had done.

I owe my ability to choose when I wanted to have children to Planned Parenthood, which provided me with free birth control until the Affordable Care Act was passed the year I met Jon. But over the years, in every setting, my gynecological exams followed a routine that felt as though it was not designed for me. When I was a teenager, as I walked home from visits to Planned Parenthood with friends, our vaginas still weeping slippery lubricant, my friends and I joked uneasily about the clinicians who had pushed their long fingers inside of us at the end of the exam. "He was *totally* fingering me," we said, unsure whether we had felt violated or aroused. We didn't really know the difference.

The pelvic exams bothered me not only for how they mimicked boys' favorite early sex acts, but also because pain and unease characterized my early sexual life. When I lost my virginity at fifteen, I mounted my kind, skinny, Christian boyfriend on his twin bed during a parent-free party, after drinking Boone's Farm wine cooler right out of the bottle. I pulled his thin bedspread over my back to cover up my body. When he entered me after clumsily slipping on a condom, I felt shooting pain. We switched to missionary, and though this hurt a bit less, there was nothing pleasant about the experience. The boyfriend went wild, and I pretended I enjoyed it; then he came. That was it. Eventually I enjoyed sex with him, but still I associated sex with knifelike penetration, something that bordered on punishment. I didn't have my first orgasm for years.

After I married, I began to feel shaken up by the way men had made further use of me later, in my twenties, before I met Jon. I began rethinking nights spent with men who had fucked me when I was passed out or semiconscious—I wouldn't have called it rape then, because it wouldn't have occurred to me that I had been incapable of consent. But I was starting to see my twenties as a string of equivocal sexual violations, mixed with clearer harms: lingering impressions of being reduced to what was between my thighs, or what my mouth could do for men, their blissed-out faces, ignorant of my own, hanging above me slack-jawed, racing toward climax. Rough physicality also hung over my sexual life—the hormonal rapture of *scamming* had turned to talk of *banging* and *nailing*. Years later, I thought of how often my body, when I had been conscious, had gone limp and taken it. I hoped that in childbirth there might be some way to restore my agency—or pleasure. In the months before I conceived, at night I had cuddled my womb alone in the bath, kneading the soft surface below my navel. I fell asleep in bed that way, my back to my husband, rubbing my belly, pushing out alcohol I had downed as fast as possible at late-night academic parties that had been all talk. I was conjuring something, but I had no idea what.

My anxiety had by then become unwieldy, cratering out space under my lungs when I woke up each morning, hitching my breath. Jon and I were drinking a lot before I made that appointment at the gynecologist to ask about my fertility, and the competitive nature and workload of my doctoral program had left me neglecting sleep and other basic needs. As I drove in whiteout conditions to campus each day to teach, lake-effect snow sheeting down while I slid across traffic lanes, salt caking on the window of our snowball-colored hatchback, I often had to clutch the steering wheel to find the tempo of my breath and keep my eyes open and on the road—to maintain control. While teaching I felt like a levitating set of vocal cords, peering out on a world I didn't understand. I sometimes had to grab my legs or a table, touch something hard, just to remind myself I was there in the room.

My frequent dissociation from my body seemed to indicate a dark history that belonged to me, but my past was just a scanty outline—a set of shameful circumstances and blackouts I did not yet have the language to explain. Later, I would learn to identify the texture of traumatic memory: patchy, disjointed, warped. But back then, though I felt disillusioned with sex and with so much violence against women in the news—campus sexual assault was making headlines regularly—I was profoundly embarrassed about my sexual life. I wanted a child in a carnal way, but I also believed that motherhood could replace the insecurity girlhood had made part of my personality. Motherhood, I hoped, might help me push away my confusion about what kind of woman I was. Perhaps I could even forge a new relationship with my disordered body by tapping into the vague power mothers seemed to wield over their children.

But as Jon and I became more intentional about conception, under the warmth of our wedding-gift comforter, I felt for the first time in my life the real oddness of sex between man and woman. Penetration increasingly felt more than vulnerable—it felt like a breach of what was supposed to be mine. Our mutual desire to have a baby, however, made coming together feel collaborative and fun at times, and Jon was kind and gentle as a rule. He *took care*, that was who he was. In high school, his mother had shattered several discs in her back when she slipped on a wet floor at her job in a nursing home. He had not only worried that he had caused the accident by stepping on cracks in the sidewalk on the way home from school but had also spent the rest of his youth learning to care for an increasingly immobile mother, debilitated by her own pain and eventually addicted to Oxycontin. He often asked if he was hurting me when we had sex, especially once we found out I was pregnant. But sometimes he also stopped himself to extend his own pleasure, halting our rhythm without asking me what I wanted, forcing me to wait while he thought about whatever men think about to stop themselves from coming. I grew irritated and refused, not wanting to be held hostage. I told him to fuck me harder and faster until it hurt.

The precipice of motherhood invited me to reevaluate my sexual life, which more than shared a border with my reproductive life, but I was also reading psychoanalytic literature at the time, in which I found an entire history of philosophers associating sex with pain. Though male colleagues in my doctoral program rolled their eyes at my insistent critiques, I was increasingly curious about the foundational knowledge on which so many assumptions about women, sex, and violence rested. Feminist author and activist Susan Brownmiller wrote in her influential book *Against Our Will*, in which she argued that rape was about power rather than sex, that "it wasn't until the advent of Sigmund Freud and his followers that the male ideology of rape began to rely on the tenet that rape was something women desired." Freudian Helene Deutsch claimed that women were masochistic by nature and that sexually mature women "put up with a bit of pain in intercourse and even taught themselves to find a bit of pleasure in it." Pointing to the pain of childbirth as evidence of women's predestination for sexual violation, Deutsch's midcentury psychoanalytic writing represented women as ordained to "a holy mission fraught with pain from beginning to end, but most particularly at the moments of labor and birth." Deutsch also argued that sex was "an essentially painful experience for an essentially passive woman."

Deutsch's writing filtered into many mainstream American publications. Brownmiller writes that Deutsch's ideas became so widespread in America that they "caused real—and incalculable—damage to the female sex, as has, it goes without saying, Freud," because they each "mistook what sometimes is for what must be." Like many Freudians, Deutsch saw women's experiences of their bodies as incontrovertible, rather than as twisted up in cultural, economic, and political ideology. She failed to consider that women's experiences of childbirth weren't inborn, but rather tended to serve a misogynist agenda—one that relied on the assumption that women's pain and suffering were to be expected, not resisted.

I didn't want anything to do with all the sexist symbolism that hovered around childbirth. I wanted my very own experience. Escaping pain, it seemed to me, was one way to forge my own path. Leslie Jamison writes in her essay "Grand Unified Theory of Female Pain" that when we talk about women in pain, we quickly "risk transforming their suffering from an aspect of the female experience into an element of the female constitution." I rejected the idea of any sort of feminine constitution, especially one that naturalized the agony of women, but I was having trouble finding a belief system about childbirth to fill the absence. Since my mother had never shared any useful wisdom with me about childbirth—she somehow remembered her two labors as blissful, even though she had a full body rash at the time I was born—I joined a natural birthing group in Buffalo, which I saw as a soft place to land. In my birthing class, held in the small backroom of a maternity clothing store, we were taught to deal with the pain of childbirth by considering its functionality. "Tell yourself," my white-haired birthing teacher said as the mothers and fathers looked on from their hard plastic chairs, "soon I will meet my baby." In the class handouts and exercises, pain was positioned as a sign of progress—a means to an end—and it had an explicit purpose: it turned women into mothers.

I liked the birthing teacher and the videos of tranquil labors and deliveries that she showed in class, even if watching them in the dark on the big projection screen, hearing muffled sounds of other women in the store sorting through clothing racks, felt like I was in some maternal indoctrination program. I also liked the books the teacher suggested, like those by American midwife Ina May Gaskin, that supposed that women did not have to suffer in childbirth. But some of the theories in these texts quickly fell apart as I read them more closely. In 2015 the popular 1942 book *Childbirth Without Fear* by the UK's Dr. Grantly Dick-Read was having a revival in the American natural birthing community for its claim that women could have ecstatic, pain-free births. The cover of my edition of the book featured a thin, fit woman reaching down for her baby during delivery with an orgasmic expression on her face. She reminded me of the woman in the YouTube video I watched repeatedly at night when I couldn't sleep, who squatted her baby out by a rushing stream without much effort. I wanted to believe I could have that kind of birth, one untouched by history.

I read Dick-Read's book hoping to pin down how in childbirth I could forgo agony for ecstasy, not knowing then that the term "natural childbirth" had been attributed to Dick-Read's early texts, in which he began his career-long claim that women feel pain in childbirth because they feel fear. Dick-Read, a general practitioner, outlined what he called the fear-tension-pain cycle and favored "removing fear through understanding," among other methods. But I was put off by Dick-Read's Fordist metaphors. He referred to "the big muscle of the uterus" as a car that needed "petrol" in the form of breath. And elsewhere he referred to the mother as a "factory" who could be made "more efficient in the art of motherhood." Women, from Dick-Read's perspective, were made to produce, and pain in childbirth was therefore not a natural state.

Drawing on Darwinism and nineteenth-century anthropological literature, Dick-Read also relied on racist and historically inaccurate depictions of what he called "primitive" women who he claimed didn't feel pain the way "cultured" women did. To combat the fear-tension-pain cycle, Dick-Read argued that women had to be initiated into motherhood through emotional discipline. "Woman fails when she ceases to desire the children for which she was primarily made," he wrote. He framed this emotional and reproductive control as a kind of liberation, claiming that a woman's "true emancipation lies in freedom to fulfill her biological purposes."

Even the more colloquial stories I encountered about childbirth when I was pregnant veered wildly into uncomfortable ideologies about women. In my last trimester, Jon's parents threw me a modest baby shower in rural Pennsylvania. The party was attended only by Jon's distant relatives, most of whom I did not know. I had by then locked down my exposure to birth stories that didn't fit what I wanted out of childbirth, even tucking Dick-Read's book away where I couldn't see it. The face of the woman on the cover now haunted me: the closer I looked, the more she seemed to be suffering. But at the baby shower, every woman wanted to tell me their birth story, whether I wanted to hear it or not. I tried to flee, but the women followed me around sharing their thoughts on feeling or not feeling pain in childbirth. Unlike the natural birthers I had met in Buffalo, nearly all the mothers I met at the shower had used pain medication in their labors and mocked my naive desire for an unmedicated birth. Holding plastic cups of champagne I wished I could drink, they spoke about epidurals like a form of revolution, and asked why anyone would *want* to feel childbirth. I timidly tried to interject my theories.

"I'm just trying not to think of it as *pain*." I'd say, flushed, hearing myself.

"Good luck with that," they said, laughing knowingly. When husbands didn't leave the conversation entirely, they joked beside the mothers, offering wide-eyed expressions of disbelief—or maybe fear. "I don't know how women do it," the men said, as children tugged on their mothers' arms and the husbands walked away.

These birth stories left me dejected. I wondered whether the mothers who didn't feel beholden to natural birthing knew something profound about pain—or choice—but I also knew they didn't have the same definition of the word "choice" that I had. Their husbands' predictable gags about women's otherworldly resilience also angered me. It was hard not to notice the "I don't know how she does it" mentality they brought to their wives' stories, and how that mentality played out in their apparent division of parenting labor. And yet, as far as I could tell, these guys didn't seem too different from the awkward, doting husbands who came to natural childbirth class, who also revealed their share of incompetent awe.

Childbirth, I guessed, was a shitty mess; so was parenthood. But mothers somehow handled it—if not with grace, then with grit. Half a decade later, in the middle of the pandemic, a Nike campaign that glorified gestational mothers as "The Toughest Athletes"—"someone who gets it done, no matter what" and "someone who deals with the pain, hits her limit, and pushes past it"—would go viral. Nike had used similar tactics before to deflect from its poor treatment of women athletes who were mothers, and the ad was generally not well received, in light of Nike's exploitative labor practices. But many still rallied behind the imagery in the commercial, as well as the narrative of motherhood championed in the voiceover: "pushing, pushing, pushing." A *Glamour* article called the ad "so empowering."

When I was pregnant I wanted to believe this was true—that there was something fundamentally empowering about gestational motherhood, and childbirth in particular. At the very least, I wanted a narrative on which I could hang my belief that childbirth was not *dis*empowering. What I couldn't fully articulate then was that our reproductive lives don't need to validate the world we live in, or even the world we wish we lived in. And even if, in the end, we cannot help but try to make meaning of pregnancy and childbirth for ourselves, it's impossible to extricate those stories from the narratives we've inherited.

"No one wants to hear a woman talking or writing about pain in a way that suggests that it doesn't end," Jessica Valenti writes in her memoir, *Sex Object*. This holds true for childbirth, frequently valorized as a marathon event that confirms women's natural predisposition to misery and to late-capitalist empowerment discourse. Birth stories are always punctuated with the boundless, instantaneous love supposedly found on the other side of the pain—an effortless bond between mother and baby, the reward for all that hurt. Childbirth, therefore, not only turns women into mothers, but also into mothers who can withstand the infinite trials of modern parenthood. That's what the whole process is good for. The productivity of women's anguish gives the whole winding saga of childbirth its shape. It also gives the assault of the institution of motherhood a biological, deterministic rationale.

My birthing-class teacher often said that everything I experienced in labor and delivery would prepare me for the work of caring for an infant. I saw some truth in this, even before I knew anything about what parenthood really felt like. Raising a child appeared to be nothing if not a state of waiting and distress. But setting childbirth up as an industrious state of torture that women brave to prepare themselves for their equally grueling work as mothers is no less troubling than a theory of women as preordained to pain and production. This perspective on childbirth and the travail of parenthood also noticeably leaves out the diverse bodies, families, and caregiving practices that can be involved in childrearing. Not all parents experience pregnancy and childbirth and this doesn't make them any less qualified for the work of raising their children.

Meaning and metaphor offer those who give birth a way to resolve the confounding story of what they have experienced, but narrative practices always risk confirming and upholding cultural beliefs as they are guided by and swallowed up by history, past and present. Though reproduction is often made symbolic of the times in which we live, as with most aspects of women's health, we know very little about childbirth. One of the most notable mysteries of childbirth is how women's bodies regulate the beginning of labor, a metaphor unto itself. Despite all this mystery, most obstetricians still routinely fish around birthing people's cervixes for information about dilation, even though these "digital" checks are unreliable for predicting labor progress. The medical model, in contrast to the midwifery model, tends to treat pregnancy and childbirth like an illness, and women like passive vessels in need of the assistance of doctors and interventions.

In *Illness as Metaphor*, Susan Sontag argues that the proliferation of metaphor around illness corresponds to a lack of understanding. We grasp for meaning when we cannot find it, attaching this to that, that to this. But Sontag observes that metaphors of the body also help rationalize cultural and political ideologies. This was particularly true when my grandmother gave birth to her four children in the early twentieth century, under the influence of what was then termed "twilight sleep," a practice that literalized the persistent belief that women's voices and bodies not only cannot be trusted, but are largely irrelevant to their capacity to reproduce. Twilight sleep removed women from birth stories altogether, offering women not just a painless childbirth, but a joyously unmemorable one. By the 1920s in America, the cocktail of scopolamine and morphine used to knock women out in childbirth had hardened cultural misgivings around women helping women through childbirth, as well as the distrust of what one North Dakota obstetrician called the "Granny 'Quack' or 'prairie midwife.'" Scopolamine—which would later be used to facilitate sexual assault in several European countries—produced an amnesiac response, causing those who gave birth to forget huge swaths of time during which they lay on obstetric tables as they were prodded, cut, and yanked open by obstetricians.

These birthing bodies spoke, even though they were unconscious. Though most women could not recollect the abuse doctors and nurses inflicted on their bodies while they were in labor, numerous reports of women howling and screaming through their labors while in twilight sleep exist. In a 1958 exposé published in *Ladies' Home Journal*, titled "Cruelty in Maternity Wards," nurses and mothers shared stories that included "women being strapped down for hours in the lithotomy position, a woman having her legs tied together to prevent birth while her obstetrician had dinner, women being struck and threatened with the possibility of giving birth to a dead or brain damaged baby for crying out in pain, and a doctor cutting and suturing episiotomies without anesthetic . . . while having the nurse stifle the woman's cries with a mask."

Despite these alarming accounts of abuse, twilight sleep was popular among women who had absorbed the belief that the pain of childbirth was an obstacle to their freedom. Dread of the physical pains of childbirth, many women claimed, spoiled their lives from youth to adulthood. Childbirth was blamed for all the emotional suffering women experienced—from troubled identifications with femininity in girlhood, to postpartum breakdowns, to widespread dissatisfaction with marriage and motherhood. Women traced their psychological discontent with a world set up to fail them not to patriarchal control but to their own bodies, and they looked to science for an antidote to what was thought to be women's essential condition: pain.

That was the rub. The practice of twilight sleep indicated that women's pain was finally being medically acknowledged and treated, rather than discounted as a figment of hysterical imaginations or a path toward spiritual penance, but the institutional acknowledgment came with a cost: it required women to fault themselves. With hindsight, it is easy to see how often women are led to believe their suffering has a pathological source within, as they are ushered away from considering external causes. But it still hurts—observing the lengths women have gone to to convince themselves that the problem is in them, rather than in the world.

The facade of unconscious birthing also caught fire in America because it disembodied women like workers on a factory line. Suddenly childbirth appeared quick and effortless; in short, modern. In the American novelist Edith Wharton's 1927 novel, *Twilight Sleep*, the schedule-obsessed, upper-class, self-optimizing New Yorker Mrs. Pauline Manford remarks that twilight sleep allowed women to drift "into motherhood as lightly and unperceivingly as if the wax doll which suddenly appeared in the cradle at her bedside had been brought there in one of the big bunches of hot-house roses that she found every morning on her pillow." Like Mrs. Manford's "bright efficient voice which made loveliness and poetry sound like the attributes of an advanced industrialism, and babies something to be turned out in series like Fords," birth now appeared whimsical instead of tragic—and so did capitalism.

In college, long before I became pregnant, I had been drawn to the history of twilight sleep like a gawker to a car wreck, fascinated by the cultural inability of both men and women to see the practice as a form of institutionalized cruelty. But I was also preoccupied by the question of what such a practice had done to a generation of mothers, including my grandmother, who suffered from a lifelong depression that no one in our family ever traced to the abuse she experienced giving birth or to her later discontent as a pill-popping midcentury housewife. Her disembodied entrance into motherhood was another reason I wanted to move through childbirth unmedicated and wide awake.

When I read *The Bell Jar* in college, which Sylvia Plath wrote in 1963, a decade after my grandmother gave birth to my mother and her twin sister under the influence of scopolamine and morphine, I was horrified by the book's descriptions of twilight sleep. The main character, Esther Greenwood, and her boyfriend, Buddy, sneak into a maternity ward and see a woman cursing in pain as she labors unconsciously. "Here was a woman in terrible pain," Esther says later, "obviously feeling every bit of it or she wouldn't groan like that, and she would go straight home and start another baby, because the drug would make her forget how bad the pain had been, when all the time, in some secret part of her, that long, blind, doorless and windowless corridor of pain was waiting to open up and shut her in again." Esther later remarks that the drugs used to induce twilight sleep seemed like "just the sort of drug a man would invent."

I knew the moment I found out I was pregnant that I didn't want any drugs invented by men. I had seen the Ricki Lake documentary

The Business of Being Born. I knew about the cascade of childbirth interventions that were the default in hospitals. While I acknowledged that "choice" was important to the broader story of childbirth in America, I feared that a cesarean would lead me into an irrecoverable postpartum depression—deeper into a hole into which I had barely avoided falling all my young adult life. After the baby shower, I committed myself to a vision of feminine power, of childbirth as immaculate wildness. I wanted to be conscious for each sensation of childbirth, even if I also wanted everyone around me to speak about what I was experiencing in the most palatable way. But I was increasingly having a hard time fixing my mind on any theory of childbirth I could put into practice without shame. Even the natural birthing world—the seeming only alternative to a surgical birth—felt muddled, hopelessly wrapped up in problematic associations between women and nature. The concept of "choice," by the end of pregnancy, felt flimsy and worn.

As Americans do, I bought a solution. In the final weeks of pregnancy, I listened to hypnosis scripts, part of a package I had purchased online. Jon rehearsed with me devotedly, dancing his fingers over my back as an Aussie woman's watery voice lulled us. She spoke to me about my cervix opening, a floral vision that frightened me, but I still replayed her voice each night, wanting so badly an unearthly— but not *Alien*—birth. "Your body opens like a flower," she said. I tried to imagine myself as a slate wiped clean, my pristine baby sliding out of me in peace. It was a vision I could never quite hold in place. Jon fell asleep, and though I elbowed him to keep up with the light-touch massage, he never budged as I lay awake trying to call to mind colored auras for each section of my body, contemplating my body's fuzzy outline in the rainbow mist I created for myself.

In the final months of pregnancy, I coached Jon through how he should coach me in labor, handing him printed pages with lines I asked him to commit to memory. "You're doing an amazing job," he was meant to say. "Remember that your body knows how to give birth, hand control over to your body." I had a hard time tracking who I was in relation to my body and who or what was supposed to be in control in these affirmations, but I expected total commitment from my husband, even if I was on the fence—about everything. I made him promise to study. To memorize his lines. To practice how he would advocate for me if doctors pushed a cesarean. He was not allowed to call my pain *pain*, lest he reify it as actual pain, and I grew frustrated with him when he bungled his lines in rehearsals.

After our last birthing class, Jon and I wandered through the maternity store, where I inspected price tags on pants with elastic waistbands. We left without buying anything after we began arguing, under our breath, about things he had said or done, like when he had the gall to suggest (only to me, and demurely) that we might just call a contraction a contraction, rather than a surge or a wave. Using the right metaphors, the right language, felt critical. On the drive home we argued about how our arguments were damaging the baby.

Maybe it was my training as a writer and an academic that led me to believe I could exert linguistic control over childbirth—that I could narrate my way out of the history of Western medicine and reproduction—but both "natural" and medical approaches to childbirth are inseparable from the storying of women's pain and from women's early role in authoring their own narrative about motherhood. I would later see this complex dance women perform echoed as I first entered America's parenting advice industrial complex: my work was to say the right things, play the right part, but in all the years I would spend trying to lean into this expectation, I would never be able to remember my lines. If there was any way in which childbirth turned me into a mother, it was in this first encounter with failure and resistance.

Nearly two days after my waters broke in the bathroom, Jon drove me to the local hospital in the early morning hours, driving fast and wild, certain we were finally on the verge of pushing. I had planned to give birth at a birth center and charge it on my credit card— to reject the medical model that would see my body as inherently faulty. But the green tinge of my waters told my doctor my baby was bathing in her own first shit. My delivery became high risk. I gripped the dashboard as our little hatchback bounced over every pothole, bringing on contractions. We were routed to the same hospital where that gynecologist and his trainee had dispassionately plunged their fingers and tools inside me. When we arrived, it had been twenty-four hours since the start of labor. I stalled out as soon as they gave me the mandatory IV in triage, having visions of doctors conning me into a C-section. It was not the agony of labor that shut me down, in other words, but the danger of what I saw as a man's hands and ideas getting to me—an impending corruption—even though, for the duration of my labor, the only man present was the one I had brought with me.

Elaine Scarry writes that telling stories about our pain helps us make the experience communal, rather than individual. In *The Body in Pain*, Scarry argues that physical pain—which she identifies as distinct from mental anguish—is a solitary state because it not only resists language, it destroys language. Pain is inescapable now-ness, that feeling of being stuck in the present moment—and in the body—which overwhelms speech and sense. How we come to understand our pain, however, is through imagination. Without the organization of language, of metaphor, and of story, the body in pain would remain adrift, without a sense of self and world. Telling the story of our pain moves us beyond it, toward recognition, and into a shared world. For this reason, Scarry argues, "verbally expressing pain is a necessary prelude to the collective task of diminishing pain."

Women have always told birth stories as a way of entering a community of mothers, but the mapping of political and cultural ideology onto childbirth has meant that such narratives also often coerce women early into certain types of motherhood, and into understanding motherhood as a key to both their own identities and our collective humanity. "Childbirth has nowhere been regarded merely as one possible event in a woman's life," Adrienne Rich wrote in a review of two books on childbirth in 1975. "Whether as a 'peak event' or as a torture rack," Rich wrote, "childbirth has been a charged, discrete happening, mysterious, polluted, often magical; in our current idolatry, a triumph of technology." But what if women's pain is purposeless?

Labor is theatrical, but aimless. Toward the end of mine, I thought only of how foolish I had been, not just in my thinking I could prepare for childbirth but also in my desire to make a child and push it out. Somewhere around the thirty-sixth hour, I remember one birth attendant saying, "I think you just haven't been in enough pain yet. We will have to work harder." Like every woman who supported me in pregnancy and in childbirth, she was gentle, good at her job; she must have been more delicate. But I knew somehow that I had to perform, to produce, or my doctor—who was growing concerned about the length of my labor—would start pressuring me into surgery. It had been nearly two days; the whole thing had gone on too long. On my knees, draped over the incline of the hospital bed, I growled, "Fuck hypnosis." I let them fill my IV with Pitocin, a synthetic hormone that induces contractions, and beating a pillow, I cried. When I stood up, blood hit the floor. Now with regularity, every few minutes a waterfall of pain coursed through my body. The blood, I was told, was a positive sign. The baby's head was making its way through my cervix. I fixated on the crimson below me. "The only way out is through," my birthing-class teacher had said in the weeks leading up to labor. *The only way out is out*, I thought now. I squatted into every contraction. I prayed for blood.

Childbirth was not the first time I had desperately wanted to get something out of my body, but it was certainly the longest process of expulsion I ever endured. Childbirth felt to me less like exercise and more like my twenties, when I was always cleansing, purging, pushing men and substances out and away, trying to reach the other side of some unrest inside. Shit the fatty food *out*. Vomit the alcohol *out*. Hurry up and cum, just get the dick *out*. At the end of the second day of labor, I hid in the small hospital bathroom, where I could be alone with my baby, my only real partner in the work. I had already thrown up, taken little shits on the floor that nurses quietly swept away, been in and out of the bathroom for hours. Alone on the toilet, I negotiated and pleaded. "Come on, baby," I whispered. Her head bucked in response. "Come on, baby," I pleaded. I could not have imagined then that my child would someday be the only thing that had been inside me that I longed to eat back up.

Someone moved me to a birthing stool, a baby's body now tearing through my own, and I saw the magnitude of what I had done to myself—of what pregnancy and childbirth did to women—along with the total failure of language to capture what that was. Of course no one had warned me. How could they? My doctor said it was time to push, and I got to work in old ways, pushing the foreign thing out. When my baby burst forth, I pulled her up on my chest. Everything felt loud and chaotic. I was later told I was calm. This new creature, for whom I was tasked to care, looked up at me as though it knew me, but I was looking at a stranger with dark thoughtful eyes, a full head of jet-black hair. Not at all what I had expected. Jon and I had been towhead blond in our youth. Had there been a mistake? I touched this wet baby, my baby, covered in the evidence of where it had been—inside of me. The nurses rubbed its warm, gooey skin with towels, and again I cried, but those absurd wet sobs were all for me, for what I had endured, and for what I perceived to be the doneness of the event. My baby cried for me, too. We recognized each other. We began.

Childbirth is often framed as a revelation, a triumph of love over agony, and a test, but labor and delivery each require a loss of the self, a loss of the body, and a giving over. I resisted this surrender for two days, while in labor, and before, in pregnancy. I had given my body over all my life, and though I feared pain, complications, surgery, and depression, what I really feared was losing control of my narrative. I didn't know it then, but this snag—between the necessity of yielding to love and the urgency of maintaining my own autonomy—was the real beginning of my story of motherhood.

In a text I studied while pregnant, "Stabat Mater," feminist psychoanalyst and philosopher Julia Kristeva wrote that childbirth is a radical catastrophe of being. But the physical and subjective catastrophe of childbirth, I came to see, unlike the sexist narratives that tend to frame the experience, is at no point a one-sided affair, even if childbirth upsets the body's tenuous boundaries between self and other, person and world. Birthing people are not passive. The body, even when it's unconscious or can't feel, keeps working, remains active. It speaks. It feels. It remembers. Labor is work, not acquiescence, not just pushing through. And childbirth, on the whole, is a total implosion of the body, a collapse of our separateness—a scary prospect in an individualistic culture.

After I pushed my baby out, the doctor tugged on my umbilical cord, told me there was more work to do. I was surprised and irritated to find that the big moment of release, the climax of production, didn't end the spectacle. I wanted to slap my doctor's hand away as she tugged, asked me to do more work, brought on more contractions. I would later learn she was worried. There was too much blood leaking from my body. But somehow, without my ever knowing, my uterus fixed itself.

With my new baby in my arms, life was fuzzier than before, further out. Once the placenta was delivered, I felt high like I had as a teen, dancing in clubs after eating colorful round pills stamped with cartoon characters. As I had been then, however, in my postbirth ecstasy I was foolish about caring for my body. I stood up on my own to pee, only to find nurses rushing at me: "Jesus, let me help you." Blood everywhere. Later, I ripped off my blood pressure cuff because it was getting in the way as I tried to nurse, which sent alarm bells ringing in my hospital room. My disorientation upset a nurse who had previously been kind to me, but she still brought me bland turkey sandwiches, which I wolfed down, dropping the first of many crumbs of bread on my new baby's hot red head.

Eventually, I was wheeled into a recovery room. Jon and I slept hard, my baby bundled by my side. A new nurse woke me up at dawn, telling me it was time to breastfeed. I hated her, but I followed orders, and a string of nurses called me "easy" as they passed me off on shift changes. They chatted about my vaginal delivery, the decent latch my daughter quickly developed, the effortlessness with which I took that first postbirth shit. I even declined the routine stool softener! Though neither the birth nor the subsequent shit had felt "easy" (and even as I sensed an indistinct animosity in the nurses' praise), I embraced their assessment of me, hopeful that my new relationship with my baby might always be that way. But as women I did not know massaged my belly, pressing hard into my uterus to help coax it into cramps that meant I was pulling myself back together, I began to see that I would not heal like my womb. The high was wearing off, and I felt blasted apart, exposed, driven to care for my baby like a wound.

When I stood up in the hospital for the first time two days later, finding my body hollowed, a nurse led me, hobbling, to the shower down the hall. I washed between my legs softly, inadequately, cupping my bulging, distended vulva, watching clots of red blood slide down the inseam of my legs, catching in the drain before breaking up and disappearing. The nurse stood by quietly, checking on me periodically. When I almost passed out trying to wash my hair, she caught my wet naked body, wrapped me up in rough white hospital towels, helped me half dress, and walked me back to my bed. I was eager to return, to be with my baby, that external lump that had once been me, or still was. Was I out there or in here? The nurse sat me down, brushed a matted nest of tangles out of my hair. I gazed at my baby—a body part of mine, now sleeping and separate. I felt like a tearful girl on her mother's lap.

PLEASURE

THERE WERE TIMES in my life when I enjoyed being touched. When I was ten I got stuck in the closet during a game of seven minutes in heaven with a boy who asked me to run out the clock. It felt like the greatest disappointment, standing there in the dark, waiting for the time to pass, wanting to be reached for, but knowing I was undesired. By middle school, boys were pointing out my washboard chest. In high school, I recall the eroticism of running my palm against the back of other boys' freshly shorn hair in math class. I wanted so badly to touch and be touched, for my body to be wanted. Desire in adolescence was a burning, and I wanted to burst into flames.

I was confused, however, about what I found pleasurable and how I might seek it. In high school I learned to get drunk, which dulled the shame I felt when boys mocked my body, my hair, my clothes, the things I said. Drinking also dulled the general emptiness of my youth. "The void you discover one day in your teens—nothing can ever undo that discovery," the writer Marguerite Duras says in her essay on alcohol. For Duras, a self-proclaimed alcoholic who always drank with men, alcohol was "linked to the memory of sexual violence." After I lost my virginity, high school was spent drunk at parties, fetal-positioning around the bases of boys' torsos, my legs folded under me, swallowed up by bedcovers that belonged to parents

I didn't know, doing what girls did at parties in high school. I held everything but my hands and mouth as still as possible, afraid to stall the desire I was stoking, to reset the journey to male pleasure back to the beginning. My toes tingled, waiting in this position, as if in prayer, for boys to cum. When we were done, I drank more to get the taste of them out. Drunkenness became for me, as it did for Duras, a replacement for a god I had never believed in, but also "the illusion of real creation," and a substitute for pleasure.

By the time I reached college, there weren't enough boys or booze around to contain my desire for self-immolation through sex and getting high. I had moved to San Francisco to get away from my mother, who was agonizing in her own ways over men and alcohol, and I had immediately fallen in love with my sprawling college campus: the feeling of stumbling off the MUNI each morning stoned, with a cloying chocolate coffee in hand; I rode the surf of students hustling toward ill-defined destinies. The campus itself also rolled up and down, buildings circling a wide expanse of lawn where baby adults lazed and smoked weed and talked about history and culture and art. The vague scent of sex and longing pulsed through the air, but in my classes I discovered another kind of burning—the heat of thinking, of piecing meaning together, making sense.

Alcohol was an intellectual lubricant as well, one which, as Duras wrote, mimics a kind of spirituality, guided by "reason going mad trying to understand why this kind of society, this Reign of Injustice, exists." I quickly developed crushes on those who shared my passion for thinking and talking and drinking, like on the sociology major whom I gave a blow job to under his desk after we talked politics. I tried to convince him to have sex with me afterward, but he asked me to leave so he could finish a paper that was due the next day. That night I walked alone through the fog that came in off the Pacific, which hung over the student housing adjacent to campus, back to the townhome I shared with roommates down the street. I smoked pot alone in my room out of a little pipe that had once been my mother's, and I tried to quiet the voices that told me it was better not to have a body than to keep carrying around the one I had everywhere I went.

My cravings for men and intellectual stimulation were intense and confusing, and seemingly at odds. I had absorbed the message that women who didn't know what they wanted were weak. A full decade before #MeToo, I had little language for analyzing the anatomy of my own desire, other than terms like "objectification." Many years later we still expect women to know exactly what they what, even though they grow up in a culture that constantly tells them how to be and how not to be; what to want and what not to want. Any confusion women do feel about what they want is frequently named as an excuse for rape and assault. But women, like all people, don't always know how to articulate, much less act on, their own wishes, particularly given that they are ushered away from self-knowledge and self-trust from a young age. "When did we buy into the idea that we know what we want?" Katherine Angel writes in her analysis of what she calls "the age of consent," *Tomorrow Sex Will Be Good Again*. Women are expected to have unflagging clarity about what they want; men, however, are rarely held accountable for their unwillingness to be curious about what women want.

The unsteady and confounding nature of my desire continually pulled me back into the mix of humiliation and hunger that was characteristic of 2000s hookup culture. When I wasn't studying I went to bars with roommates, where we took shots named after body parts, dipping our tongues performatively into the foam that topped them. Chasing drunkenness made me both more masculine and more feminine—tough yet available, always in pursuit of an indistinct rebellion. I spilled liquor on my spandex dresses, threw up in the bar bathroom, drank more, as all the girls I knew did. These nights kept me from hiding in my room reading and smoking pot alone, where I felt more comfortable, and my mother, who lived hours away from me in Los Angeles, was not yet sober, so there was no cloud of potential addiction hanging over me yet.

When I moved back home to LA after two years of college, I further fashioned myself with wine and beer and tequila into the kind of woman who ended up confused about what had happened to her. Drinking was never just a means of escape, but a way of taking ownership of what I could not otherwise guarantee. If I was to live in a culture that perceived me as an object, I could at least pretend I was choosing to be one. I used terms like "sex positive," that mostly depoliticized brand of sexual liberation that was a precursor to what Angel calls "confidence culture," a discourse of empowerment that took hold in the 2000s and 2010s and taught women to see their "insecurity and lack of confidence as ugly, abject and shameful"—and instead to take charge. It was a kind of lean-in sexuality. Given the choice between presenting myself as a slut or a victim or a sex-positive feminist, I chose the latter. I pretended at what Angel characterizes as an insistent strength, one I hoped would make me "almost heroically invulnerable," tapping into qualities I perceived as preconditions for successful womanhood, but also for being a feminist.

In Los Angeles I honed the art of seduction, working for the want of men who were blah, like the drummer with the little dick who had Neil Strauss's book on pickup artists, *The Game*, by his bedside, as if the book itself spoke to his sexual prowess. I got used to voided nights, to temporary losses of memory, to regret, and though it was all beginning to concern me—more so as my mother's own struggles with alcoholism reached a breaking point—I liked seeing men's gratification hang in the balance, me the only agent of its fulfillment. Drunkenness was the door into that culture of hedonism and false freedom. But after blurry nights of sex, if men stayed long enough for me to piece together what had happened the night before, I wouldn't have been able to name how I felt about who or what I was becoming, much less articulate whether I was feeling real pleasure. Like many men and women of my generation, I believed that, as Angel writes, "sex *is* something into which women don't enter willingly; something into which they have to be persuaded or coerced" whether through "alcohol, pills and persuasion" or some other means.

Eventually, I dabbled in other substances. After I'd met a former child star at a bar in Long Beach and watched him sing Dave Matthews Band cover songs, we sniffed powder off his kitchen island, and I pictured myself marrying into his life: living in his massive Studio City home, making friends with his brothers, also child stars. But that night he sent me below his fluffy white comforter, down where I could pleasure him without, I assumed, him seeing my face. Did I beg him to have sex with me? I did that sometimes. Wanting to be wanted. Either way he drove me home mostly in silence the next morning in his yellow sports car, driving fast on the 101. I sat in the passenger seat, nursing a headache in the almost-sun of first light, my knotted hair stinking of him and his oblivious satisfaction. Weeks later a friend of his invited me over to his house and poured me absinthe, leading me to believe the former child star I liked might join us. I drunk-dialed the child star compulsively, wanting desperately to see him again, but he never answered his phone. When the night had almost turned to dawn, after drinking and dialing for hours, the child star's friend took me into his garden and kissed me. I made up some excuse for leaving and asked him to drive me home.

On nights I spent alone in my apartment in North Hollywood, I emptied bottles of wine and smoked cigarettes outside in the warm dark night, feeling like a slut and a drunk, dreaming of another life. My mother had recently gone into recovery, and now I saw myself as a replica of her. For years, when men were not around she had drunk and smoked on our back porch, feeling ashamed of herself. Other nights she had primed herself with coke for men who used her. When the men and drugs were gone, she drank bottles of wine alone outside, but alcohol was a poor bedmate for both of us. It left us empty. "Alcohol is barren," Duras writes.

I would not quite say I hated myself then. I might have even been "happy." With some men I even felt a pleasure that, once I became a mother, felt impossible to retrieve. Before I met Jon, I had a dramatic affair with an actor who worked with me at a restaurant in Burbank, the Los Angeles suburb where I grew up. We played house together off and on for a few months in an apartment in Glendale that he was borrowing from friends who were traveling to film a television pilot, but we kept our relationship quiet among those we worked with—he was beholden to a long-distance girlfriend, which added to the theater of our affair. At work we touched covertly, and he called me "trouble" as he fingered me through the hole in the crotch of my worn-out jeans while we were doing side work after shifts, licking my juices off his fingers, or rubbing them on the forks and knives we wrapped up in cloth napkins—an act of revenge on our asshole customers. When the restaurant was busy, we tumbled down the stairs to the basement that ran underneath the big dining room, holding hands, making out in the liquor storage room while our customers waited for drink refills.

After shifts, at the borrowed apartment where we stayed together, we drank whiskey on the dark patio and talked into the morning hours about our restless artistic ambitions. We both wanted to live a life consumed by art. The unconventional nature of the love we shared fed that fantasy. And in bed, he never pushed me down where he couldn't see me. He kissed me, lingered on my face, watched me as he trailed his mouth down my torso. Our hunger for each other was limitless, effortless, but also full of mutual intellectual admiration. I left him after late nights to write at a coffee shop in Toluca Lake, and he admired this about me—how my writing came before him.

I was, however, privately pained by living on the other side of infidelity. I wanted him to see me as a potential wife, as motherly. One night I ended up naked on the bathroom floor of the borrowed apartment, throwing up whiskey after we had sex. He came behind me and held my hair, and we drove to work together the next morning, laughing it off, but I knew that over the years, in all my efforts to make myself into a woman that was hard and strong—empowered and liberated—I had somehow become everything a woman was not supposed to be. That actor would go on to marry a younger, Christian hostess, who had been a star cheerleader in high school, and I knew the way he must have compared us: she, so young and pure; I, so wanton. There was little maternal promise in me then.

Maybe because I knew this, around that time my pattern of shaping my life around drinking with men shifted. Not long after the actor and I broke up, I woke up naked at a friend's house in Santa Monica, in a bed tucked in an upstairs loft, and I reached down to find a stranger's fluids between my legs. When I descended the stairs, my friend was there. I remembered hardly anything from the previous night after meeting a man at the tiki bar near her house, sharing a drink beside him, moving to some other corner of the bar, my friend disappearing into the crowd. That was the same man, I assumed, who must have helped me up the stairs to the loft, but I had only imprecise flashes of his face, of flirting and walking together on a street, fog on the sidewalk, bedsheets, shivering, feeling sick and dizzy while he moved above me, trying not to throw up.

"You were so drunk," my friend said. "Don't you remember?"

I was hot and shaking, embarrassed, nauseated. I told her I hadn't drunk that much, counting drinks in my mind. I told her I thought someone had put something in my cocktail, but it didn't register. I wondered whether I was making excuses for my poor behavior, counting again. She rattled off embarrassing things I had done. The incident would repeat itself later on a trip to New York, after I met up with an old high school friend, a boy who had a crush on me when we were younger. I met him at a bar on a rooftop, where we all wore red robes to keep warm against the fog. He had become a wealthy finance something, gained weight, bought bottle service that night, and though I was with a friend, I must have begged her off, or he did, or he let me, because I woke up at his apartment, in his boyish bed, walls decorated with sports paraphernalia, feeling the evidence of him on and in me. I dressed and rode the elevator down without waking him, re-pinning a flower I had worn in my hair the night before, which I had found tossed on a low-lying table of athletic trophies. The apartment building was unrecognizable. I went digging inside myself for clues about what had happened.

Though friends of mine shamed me for what was understood to be my poor behavior in those years, and for my sloppy pursuit of pleasure, I can't blame those young women for the actions of men. After all, I, too, had internalized the belief that women were responsible for their own violation, and it wasn't until years later that I really began to rethink that perspective. One month after Jon and I moved to Buffalo, Trent Mays and Ma'lik Richmond repeatedly sexually assaulted a teenage girl in Steubenville, Ohio, while she was unconscious, documenting their night on social media and in text messages with the help of onlookers. Steubenville was one of several cases that marked an increased awareness in America about boys sexually assaulting girls. CNN's coverage of the trial, however, featured three pundits talking about the tragedy of the boys' lives being spoiled by one bad night. The journalist Poppy Harlow said it was "incredibly difficult" for her to observe "these two young men that had such promising futures, star football players, very good students," as "their lives fell apart." The victim's "promising" future did not share that air time on CNN, but "alcohol-fueled parties" did. Soon a flurry of think pieces about drinking drowned out critiques of rape culture—the many social attitudes that had taught boys to find humor and fun in sexual violence, and that also led news commentators to barefacedly center these boys' stories over the stories of the girls they had abused.

I restructured all my writing classes around rape culture. That same year, fourteen-year-old Daisy Coleman accused seventeen-year-old Matthew Barnett of raping her, then leaving her, passed out, on her porch in freezing temperatures. Like Mays and Richmond, Barnett was a star football player but also grandson to a former Republican congressman, adding to the Americana of the case. Coleman would later take her own life after years of harsh victim blaming and shaming. Overcome with grief, Coleman's mother would take her life as well four months later. Barnett was never convicted of sexual assault, but instead received probation for child endangerment. In one essay I taught frequently in those years, Roxane Gay responds to an essay typical of that era, by the writer Emily Yoffe, titled "College Women: Stop Getting Drunk." In her 2013 essay, Gay writes, "We have to talk about young women exercising better judgment to reduce their risk because it's such a seductive fantasy: If we're good enough girls, maybe we won't get raped." But girls can never be good enough to not get raped in a culture that normalizes the exploitation and abuse of women and sanctions the control of women's bodies—and that doesn't believe what women say when they do come forward after they have been assaulted. Gay notes, referring to the diversionary think pieces that explored the role of alcohol in campus rape culture around that time, that even so, "these pieces continue to get published because they satisfy the cultural narrative that victims are ultimately responsible for their own violation."

Many of my male students—most of whom came from small towns Upstate—openly accused women of sending confusing signals out at parties. They didn't seem to believe consent was something they could authentically obtain from women. I found myself frequently shutting down our conversations as they threatened to become completely unhinged: I lectured the class about why, after high-profile campus rape cases, the conversation usually turned to what girls and women had done wrong, to what terrible choices they had made, rather than to question why young men were raping unconscious girls who obviously could not consent to sex. "It's so hard to tell though," some male students would say, throwing up their hands. "Girls are so misleading. Girls don't know what they want." Heads would nod along.

Accusing women of not knowing what they want—as though that were not only a moral offense, but reason enough to be stripped of autonomy and protection—is one method boys and men often use to distance themselves from basic sexual responsibility. It also helps to culturally normalize rape as something that is just bound to happen to women because their minds and bodies are so untrustworthy—which in turn validates a range of legal and cultural mechanisms that reinforce distrust that women can account for their own reality. All this places the burden to prevent assault and rape on girls and women, a burden that is hard to shake, even when they know it's illogical. In my second year teaching the rape culture material, a female student came to me, sharing that she had missed class because her friend had gone missing at a party the night before. She later found out the friend had been drugged and assaulted. I told my student to protect herself, to not to get too drunk, to watch her drinks, to look out for her friends. Then I watched her walk away and felt immediately regretful of the responsibility I had saddled her with. The voice that came out of my mouth, not my own, contradicted the lessons I was teaching in class about men's responsibilities to not rape women, and women's right to be imperfect without having to worry they might be assaulted—as though I were ventriloquizing the texts I was teaching my students to question.

When I came home to Jon in those early years of marriage after having these sorts of conversations in and out of class with students, only a few years before I would become a mother, I saw everything about my marriage through the lens of the sexual culture around us. Jon had told me stories about his own youth: growing up masturbating to pop stars, or to his mother's catalogues of women's clothing. I didn't want to shame him for his adolescent sexual curiosity, but his sexuality, reliant as it was on the objectification of women, implicated me. Sometimes he scooted next to me in the kitchen and eyed my ass, commenting on how good it looked in leggings. He made hungry noises for me, sidling up for a kiss or an embrace. How was he not consumed with rage over sex and violence, these things between us? He knew nothing of my world. But maybe neither did I. So much of what I thought I knew about pleasure and sexuality was now unraveling, as I observed more closely the pressing culture of sexual violence in America. What did any man know of what it felt like to witness violent rape and assault in the news, year after year, all of one's life, forced to relive my own unprocessed abuse, much less with a husband at home smacking his lips?

I began pushing Jon away. The transition from endless sun to harsh winters had been hard on us, and on me especially. I was enchanted by the first snowfall in Buffalo, but I was West Coast. Amid my growing frustrations, we did our best to settle in. We learned to wear oversized scarves. We met other writers and academics with whom we talked and drank. We went to poetry readings in abandoned grain silos. We threw a "cookies and cocktails" party each winter, and I carried around a big goblet of red wine all night, which made it easier to hug new friends and colleagues at parties, to playfully rest my hand on an arm in conversation, to estimate pleasure and creation. But most nights I eventually climbed upstairs without saying goodbye to anyone and passed out alone. Someone broke our green couch at one of those early parties, the first sofa we had ever owned, purchased at the Salvation Army, and it stayed broken until we left that apartment; propped up on one side with books, teetering to one side whenever we sat down. When Jon and I were alone, we drank wine and Canadian beer together, which made it easier for me to give myself over to obligatory marital, and when the illusion failed and I wanted to purge, we ran mile after mile together on salted sidewalks, winding through the local cemetery, observing families buried together and stray headstones standing all alone.

In my second trimester of pregnancy, while I was completely sober for the first time in years, more news of campus sexual assault filtered into our home. In January of 2015, the same month I found out my baby would be marked *girl* at birth, the Stanford rape case made headlines after Brock Turner assaulted Chanel Miller at a party while she was unconscious. Miller's case was legally fraught by her inability to remember details of the assault, but her victim's impact statement, which went viral after it was published the following year under the name Emily Doe, revealed the incredible detail she did recall about waking up to find that Turner had assaulted her.

"The phrase, sexual assault, is a little misleading," Miller writes in her memoir, *Know My Name*, "for it seemed to be less about sex, more about taking. Sexual assault is stealing." Miller's case urged me to reassess much of what men had done to me, not only because I began to understand that assault had more shapes than such a phrase allows, but also for the questions about drunkenness, memory, and consent that the case raised. "One-sided wants" is how Miller describes assault—"the feeling of overriding the other." That feeling had so often characterized my sexual life that I had lost my own intuition about my body, about naming when it had been violated or wronged. But now that intuition seemed to resurface as a kind of ambient rage. "Sometimes I'm too angry, seething after reading a rape story," Miller writes, "*I need to slice a dick off.*"

Though many of my sexual experiences before marriage had been tainted by a culture of men taking what they wanted with or without consent, part of why I fell in love with Jon was because he always put my desire before his. We met in graduate school, in a writing program on the outskirts of Los Angeles. I was reading French feminist theory, critiques of Freud and Lacan, essays on female pleasure, but I held on to a clandestine desire for conventionality, believing that a husband—and a family—might make a better story of me. I had heard the gossip that Jon cried in a writing workshop while reading one of his own poems aloud, unsure whether this was a turnoff or a central element of my attraction to him. His eyes were shy and full of feeling behind his wide-framed Dahmer-style eyeglasses, his smile consistently conciliatory. I saw his chin-length hair, his sensitivity and modesty, his interest in the self-emasculating performance artist Vito Acconci, Jon's whole *vibe*, as a resistance to gender, just as he did. But I could also see that generosity and kindness were embedded in him, part of his makeup, something rare in men I had known.

On our first real date, he took me to the Barragan's Mexican restaurant on Sunset. We sat across from each other on the patio sipping syrupy margaritas, talking about performativity, chomping chips. "Everything I do," I said, "feels like such an act." He looked at me across the table, offered a knowing smile. He didn't try to push more drinks on me or rush through the meal and off to bed. He wanted to look at me, to know me. Nothing about him was an act. Or maybe it all was, but only ever in service of others. We got headaches. He paid with his credit card, adding a $60 bill to a pile of debt that would follow us for years. We walked back to his apartment, holding hands, discoursing on art. It was a love I had never known before. I immediately dreamed of marriage.

By my late twenties, matrimony and reproduction—what some call "settling down"—looked like a respite from the imbalances of sex. I had subscribed to a belief many women held in the early 2000s—that I was meant to "experiment," to "enjoy" my youth. I believed having lots of sex would prime me to be a better partner, a better woman, whenever this wave I was riding finally crested. My mother had taught me to be skeptical of men and fairy-tale endings, but I had found a way to believe in them anyway. I was sure that all that giving over had been in the pursuit of something real—of love.

The first spring Jon and I spent together in his studio apartment in Echo Park was hot, like every season in LA. He invited me over for underwear dance parties, assuring me we did not have to go to bed, but I was so used to asking for love by giving sex, that we did anyway, then we lazed around holding each other, talking about *family*, which we associated with adult life. He wanted the stability his long-married Christian parents gave him; I wanted a sense of normalcy, something I never had growing up in a home tense with addiction and financial precarity.

Amid all this dreaming of middle-class life, though, there was also real pleasure. The year we met, Jon was working on a project for which he regularly photographed himself mouthing dildos. He kept his box of variously colored silicone dicks above our efficiency kitchen, and when he showed them to me for the first time, I saw his aesthetic submissiveness as subversive and safe. I asked him to penetrate me with every color, one by one, my body splayed open in the midday sunlight of his undressed windows. My favorite was a violet one we called the purple beast. I was wide awake, completely sober, listening to the sounds of the LA Metro bus calling out its stops right next to our window. Later, I let him throw me up against a bathroom wall during a trip to Atlantic City that we also paid for with credit. We fucked to the sounds of other people pissing. It was always my pleasure, however, that turned Jon on most, and while later his piercing gaze would come to bother me for the way it seemed to demand that I turn him on by showing how turned on I was, when we first met he seemed to offer an invitation to center my own desire for the first time. Two years later we wed at a discount party venue in Culver City, the closest to the beach we could afford.

After giving birth, the shock and awe of new parenthood runs up against the quiet demand that we go back from whence we came— that we get our bodies back, our sex lives back, and that we do not forget our husbands. New mothers (assumed to be married to men) are encouraged by parenting websites, marriage books, and popular media to hastily revive their sexuality. Not doing so, women are told, could send marriages into peril. Listicles of tips for reviving postbaby sex drive abound, even though nearly all women feel pain the first time they have sex after giving birth. Advice pieces on postpartum sex occasionally try to remind men to be patient with their wives, addressing husbands as though they are impatient children sitting on their hands, trying desperately to hold back a force beyond their control. "Fight the urge, boys," one 2015 dad's guide to postpartum sex says, "and take it slow."

On the other hand, despite the embodied nature of caring for a newborn—the work is nothing if not visceral and wet—American women are at the same time expected to detach from their sensual and sexual lives once they become mothers. They should take pleasure in their babies, but not *too* much pleasure, lest they forget the husbands. As Adrienne Rich observes, "The divisions of labor and allocations of power in patriarchy demand not merely a suffering Mother, but one divested of sexuality: the Virgin Mary, virgo intacta, perfectly chaste." This simultaneous mandate for and rejection of sexuality in motherhood may appear paradoxical, but they are just two sides of the same coin: women are meant to serve men, marriage, and motherhood; they're not supposed to receive any pleasure themselves independent of those institutions or the responsibility of serving them. Silvia Federici writes in her 1975 essay "Why Sexuality Is Work," "The law, medicine, and our economic dependence on men, all guarantee that, although the rules are loosened," women's sexuality remains controlled as one duty in a catalogue of jobs for the housewife. "Sexual liberation" has only intensified that work: "Now we are expected to have a waged job, still clean the house and have children and, at the end of the double workday, be ready to hop in bed and be sexually enticing."

But after giving birth, bodies change. There's the existential and personal upheaval, the difficulty of tracking where the parent's body ends and the baby begins. The chest is supposed to be offered up on demand, as are sore arms and hollowed-out torsos and achy legs; the genitals hang heavy—in tatters—and throb. Hormones also dip and swing and surge, while brain chemistry is fundamentally altered by the work of caregiving. Then we must reckon with how our new figure compares to cultural standards of beauty. My body image was torn apart by my new stretch marks, my pooch, my massive, hanging breasts. My sexuality was also reshaped by motherhood because my sense of pleasure was now completely wrapped up in my new baby.

I relished skin-to-skin contact, my baby's warm wrinkly skin on mine, her fingers looping around my thumb. Every interaction felt invited. When we came home from the hospital, there were still printed black-and-white images of uteruses on our walls, each emblazoned with blooming roses meant to represent cervixes widening with the force of a baby's head. I had taped these up all around our apartment days before my due date to support my dream of birthing outside history, imagining myself like the woman in the YouTube video I had watched so many times who pushed her baby out in ecstasy. I had forgotten to use these images as planned, as some mandala on which I might meditate as my cervix dilated, but now I gazed at the representations of my reproductive organs with a goddess pride. My body was odd, stretched out, bleeding; but I was a deity.

I spent most of those early days on a red velvet couch we had inherited from the apartment's previous tenants, who had cats that scratched up the smooth skirt and arms of the sofa. We had repaired the frays with packing tape, and now the lush fabric cradled me as I cradled my new baby and crackled under my weight when I shifted or got up to fetch frozen maxi pads to replace those that had turned warm, yeasty, and wet with blood. Unwrapping the pads I found the cotton edges crystallized from our too-cold freezer, but I still stuck them on the weightless full-coverage mesh underwear I had stolen from the hospital, squeezing the ice between my legs. The pads burned and soothed.

My daughter's arrival conferred the disappearance not just of sex but of much else in my life. She gave me permission to let my professional life fade away—and she came at a time when I needed that permission. I saw motherhood as a refuge from a world into which I never quite fit, an intellectual culture that had once fed me but ultimately felt charged with a hierarchical, sexual politics that left most women I knew feeling unsafe, paranoid, and unequal. Now, life revolved completely around the care of bodies—my baby's, but also my own. Every movement was intentional, purposeful, animal, and I wanted no intrusions. I made Jon promise that no visitors would be allowed in the apartment for at least a month, and I took few phone calls—my own version of a lying-in period.

We named our baby Hannah after female artists and thinkers—philosopher Hannah Arendt, artist Hannah Wilke, poet Hannah Weiner—whom I had studied during pregnancy. I nursed naked because the lactation consultant at the hospital had promised on her short visit to my bedside that it would give my baby a higher IQ. "Skin-to-skin is in," the nurse had said, waving around a clipboard as proof. Hannah nursed vigorously and without resistance, a small apology for her lengthy exit from my body and a preview of what would be her nature—attached and determined. In breastfeeding, I felt determined, too, thinking that I was giving my baby the best. She rooted around for gold pearls that beaded on my nipple when I squeezed my breast into her mouth, her warm skin pressed into mine, and I felt the way I had right after delivery, as I had in my teens dancing around clubs in Hollywood, ecstasy melting on my tongue, the all-over buzz of breastfeeding so like that liquid-body high. As Hannah drank from me, I pulled her in close, taking in her sharp, earthy scent. We hadn't bathed her since we left the hospital, something I had seen suggested online, and she still had a scab-like chunk of something in her thick head of dark hair, which I worked to scrape out over time with my fingernails—my first experience with the carnal gratification of grooming my child. In time, my milk came in, and when it did, it spilled down the corners of Hannah's mouth. I snapped a photo, proud of my productivity.

Jon and I had no paid leave but enough credit available to hole up for a few months, and this felt like great wealth. We made less than $15,000 each a year from our teaching positions, but because the cost of living was so low, and we could never find work in the summers anyway, we had this time together as a threesome, something I knew many parents in America did not have. I vowed to cherish it. I lay topless every day on my crimson tufted throne, under the large living room window. With no air conditioning, and with the constant breastfeeding, sprawling nude was the only way. I was sticky in the humid summer heat, my sleeping, diapered baby an appendage that Jon and I peeled off and passed back and forth from shirtless chest to shirtless chest. Jon delivered portion after portion of the fatty food I had cooked and frozen in trays before I went into labor, and we rewatched the whole series of *Friends*, the droning laugh track fading in and out of sleep and feedings. When Jon and I found ourselves dumbfounded as Ross was asked to imagine himself as a birthing mother, opening like a flower in a Lamaze class he attends with Carol and Susan, we worried the show was implanting visions of monstrous women in Hannah's mind.

"When should we stop watching TV around her?" Jon said. We studied our baby. Her eyelids were thin, closed, her breathing heavy. Sounds of an explosive shit broke the anxiety. We laughed and clapped, and Jon changed the diaper while I searched for something else to watch, trying to find a truly neutral narrative.

While Hannah suckled, I looked out on the porch, trees rustling, neighborhood kids playing in the street, cicadas singing—their summer song was the only element of the Buffalo summers I had ever really enjoyed. Hannah was born over Memorial Day weekend, and soon everyone in town had burst into the streets, frenetically worshipping the summer sun. I savored my position at the boundary between home and world. My baby was a sweet, warm, new project. She could be the world as it had never been before, and she would discover that new world in me. Audre Lorde writes about the erotics of motherhood—of the child coming to know the world through the mother's body and breasts, and through the mother's passage of language. "I am a reflection of my mother's poetry," Lorde writes. This embrace of the power of the mother may appear to veer back into biological essentialism—into the idea that women are made for making babies—but Lorde distinguishes in her writing the powerful work of care, a labor that need not be gendered. Lorde views caring for a child—a mix of linguistic and sensual work—as a form of radical creativity.

I took pleasure in the hypervigilance and in gazing at every curve of my baby's body. Motherhood was a creative puzzle, one I thought I could understand in time, or maybe already did. But as with childbirth, I quickly saw myself slipping into preordained narratives. Breastfeeding felt like a bottomless, unpolluted intimacy. Each day Hannah's small body tucked farther into corners of my own and her hands soon became strong enough to squeeze the engorgement out of my breasts to get what she wanted, to pull herself in. I attributed her growing strength to my milk production, and I was fascinated by the benefits of breast milk and by my body's ability to nourish the child I had grown. In the 2015 essay that led to the publication of her book *Like a Mother*, Angela Garbes writes that "breast milk is much more than food: It's potent medicine and, simultaneously, a powerful medium of communication between mothers and their babies." I was enthralled by the magic and science of breast milk, the way it mended not just my baby's emotions, but all minor sicknesses and injuries. Whenever I encountered some new ailment on my baby, I turned to my breasts, squirting milk in her clogged tear duct, on her rashy labia, and on her finger when I—crying, hysterical—realized I had cut a chunk of skin off while trying to trim her soft, thin nails. I picked Hannah up and latched her on, the reunion of our bodies, and the euphoria of my milk, the only ritual that could calm either one of us down.

I enjoyed breastfeeding, but I also felt the gravity of my body's need to produce at the cost of my child's future intelligence and emotional well-being, responding to popular-at-the-time slogans like "Breast is best." For many women, the pressure to breastfeed becomes the first deep denial of their bodies' needs and desires in motherhood. Clinical and colloquial conversations around breastfeeding rarely emphasize consent or autonomy, or consider a parent's prior relationship with their body, assailing them instead with injunctions to just relax. Not to mention the absence of attention given to just how much time and effort breastfeeding takes. "Heaven forbid," Kate Manne writes, "that whatever putative benefits breastfeeding has for the infant should be soberly weighed against the pain, exhaustion, and lack of freedom it entails for many of those who try to do so." There is no neutral narrative, in other words, about breastfeeding. And as with most expectations of mothers in America, there is a lack of support in meeting high demands—including no national paid parental leave, minimal lactation education, and no protections for nursing parents pumping on the job.

My love affair with Hannah, however, still felt cleaner and less threatening than anything I had experienced with men. And Jon— though I was thankful to have him there—was an outsider in our romance. When I nursed, he fell away, his voice drowned out by my baby's rhythmic swallows, a mix of gulping and sighing, meditative and hypnotic. Before giving birth I had read that breastfeeding was considered by some to be an extension of the sexual act. I felt this as my head rolled back, oxytocin coursing through me. My feelings for my baby were like those I had felt falling in love with men—that deep want of contact all the time, the world falling away, how time stopped for us. Maggie Nelson writes of one sidebar in Dr. William Sears's *The Baby Book*, in which Sears assures mothers that any "sexual feelings" they get from breastfeeding are because "you're basically hormonal soup, and because the hormones unleashed by breast-feeding are the same as those unleashed by sex, you could be forgiven for the mix-up." As Nelson points out, it's hardly a mix-up. "It isn't *like* a love affair," she writes. "It *is* a love affair." I never felt the two—orgasm and breastfeeding—to be indistinguishable, but I understood their affinity.

Before the affair becomes "unrequited," the relationship between mother and child is "romantic, erotic, and consuming."

My relationship with my infant felt unspoiled, too, because there was no gendered power struggled passing between us—no "tentacles," as Nelson puts it—at least not in the beginning. My baby had no history of masculinity with which I had to contend. Of course I wondered: How much of the pleasure I felt as a new mother was related to a relief from the patriarchal pressure to have a child? I had done it, yes. Perhaps I was a real woman now. But in the early days of motherhood, this was not the sentiment that pulsed through my body. Instead, I thought often of something I had read, written by the artist and mother Mary Kelly, in which she describes new motherhood: "Yes, sensual," was the phrase I remembered and repeated. I loved her awareness of the audacity of her observation as much as her audacity to say it. And I whispered the phrase to myself as Hannah slept on me, as I breathed her in, as my milk flowed into her belly. *Yes. Sensual.* A surprise, and an allowance.

Soon, though, my relationship with my baby was thrown off-kilter. As Hannah grew, breastfeeding became less idyllic. She took me in, guzzled and cooed one moment, hated me the next. When my breast slipped from her mouth, or the milk didn't pour down her throat fast enough, she beat my chest, mauled me. I thought of the psychoanalyst Melanie Klein's theory, which I had first read while pregnant, in which she argues that the mother-child relationship forms every person's early sense of self. Klein in some sense blames the mother for all the troubled contours of the human psyche—an American tradition, especially in the field of psychology—but she also introduces a sense of power into the psychoanalytic saga of the mother's purportedly passive body. For Klein, the mother's breasts are the first objects the infant encounters with passion. They are also the first tools of power, and they begin, in the child's mind, as two confusing, fragmented objects: a "good" breast that gratifies and a "bad" breast that deprives and tortures.

I had found this all confusingly abstract before I breastfed. Was one breast fuller? The other with a low milk supply? I had interpreted the theory literally, finding it hard to understand an infant's perspective, which is that the good and bad breast are, bewilderingly, one and the same. Watching Hannah nurse, I could see now how the mother's body teaches the infant about nourishment and the threat of its denial, about giving and taking, and soon, I would learn to identify the potential there—the possibility of teaching my child about consent. Klein called the early phase of infant development the "paranoid-schizoid" phase—a time when the child understands the mother as two beings, a giver and a withholder of pleasure. As the child grows, however, it learns that the mother's breasts are two aspects of the same presence, and that the mother is a being unto herself.

When I was still reeling from childbirth, I didn't yet see this period as an opportunity to provide my child with her first lessons on autonomy. Instead, our breastfeeding relationship became increasingly one-sided. I lost any strength to resist her demands, to say no, to refuse her, not only because she was needy and helpless and it was my job to care for her, but because the advice I consumed in the early years of motherhood—in books, online—told me our relationship should be this way. Learning to see the mother as a whole person, one with the power to teach the child a range of human emotions, I found, takes a very long time—but even longer in a culture that tells women that they no longer belong to themselves after they have children and that their time for freedom is over, if it ever had a chance to begin.

Even so, years later, when I think back on that time of giving myself over to my baby completely, I do not feel remorseful. I yearn for the short-lived decadence of the first months, for the license I gave myself to fade from public life, to devote myself to my baby, to the creative work of caring for her, and for myself. I sometimes long for those days—before I began to see how my love and my labor as a mother were deeply entwined with my own disempowerment, and with a world built on one-sided wants. Before I began to fight, but also before my baby began to move away, as all babies do. I don't wish that I had never woken up to the culture of motherhood that was thrust on me, but I do sometimes long for that brief time when everything felt like a choice, even if, perhaps, it wasn't. *Yes, sensual.* The certainty I felt in that phrase. How I miss it. I was unearthing something in those words I muttered to myself: an understanding that submission is not the same as studying the other, as giving one's self to a child as an act of care, even if, in motherhood, they can feel indistinguishable.

WORK

I RETURNED TO WORK when Hannah was three months old, brokenhearted that our honeymoon period was ending so soon, but determined not to fall apart. The first day I went to campus to teach, Jon shot a photo of Hannah on the floor with a piece of paper laid upon her—a sign he had made that read "I'm proud of my working mom!" We both wanted to believe we could manage. Recalling my daily flow as a nanny, years earlier, the swift momentum built into every hour, I developed schedules and procedures, logged them in my phone, and shared them with Jon. I organized our days around naps and diaper changes, laundry cycles and dishwashing. I set the house up to enable maximum domestic productivity too: baskets for dirty clothes nested in each room, toys and books set in more baskets, to be used at various times of day.

I hated the breast pump, which hurt and turned my nipples wide and flat, only to eke out a few drops of milk. Nursing was easier, had less variables, and felt good. So I structured my professional routines around the labor of feeding: I taught in the mornings, worried about milk leaking through my shirt, sped home after class, ran inside to Jon on the floor with Hannah on his lap, a basket of just-read books beside them. He passed her off to me, she drained my engorged breasts, Jon hurried off to teach a few classes, and I put Hannah down for a nap. I started laundry, washed dishes, staged the living room for Hannah's impending wake-up, nursed again when she woke up. The relay race went on for a year.

When I was home alone with Hannah, ancillary work tasks—grading papers, writing my dissertation, finding more lucrative work so we could one day afford daycare—tugged at me, but I didn't do them. I lay with Hannah on the floor, she on her back, feet jutting into the air, arms levitating toward the sky. I tried to stay busy, picking up toys she was too young to use, putting them in a new spot to entice her. I waited for her to roll over. I sat on the couch and stared, afraid to leave her alone, afraid she had spent too much time on her back. Clearly she was getting a flat head and would need a helmet if she stayed that way much longer. I flipped her. Now it seemed she had spent too much time on her stomach, her neck was giving out, she was whining, this was child abuse, her sounds so muffled with her face smashed into the filthy carpet that way. Could she even breathe? I contemplated vacuuming. Too much time in arms or too much time on the floor. Was I smothering her? I looked it up on my phone. Too much time hearing my voice; not enough. Flip-flop, here's a toy.

This was my most valuable work: attending to the child. But life had become one interminable cycle of worry and maintenance. I tried leaving the house with Hannah more often when Jon was away at work, to create an interlude in the day, pushing her down the street in her stroller toward the wide traffic island at the end of our block and setting us up on a blanket in the grass. The sun danced around us. I watched her kick and squint. I described the nature of trees and light, then worried over sunburn aloud, moving us under the big elm where the locusts sang. We pressed big palm to small palm, and I talked about hands, as she gripped mine softly. We nursed. I packed up. We walked back to the apartment.

Back at home, on our velvet couch, I sat with Hannah on my lap, each of us staring out the large picture window at the street. By the end of that academic year, she would crawl off me, pull herself up, peer out into the world. For now, she was just a heap, a hunk of meat, perceiving. I checked the time, estimating how long until Jon would be home. He was working more than I was, teaching multiple classes at the university as an adjunct so that we could afford our rent. It was just a temporary arrangement. Hannah was still so young. I looked at my phone, located information about sensory development—how far could she see? I put my phone away, remorseful about my scrolling, and told stories instead. "Those are leaves. Those are trees. It's fall. The leaves are falling." I wondered if, just by hearing my descriptions, her vision might be more clear than other babies'; I patted myself on the back for my good work. We listened to music and swayed. She squealed and cooed. When Jon finally came home, I told him her sounds had been like singing, her little ballad the most momentous event of the day.

In 2015, my first year of motherhood, I had not yet heard of "intensive parenting," a trend of relentless parental involvement, usually practiced by white middle-class parents. Drawing on the work of Sharon Hays, who coined the term, Darcy Lockman calls this kind of parental overwork "a gendered model of childrearing that is child-centered, expert-guided, emotionally absorbing, labor-intensive, and financially expensive." I fell right into it.

Intensive parenting emerged as women entered the workforce in higher numbers after the Second World War, as a response to the widespread accusations of feminine idleness many believe were a primary influence on women's increased workforce participation. Midcentury Americans often blamed domestic technology and housewives' economic influence as consumers for creating freeloading housewives, who were depicted as parasitical "little women" at home and as direct threats to men's power outside the home. Some women went to work outside the home to prove their value, but for housewives, the question became how to make their labor in the home more visible.

By the time I became a mother, women were no longer expected to stay busy either at home *or* at work, but to be busy in both realms at the same time. Jon's expectations for me also began to shift as soon as we agreed that I would start teaching again. Although Hannah and I had once been a twosome on whom he waited, now I was expected to feed and water myself and also do an equal share of work around the house—more on days when he worked. I also ran the flow of the home, and even when Jon was around, Hannah wanted only me. Her needs eclipsed my own, and the support I experienced in the early months dwindled. I felt unmoored by the transition into working motherhood, even as I had more luxuries than most: a part-time job, a partner who didn't work full-time and so had odd hours for childcare. Nevertheless, the early trance of parenthood turned into round-the-clock work.

Hannah was also sleeping less and her behavior was becoming more erratic, putting Jon and me on edge. She was overtired, or not tired enough. We were tired, too. I looked for daycares, but the cost of childcare would have canceled out one of our incomes. So I tried again with routines, tweaking Hannah's naps, going on to Jon about what needed to change in our home to make things more manageable. I spent hours on my phone reading about sleep regressions and nap transitions, and still more hours angry with Jon that he didn't also devote all his free time to workshopping our domestic lives. I wanted him to care the way I cared, to share in what is now commonly referred to as the "mental load" in the house—the emotional and psychological strain of keeping an overtaxed American home together. Back then that load just felt to me like an amorphous set of responsibilities. And I still believed that we could transcend the conditions in which we found ourselves, if only we thought our days out enough times.

No matter how I tried, though, I could never get a handle on it all. I lost my grip, and we left New York in May on Hannah's first birthday. We had found a two-bedroom apartment to rent ten minutes from my mother's apartment in a suburb of the Bay Area, where she had moved years earlier to be near my sister and her two children. I flew to California, babe in arms, while my mother decorated our new apartment with pink and yellow polka-dotted towels, a handmade welcome sign, two blue plastic Adirondack chairs to fill the furniture-less space, and a blow-up mattress on which Hannah and I would sleep for a week until Jon arrived with the U-Haul. He drove the packed truck across the country alone, our anxious cat in a cage beside him in the passenger seat, yowling and pissing the whole way. He was stoic in his new role as dad.

After five years living in the chill of western New York, moving back to the warmth of California felt like a potential homecoming, but also like the only option. We needed childcare; my mother promised to help. That first week she organized the apartment with me and read to Hannah, who was now waddling around, a stubby white ponytail atop her head. I unpacked and stacked books. My mother and my daughter's love bloomed fast, and I welcomed the extra hands. But as we settled into California, my mother—who had no retirement funds and would have to continue working full-time long after she qualified for Social Security—didn't have the time to watch Hannah much beyond the weekends.

I had already lost ground professionally, and the long-term effects of my pulling back on work for a while longer seemed abstract and ill-defined. I couldn't qualify for full-time teaching positions in California because I hadn't yet finished my dissertation, a project I couldn't finish without childcare, and I calculated that, even if I were to pick up a few classes on a part-time basis, the work would not be lucrative enough for me to afford the daycare I would need to show up to teach. I applied to other gigs at nonprofits and arts centers, but nothing panned out. I tried to write for money, pitching story ideas to a few millennial women's magazines, and even got one piece accepted for $35, but I didn't respond to the email for days because I forgot I had sent the pitch out. I tried to write more serious essays, hoping they might lead to more money. But how could I write anything well considered with my child crying by my side and banging on my laptop?

It all brought me back to the same problem: I couldn't make enough money to send my child to daycare without my child in daycare. In 2016, my situation was hardly unusual. One 2019 article called the 2010s "the decade that made childcare unaffordable" in America, with costs steadily rising, and daycare-center-based care costing families on average one-third of their income. I read online advice written by mommy bloggers I found on Pinterest about how to keep kids busy and make money at home. "Give them a pot to bang on," some said, understanding that, in many ways, caring for children alone requires endless creative distraction. But other tips were more sadistic, like the suggestion that I work during my child's naps. Most often, however, the bloggers suggested paying someone else to take care of my kid. "Get away," they all seemed to say, "however you can."

Jon also had a hard time finding work, but eventually landed a job as the director of a corporate tutoring center in an affluent part of Oakland. As part of a cagey, two-month-long interview process, during which we ran up our credit-card balances and begged family members for cash, he was required to take a Caliper Assessment that reported he was passably fit for management. He was not, however, devoid of red flags: he scored way too high in the category of empathy, a quality he was unwilling or unable to hide, and which gave the hiring managers pause because it directly conflicted with the job's duties.

I felt badly for Jon, who had taken a string of jobs he didn't like since we married. When we first moved to Buffalo so I could pursue my degree, he didn't have a job yet and had an unmanageable amount of credit card and student loan debt on which he was now defaulting. The first fall we spent in New York, I came home each night to find Jon sitting where and as I left him: huddled over his computer at the kitchen table, a fleece blanket draped over his shoulders, his body underneath wrapped in the green Snuggie his mother had given him the previous Christmas, looking for work. Our apartment in Buffalo—a city known to some for its literary history, and to more for its snow—was cold, both concretely and metaphorically, that first winter, and we had to be careful about running up the heating bill. Jon shuffled around the apartment in his double-blankie getup, sometimes hooking the blanket over the top of his head to try to stay warm, his coverings like a thickly layered cape trailing behind him. "Nothing yet," he'd say when I came home, standing to fill his coffee cup. A fixture.

That first winter in Buffalo, Jon took a seasonal job at UPS after flopping an interview at Geico. During one UPS shift he looked on as the senior delivery man, Geoff, with whom he shared a route, in a fit of anger threw every box off the truck into the snow just two days before Christmas. Jon came home and told me about the meltdown as he removed his black beanie and his regulation brown jacket. He was shaken up, but also felt for Geoff, who had been working the position for many years, and with whom he had developed a partnership. They had a method: Geoff would sort the boxes, then toss one at a time to Jon, who ran the deliveries up the steps of old Victorian porches, trying not to slip on the ice that dotted the sidewalks. "He went postal," Jon said to me the day of Geoff's meltdown. He was punning, playing it off, making light, trying to inject a little poetry into the moment. Jon had worked manual labor before, construction and pavement-laying with his brother before we had met, so he had experience, he said, with the feeling of a job needing to get done and there being nowhere near enough time to do it.

I was turned off by Jon's stints with joblessness, but felt responsible. I supposed I had put him in that position in New York, by asking him to move. Now, in California, he mentioned feeling as though he had again relocated for me, even though it was a move driven by shared parental desperation, with hopes we could lean on my family for childcare. We were increasingly unable to parse out whose decisions had led us to where we now found ourselves: with such a limited set of future choices. And the job he took in California felt demoralizing for other reasons: the tutoring franchise's owners felt that the best method for convincing parents to enroll their children in supplemental learning programs was to pinpoint and exploit what they called parents' "point of pain." As an administrator, executing this tactical assault against insecure parents—mostly middle-class or wealthy parents, but also those with low incomes who took out loans to keep their kids from falling behind in school—was Jon's primary role. But the job offered a modest salary, so he took the position and became the breadwinner, while I committed to staying home with Hannah for a little longer. These were decisions, we told ourselves, made by two adults who understood how women get pushed out of their careers by motherhood—another temporary arrangement—and we wouldn't let it carry us away.

Kim Brooks writes in *Small Animals: Parenthood in the Age of Fear* that the early 2000s emphasis on choice turned parenting into a branded identity, leading many to defend their own parenting styles more vehemently than ever before and creating a sense of obligation to "do it right," after they had agonized over the choice of whether to do it at all. Middle-class white women felt particularly compelled to study up not only on how to have the best birth possible but also on how to produce the worthiest children, with the most advantages. And yet, there remained so many elements of parenting—a labor that extends over decades—that were both beyond parents' control and were controlled by others. Brooks writes that she, "without ever formally deciding," became a stay-at-home mother, something that is often talked about as "a deliberate choice, an issue that's black or white, either/or," and that is supposed to tell the world something about who we are as women and mothers. In truth, for many women, staying home is "more of a response to circumstance and lack of alternatives."

The idea that living in an era of "choice" had not ultimately made my circumstances much better than those of generations before me was hard to sit with. But despite the abundance of choice sold to parents in terms of parenting style, choices around childcare and reentering the workforce are still an illusion for many parents, especially those without economic privileges. Not only is consistent childcare out of reach for most parents who are poor or working class in America, the absence of federally funded parental leave policies has a cascade effect, worsening inequality in and out of the home, especially for low-wage working women. In New York, as an adjunct and a student, Jon and I qualified for no governmental support in the transition to parenthood. Had we qualified, my experiences as a mother, and Jon's and my respective relationships with Hannah, might have been radically different. But the absence of federal leave and affordable childcare in America had been so normalized, such questions felt moot. "If I had been a citizen of one of the forty-one industrialized nations that offer parents paid maternity leave—to say nothing of subsidized childcare, quality early childhood education, or a host of other family supports—I might have made a different choice," Brooks writes. "But I lived in America, and so the calculation was simple."

"Choice," nevertheless, is consistently weaponized against women seeking control over their own bodies. Thought experiments that ask citizens to imagine who an "unborn" child or a "promising" young rapist could have become if only, for instance, a woman had not had an abortion or not spoken up about a rape are each common rhetorical exercises in so-called pro-life discourses and American rape culture, which both police women's voices and behavior, while excusing institutional and interpersonal abuses against women. The question of who rape victims or people with uteruses might have become had they not lived in a culture of violence and limited choices is less frequently entertained. "Anti-choicers like to pose hypotheticals about the remarkable baby a woman could have if she just didn't get an abortion: what if they cured cancer?" Jessica Valenti writes. "None ask if that woman herself might change the world. They never consider that we could be the remarkable ones, if only given the chance."

Given what we know about women's workforce participation after women become mothers, and the penalties they face if they do continue working outside the home, such questions are more than reasonable to ask. As journalist Katherine Goldstein argued during the pandemic, the 1.6 million women who left the workforce between 2019 and 2020 did not just "drop out" of the workforce of their own accord, as CNN, CNBC, and the *New York Times* all phrased it. As Goldstein put it, it would be more accurate to say that they were "'forced out,' 'pushed out,' or, my favorite, 'thrown out of a five-story window.'" The economic problem for new mothers is not that we have too many choices, but that we do not have enough decent ones, even if we are constantly sold the fantasy that we do.

Unequal access to childcare is a major part of this narrowing of the road. Just a few years after I made the "choice" to stay at home for a while, Anne Helen Petersen wrote, during the pandemic, that early childhood education in America was "a total market failure, and has been, whether we realized it or not, for decades." Over 90 percent of early childhood educators are women, and nearly half are women of color. Paid care work remains unpopular with men, which can be linked to male entitlement to caregiving by women and to "more traditional masculine jobs." The pay for those working in childcare is also low, leaving just over half of childcare workers on government assistance. And due to a high demand and low supply of workers—a problem that could be eased if more men pursued childcare positions—children-to-caregiver ratios are so high that early childhood education work tends to be furious and strenuous. Many flee the field because of these poor conditions.

Childcare costs remain high, and pay remains low, because American policymakers have never recognized childcare as a public good. Childcare is not just a shared, public necessity because it allows parents to work; children are also future laborers, the bodies and minds that will contribute to a robust workforce. Parents are nevertheless left to quietly hammer out individual solutions, often patchworking care between home and daycare centers, preschools, public education, private and community programs, and family members. Parents wind up feeling run into the ground, physically and emotionally taxed beyond measure. Women tend to shoulder that burden. As Jenny Brown writes, "Here in the United States, the labor of bearing and rearing children is done cheaply, with the costs pushed onto the family, to be paid out of our strained wages or added to women's unpaid workload."

In the late 2010s, parents like me didn't always see this as a systemic issue. We held ourselves responsible, figured it out, made it work, or didn't. We exchanged platitudes to make sense of what we were doing: "They're only little once," mothers often said. We laughed off the hectic days or cried alone after putting kids to bed. Drawing on Evelyn Nakano Glenn's book *Forced to Care*, Petersen notes how demoralizing things are for parents and caregivers underneath all the individualistic gusto about making difficult caregiving situations work. Petersen writes, "For so many people, this lack of options—this *coercion* to care—breeds intense resentment of a role that, when chosen of one's own volition, might feel incredibly satisfying." There were elements of that early period of motherhood I found satisfying, even as I felt myself losing control of my life: I loved not only the idea of being around my daughter while she was young, but also the way it fused us. I studied her and taught her how to talk about her feelings, her world; how to give and receive love; how to laugh and sing and color and ask for help and do it yourself and be held. I enjoyed being of service to her.

But in the same way I came to view my confusing early sexual life as something I had brought on myself, I internalized the chaos of those early years of motherhood as a sign of deep personal failure. As much as I knew I was a "good" mother, doing my best work, I felt that I was a bad one. And this only made me increasingly rationalize everything I was doing as *the* right choice, to defend my so-called choices, which I felt had been mostly poor and wrong. In her book on the burgeoning parental anxiety that took hold in the early 2000s, *Perfect Madness: Motherhood in the Age of Anxiety*, Judith Warner writes, "If you have been brought up, all your life, being told you have wonderful choices, you tend, when things go wrong, to assume you made the wrong choices—not to see that the 'choices' given you were wrong in the first place."

That first summer in California I dove headlong into the work of running our apartment as one way to prove both my productivity and my worth. I submerged myself in Pinterest, where I saved tips for reorganizing and redecorating. I read about postpartum mood disorders, most of which I felt I had but feared admitting to, especially since I had long passed the agreed-upon period for diagnosis. I created a whole board dedicated to recipes for green smoothies, along with another I titled "this week" for healthy dinners I wanted to cook that very week. When I felt motivated toward action, or zapped of energy, or fat, I saved workouts and diets. As I had done in pregnancy, I considered how I might make myself better at motherhood by focusing on bodily efficiency. When bills went unpaid and I was reminded of the unsustainability of our financial life, I searched for side hustles and couponing strategies.

I tried to find joy in housework and the general aesthetics of our home, but I also committed to besting myself in caregiving. In the mornings I fitted lettered blocks into cupcake tins for Hannah, then set them out for her to explore. I assembled baskets of color-coded household objects, arranging every yellow item I could find in the house neatly, enticingly, so that when Hannah woke from her nap she would find them clustered there, in the center of the living room carpet, beckoning to her to touch. I imagined one day I would create an elaborate set of something called "busy boxes," plastic containers filled with carefully selected toys and educational challenges that would occupy Hannah for hours, while I wrote or applied for jobs beside her. I would stack my organized, assorted offerings high in the hall closet, where Hannah could retrieve one box each day in the morning, neatly returning it hours later when each of us had completed our shared workdays. I got into Montessori—and the premise of the independent child—and I made lists on my phone of art supplies I never had the time or energy to procure from the Dollar Store. When I felt low because I had lost my temper or yelled, I aggregated inspirational mantras and language to use to help calm Hannah down during tantrums.

Life felt almost manageable when I made plans to do things better. The endless streams of aspirational content that supported this imaginative, futural work also brought me the promise of a home unlike my own—one where everything was beautiful, orderly, spotless, easy. A home I might achieve, someday, if I kept up hope and put in the work. But then I would stumble on a post guided by biblical verse and feel goaded, tricked by the culture of motherhood I was consuming. Throwing my phone down like it was contaminated, I thought about all the images I studied. My life was fading into a string of compulsions, and I could no longer distinguish between what I was doing because I felt it was the right thing to do and what I was doing simply because it fulfilled some image of motherhood at which I had gazed wistfully and for too long.

Women have always been the default domestic engineers, tasked with creating for husbands and children a respite from public life. In this social arrangement, domestic harmony, not just in terms of relationships but also on the level of the senses, becomes a primary measure of maternal success. In her essay "House and Home," Marguerite Duras catalogues the "fantastic challenge a house represents" and how rising to that challenge is understood as a reflection of one's success as a mother. "From the man's point of view," Duras writes, "a woman is a good mother when she turns this discontinuity" between the requirements of childcare and those of household management "into a silent and unobtrusive continuity." The work of converting the mess and chaos of domestic life into comfort—into something called "home," with this labor of upkeep rendered invisible—has long been inseparable from the concept of the "good mother."

Viewing housework as one arm of motherhood is a feature of Western culture, as is men's abdication of responsibility in the domestic sphere, even though, really, cleaning house has little to do with caring for children. In antiquity, however, a man's access to the "good life" of the public sphere—and it was only men who had access to the freedom contained in the polis—depended on the degree to which his body was unencumbered by the labor that took place in his home. This was how servants provided men with freedom: by emancipating them from domestic life. In the Middle Ages, the "soft delights" of home were also intended to counteract the "hardness" of men's work, and women were purveyors of this rich, textural domesticity.

Late capitalism has only made the imperative of achieving domestic cleanliness more urgent, and domestic aesthetics are now wrapped up with personal branding. When we feel under threat, we cling to the security of home, itself eternally linked to the woman's body. As sociologist Kathryn Jezer-Morton has written, our obsession with cozy homes has only "grown in step with our growing feeling of collective precariousness—economic, environmental, social." And the volume of work required to conceal domestic discontinuity has also grown under late-stage capitalism. More stuff amounts to more labor. Housework today involves covering up and dealing with the mess of American hyper-consumerism and waste. Cleaning up, throwing out, and organizing is practical in an era of stuff, but it also remains symbolic and highly gendered. A woman's ability to deal with excess possessions around the house reflects her capacity to provide emotional care to the children and spouse who live there. Mess, on the other hand, is often seen as indicating that something is amiss with the little woman at home. As Duras writes, "A dirty house" can be thought to signify "that the woman is in a dangerous state, a state of blindness."

The moralization of cleanliness has always been gendered—a pure woman has a wholesome home, a wicked woman a filthy one, likely with cats—but the phenomenology of cleaning, and what it offers in the form of domestic catharsis, can also feel, to the homemaker, like a form of rebellion. For many women, Adrienne Rich writes, "Furiously and incessantly cleaning house, which they know will be immediately disorganized by small children," is one way to deal with "the hopelessness of any control of her life which is indoctrinated into so many women." In my first months in California, I didn't rage-clean—my feelings about the world and my life were too nebulous to call it that—but I did use tidying and scrubbing to escape the confines of our apartment, in which I felt increasingly trapped. If I sat down, Hannah would climb all over me, yank my breast out of my shirt. Cleaning was a way to keep my body busy and unavailable—to regain some physical autonomy, or at least the momentary illusion that I could still move about the cabin, and that I was in some sense still free.

Hannah busied herself as I mopped the floors and scoured the old linoleum of our apartment on my hands and knees. I sometimes thought of the feminist artist Mierle Laderman Ukeles, who wrote in her "Manifesto for Maintenance Art 1969" that "maintenance" work, the life-sustaining labors we all must do to keep showing up for collective life, is "a drag" because it "takes all the fucking time." I had studied Ukeles's work before becoming a mother, but now my only outlet for intellectual stimulation was to apply her theories to what was before me. Maintenance work *was* a drag, but mostly because our "culture confers lousy status" on it: "maintenance jobs = minimum wages, housewives = no pay." I tried to take pride in my work at home, to remind myself my labor was valuable, creative, even if it was underappreciated and unpaid—even if this work, historically done by women, had been erased and denigrated. I even got excited about surprising Jon at the end of his disheartening work shifts with my supernatural ability to produce the illusion of composure in our lives, despite knowing things were spinning beyond our reach. He, too, had been pulled into a life that was making him unhappy, a job that would push him further away from both housework and childcare responsibilities, causing a deep rift in our marriage. But we tried to have fun with the absurdity of what our lives had become.

"Honey, I'm home," Jon would say as he tiptoed in late at night. I liked hearing him gasp and tell me how great the apartment looked. But actually, the sly introduction of '50s gender roles into our home made me increasingly depressed, and the pace of keeping up with the mess was backbreaking. Duras offers a sample of a midcentury housewife's day, one that looks a lot like my days in 2016: "In a morning five hours long, she gets the children's breakfasts, washes and dresses them, does the housework, makes the beds, washes and dresses herself, does the shopping, does the cooking, lays the table. In twenty minutes she gives the children their lunch, yelling at them the while, then takes them back to school, does the dishes, does the washing, and so on and so on. Maybe, at about half-past three, she gets to read the paper for half an hour."

The work of quelling what Duras calls the "discontinuity" caused by children felt like an infinite labor. Hannah became more mobile and active. She walked around and pulled things off shelves, laundry out of drawers. When she ate at her highchair, she chucked food over her shoulder. "Lots of women never solve the problem of disorder," Duras writes, "of the house being overrun by the chaos families produce." I couldn't imagine how, in the modern American home, *anyone* solved the problem of the home, and its endless need, ever. I couldn't follow Hannah around fast enough, and I grew frustrated with her childish carelessness. It felt like a sign she didn't value myself, which was quickly becoming an extension of our domestic space.

But that was the goal of cleaning, wasn't it? To disappear myself? When everything runs smoothly, the housewife fades away—becomes the background. Cleanliness maintains the ghostly character of women's work, keeps it systematically hidden. Even critics of capitalist work have failed to take note of the labor that takes place beyond the factory gates. The political philosopher Hannah Arendt pointed out, for instance, that Karl Marx, following public opinion at the time he wrote, characterized the work that took place in the home as unproductive labor, which left "nothing behind." Arendt noted that Marx and many other male philosophers exalted work performed outside the home as the only real form of work, while they characterized domestic work "as parasitical, actually a kind of perversion of labor" because it "did not enrich the world."

Arendt saw this hierarchy of work as a fundamental misunderstanding of what happens in the home—a misunderstanding that arose from the unique temporal features of care work and housework: the labor performed in the home moves so quickly, and produces so rapidly, Arendt wrote, that "its effort is almost as quickly consumed as the effort is spent." Ancient political philosophers, Arendt writes, at least recognized the vital productivity of their servants, who, they believed, left behind "nothing more or less than their masters' freedom or, in modern language, their masters' potential productivity." In antiquity, the work performed in the home was understood as constant, life-sustaining work that always produced: indeed, it produced the very possibility of public productivity; it created the possibility of shared communal life outside the home.

After we moved to California, I started to notice how much of America society was, on the contrary, built around a complete disregard—almost like an intentional erasure!—of women's work in the household and the fact that it bolsters and makes possible all other work. How well hidden was the incredible volume of labor it took to maintain a home and raise children, to keep a society moving—so well hidden, in fact, that I never saw all the labor coming. I expected parenting to be challenging, taxing, life-altering, but in ridiculously minor ways: perhaps I couldn't travel as much or stay out late partying; perhaps I wouldn't get to watch so much TV. Even as a young feminist who researched and studied representations of so-called women's work, who knew such work was undervalued societally and economically—even as the daughter of a single mother who struggled under the weight of motherhood right in front of me—I didn't understand, before I became a parent, how significantly every aspect of society was designed for men with wives.

The paradigm of careerism alone, which requires the complete absenting of children from adult life for approximately forty hours a week, now felt outrageous. But I had seen glimpses before I got pregnant, outlines of a systemic exclusion that now looked darker, more well-defined. Academia, for instance, with all its attendant disembodiment and intellectual competition, was a masculine arena. Many of my colleagues had suffered ailments of the body in their extreme commitment to the life of the mind—boils on ass cheeks, depression, anxiety, mysterious digestive issues. Everyone had houses run amok with unclean laundry and fast food, and everyone drank too much—including me—trying to shut their bodies up so they could work. Intellectual work *required* a denial of the body and home in favor of the mind, a tradition rooted in that ancient separation between political, intellectual life and domesticity. Women in my old department—I learned through emails after we moved to California—were often advised to defer having children if they wanted to get jobs, or to consider not having them at all if they wanted to pursue tenure track positions. Some, whether they had children or not, were receiving guidance to hire domestic workers to clean their homes so they could get ahead.

As a mother I guessed that all this physical movement put toward taming our home was supposed to add up to a life, an identity, but it was a life that seemed, as Duras puts it, "to have been written down and described already"—a role I was playing "inevitably and almost unconsciously." Of course the role had been written long ago. Silvia Federici argues that women's desires for marriage and motherhood are not informed by biological or sexual destiny, they are coerced. Under capitalism, Federici writes, women are taught to pursue their sexual development by marrying and bearing children, rather than through pursuing their own pleasure. This gets capitalism "a hell of a lot of work almost for free." Rather than organizing against their own exploitation, women are taught to view the work performed in the home as a condition of femininity, and are encouraged by the mythology of love to seek out heteronormative family life as "the best thing in life." But both Wife and Mother are forms of work, not identity positions. And although we often develop loving relationships on the job, because women are pressured into marriage and motherhood from such a young age it can be hard to see the difference between what we long for and what we have been told will make us good.

It can also be hard to disentangle the love we find in such roles from the work those roles require. Before Jon and I had Hannah, we often griped about how the parents we knew complained about caring for children. We swore to never treat our children this way—like they were such a problem. Once I became a parent myself, though, I saw these complaints as part of a hidden labor struggle—as complaints not about children, but about the daily grind of American parenthood, which is not an inevitable part of raising children and has nothing to do with the love we have for our children. American parenting in particular has been set up to manipulate and abuse women's bodies and psyches, to put them to work for free and call it love, then to gaslight them into thinking they have done something wrong that led them there. But women's powerlessness has always been the point.

Not long after I lost my virginity in high school, I had a crush on a shy but popular football player who never showed much interest in me. At a party one night I ended up in a bedroom with him, on a mattress that was for some reason unmade, without sheets. I knew he was a virgin, and I felt I had been chosen for a special role, one that I thought, if I played the part right, could improve my marginal social status and pull me out of the loneliness I so often felt. I imagined us holding hands at school at lunch, popular girls looking on. I imagined us falling in love, holding each other close, laughing and talking. But in the bedroom that night, he didn't kiss me. He just hovered over me and thrusted, and I focused on the feeling of the rough mattress underneath my back. After he came, I smiled demurely as I dressed, but he never spoke to me again, not even later at the party. It was a plan, I later realized, that had been concocted by his friends, other boys who knew how much I liked him.

American motherhood felt like that: like a plan devised by men. Something I wanted, then got, only to find I had been lured in by a group of boys who didn't care at all how I ended up and who were nowhere on the scene. Sure, I had consented to motherhood. I had *asked for it*. I had even desperately *wanted it*—in the same way I had craved the touch of that boy. There was even pleasure involved in putzing around the house with Hannah, and in the laughs I shared with her as we splashed around the water table on our patio—a purchase I had made hoping to keep her busy when it was just the two of us, at home alone. But my housewifery also felt forced, compulsory, staged. And the experience of getting what I wanted was immediately tainted by what I hadn't known before consenting.

Motherhood feels like a script written for women by men because it is. The American economy has for centuries been shaped around the exploitation of unpaid labor, which has benefitted men not only in their ability to excuse themselves from the hard and dirty work of taking care of kids and the home, but financially. "Capitalism thrives on women's unpaid labor in the home because women's care work supports lower taxes," Kristen Ghodsee writes in *Why Women Have Better Sex Under Socialism*. Offloading the cost of childcare and the social safety net on to families has historically hurt women most. But for men, the economic advantages abound. "Lower taxes mean higher profits for those already at the top of the income ladder—mostly men." Meanwhile, women with children remain systematically cut out of the income ladder. "Choose your data source, and you find the same story," Ghodsee writes. "Unemployment and poverty plague women with children." Yet if American women's labor around the house and caring for relatives were compensated it would be worth an estimated $10,900,000,000,000,000.

Capitalism "created a true masterpiece at the expense of women," Federici writes. In the transition away from feudalism to capitalism in Europe, enclosure eliminated the commons, which were foundational to female social and economic life. Women found themselves "increasingly confined to reproductive labor at the very time when this work was being completely devalued," writes Federici. The "unity of production and reproduction" that had been typical of subsistence economies in Europe ended, and these forms of work were sexually differentiated. No longer "the village midwife, medic, soothsayer or sorceress," seeing their own disempowerment, "women holding pitchforks and scythes" protested this new economic order in huge numbers, which led to the elimination of legal protections they previously experienced under their husbands, and to the arrest and imprisonment of many women involved in the resistance. Unruly women were a lethal threat to capitalism, and their lives were continually restricted, as evidenced by the witch hunts, which reached their peak between 1580 and 1630—an era of gendered punishment that pushed women further out of public life and into the home and that destroyed relationships between men and women as well as "a universe of practices, beliefs, and social subjects whose existence was incompatible with capitalist work discipline."

"How much does this really have to do with capitalism," Rich asks, and how much has to do with the system of power that "predated capitalism and has survived under socialism—patriarchy?" Most intellectual paradigms, Rich points out, including Marxism and psychoanalysis, have historically "assumed the traditional division of labor within the family," leaving them unable to account for the timeless problem of "the attitudes—acknowledged and hidden—held toward women by men." Those attitudes continuously affirm that women are "first of all Mother who has to be possessed, reduced, controlled, lest she swallow him back into her dark caves, or stare him into stone." Even before the transition to capitalism, philosophies about women's natural predisposition for different types of work proliferated. In her cultural history of touch, *The Deepest Sense*, Constance Classen writes that in the Middle Ages women's bodies were considered to be colder than men's, "like uncooked dough," so women were advised "to stay warm indoors" performing domestic work. Martin Luther thought women's broad hips and wide haunches made their bodies ideal for sitting at home.

The division between reason, understood as masculine, and the senses, seen as feminine, helped justify women's subordinate position in society and supported links between women and domesticity. Even the senses themselves were divided and coded by gender, as premodern bestiaries confirm. The eagle and the stag, associated with the higher-order, external sense of sight, were masculine, whereas the tortoise, associated with the supposedly lower sense of touch, and therefore with women, "suggested the quintessential homebody, the woman who never leaves the walls of her house." The spider represented woman either "as housewife, spinning and homemaking," suitably using her "covetous touch" to care for the home, or "as temptress, trapping her (male) prey in a silken web of seduction." Without her even trying, the woman's body posed a "tactile threat to men—the mere fact of its being pleasurably touchable made it seem a peril." Homemaker or slut, we have only ever had two options, both of which urge our bodies into shadows of domesticity.

As Rich notes, socialism hasn't treated women much better than capitalism, given that "in no socialist country does the breakdown of the division of labor extend to bringing large numbers of men into child-care." But other countries have done better than the United States in terms of de-gendering childcare and housework, especially in the past few decades, creating leave policies that encourage men to be more active caregivers and that de-stigmatize part-time work for parents of young children. Women in the US, however, still live with two sets of impossible demands, trying to appear as both "the unencumbered worker and the ever-present mother." In the UK, Jacqueline Rose writes in *Mothers*, "participation of mothers in political and public life [is] seen as the exception." But why, Rose asks, is "being the props of neo-liberalism"—whether by recommitting ourselves at home, or by "leaning in" at work—supposed to be "the highest form of belonging and agency [women] can expect"? Feminist sociologist Angela McRobbie calls these limited aspirations the "neoliberal intensification of mothering," epitomized by those "perfectly turned-out, middle-class, mainly white mothers, with their perfect jobs, perfect husbands and marriages, whose permanent glow of self-satisfaction is intended to make all women who do not conform to that image (because they are poorer or black or their lives are just more humanly complicated) feel like total failures."

Perhaps because it's so difficult to envision a society in which the personal and the public are not assumed to be separate, and are not coded by gender, women continue to struggle with how they might break free of centuries of associations between their bodies and the home, without simply leaving the domestic scene altogether. In the 2010s, seemingly successful working mothers helped position free enterprise as a fantastical path toward femme freedom, offering an escape from the cataclysm of American motherhood under patriarchal capitalism without ever having to speak patriarchal capitalism's name, much less question the economic system. But the system itself stayed largely the same. In a 2012 article for *Salon*, Rebecca Traister argued presciently that the concept of "having it all" upon which that era rested should be struck from the feminist lexicon forever, because it was "a misrepresentation of a revolutionary social movement" that was "conflating liberation with satisfaction" on the individual level. Such a conflation encouraged women to blame feminism or themselves when they felt disempowered, unsupported, or "tugged in ways that she perceives her husband does not." And yet she—the illusion of the self-satisfied working mom—persisted.

While I was struggling with my own "choices" around work and motherhood in the mid-2010s, "women's empowerment" reached a peak, with marketing experts "sanitizing" the term "empowerment" away from its radical roots and making it instead, as Koa Beck writes in *White Feminism*, "transactional—something you could buy, obtain, and experience as a product rather than an amorphous feeling that rushed in from challenging power." Feminism ceased being seen as a collective struggle, and instead was viewed more often as an individual quest for fulfillment, sometimes pursued without accountability to others. The effect was that the postfeminism of the 2010s picked up where midcentury anxieties about feminine idleness had left off. Careerist empowerment was all about self-discipline, the performance of productivity and busyness, with work outside the home seen as the ultimate source of freedom—something all women could achieve if they just threw their backs into it. The internet eventually even brought a certain sparkle to the hustle. But as Anne-Marie Slaughter wrote in a cover story for *The Atlantic* in 2012, a larger problem would remain: "the way America's economy and society are currently structured."

Bubbling under the surface and not getting quite as much airtime, according to Traister, was "a story that academics and feminists, including Arlie Hochschild, Linda Hirshman and Leslie Bennetts, have been telling for years about the distances feminism has yet to travel when it comes to reforming the domestic sphere and changing retro-male workplace culture." Feminism was not to blame, even though the movement was often demonized, as evidenced by the "sad white babies with mean feminist mommies" trope that seemed to inspire the *Atlantic* cover for Slaughter's essay—a faceless career woman carrying her toddler in her leather briefcase. Our economic system makes good "money out of our cooking, smiling, and fucking," Federici reminds us, and our participation in that system has been the result of limited options, not the failures of feminism. Women have participated in such an economy not because it was our nature, but "because we did not have any other choice."

The structure of the American family has always placed Dad on top and Mom somewhere near the bottom, but such a hierarchy is not inherent to the work of raising children. Long before the days of Instagram-perfect homes, Pinterest organization boards, and intensive parenting, the homemaker was a boring, busy lady: "the ideal woman and wife—passive, obedient, thrifty, of few words, always busy at work, chaste." Put in her place by the eighteenth century, after two hundred years of state terrorism against women, the housewife was principled and hardworking, the inverse of the image of women during the witch hunts—"mentally weak, unsatiably lusty, rebellious, insubordinate, incapable of self-control." Housewives went to work in service to the family, which was not a precapitalist structure but, in Federici's words, "a creation of capital for capital," created on the heels of epidemics, overwork, and proletarian struggles in Europe in the nineteenth century, which made it clear that a "more stable and disciplined workforce" was needed.

As that institution, however, met its crisis in America in the middle of the next century, Black feminists often looked at the vital intimacy of the family in different terms. In "Revolutionary Parenting," bell hooks wrote in 1984 that if Black women's voices had been more central to the second-wave feminist conversation, motherhood "would not have been named a serious obstacle to our freedom as women." Whereas white feminists tended to be concerned with making demands relating to paid work and the desire to break *into* work outside the home, Black feminists saw domestic and familial work "as humanizing labor, work that affirms [Black women's] identity as women, as human beings showing love and care, the very gestures of humanity white supremacist ideology claimed black people were incapable of expressing." Black women had always worked outside their own homes, and saw more liberatory promise in kinship. Most second-wave women's liberationists, however, as hooks wrote, didn't yet see waged work as alienated labor—as disaffecting, extractive, and devoid of care.

But another major sticking point in second-wave feminism that stuck around through the late 2010s was the underexplored concept of choice. How much of our lives was in our control and how much was shaped by the institutions we had inherited? My own frustration with this question radicalized me further, as I began to see how unhinged social and economic structures were from the material conditions of parenthood in America, and how those structures were nevertheless shaping my life. Valerie Solanas began her cutthroat 1967 invective against male control, *SCUM Manifesto*, declaring, "Life in this society being, at best, an utter bore and no aspect of society being at all relevant to women, there remains to civic-minded, responsible, thrill-seeking females only to overthrow the government, eliminate the money system, institute complete automation and destroy the male sex." When I first moved back to California I spent a lot of time blasting upbeat nursery rhymes in the car while driving to parks, feigning interest in pretend play, and designing cutesie toddler activities at home, but through this cloud of artificial joy, I also began to feel that a total war on society might be the only answer to the complete erasure of domestic and reproductive labor and to the disillusionment I also felt with work outside the home.

Motherhood radicalized me, but I was too caught up in trying to get by to institute any rebellion. That year I started working at my sister's home daycare for $12 per hour (roughly matching the national average income for childcare work) and doing school drop-offs and pickups for my sister's kids for $10 per hour, sometimes driving around town for more than two hours a day. Driving home after hard days taking care of six or seven kids in my sister's condo, listening to galvanizing pop songs about never giving up, I sometimes found myself weeping quietly in the driver's seat, overcome by unfulfilled ambition and an unlocatable urge to get free of the confines of my life. I wanted to think. I wanted to write. Really, I wanted to do anything that felt like a life I had chosen. Peeking into the rear-view mirror, seeing Hannah looking out the window and taking in the world, I thought about how to start again, how to not give up, how to stay with her, or to leave. "Your kids are watching," one meme had told me. Motherhood also, for a time, broke me.

For a while I imagined I might start a little bakery out of my home. I would call it Smash Cakes, and make only those little milestone confections into which kids face-planted when they tasted sugar for the first time on first birthdays. Smash Cakes wasn't such a terrible stretch. Sometimes, when the discontinuity of our home became too much, I let Hannah scoop and measure sugar, dump it in our one, too-small, aluminum mixing bowl, then hold tight to a hand blender that skittered around as she creamed the sweetened butter. We rarely baked cakes, but we had mastered a cookie dough recipe for which we used both salted butter and added salt. I worked hard to let myself embrace the mess, flour snowing down all over the kitchen, sticking to the soles of our feet.

"Keep it in the bowl," I'd say, rushing in to hold Hannah's little hand in place as she steered the rogue mixer. When the dough came together, she stirred in the chocolate chips, then plunged her hands into the bowl, happily licking the sticky-sweet webbing from between her fingers as we thwacked malformed balls on to a cookie sheet. When I was a girl, my mother and I made break-and-bake cookies. She always worked late hours outside the home, jobs she hated for men she also hated. She had very little time for me, and while, so many years later, I could not fault her for how she tried to make a life for herself in a man's world, I wanted something else for myself and my daughter. I wanted to fill my time with Hannah with sense memories I did not have, and I loved making cookies with her, smelling her dirty hair afterward.

But I loved other things, too. In a section of her manifesto titled "Personal Part," Ukeles wrote: "I am an artist. I am a woman. I am a wife. I am a mother (random order). I do a hell of a lot of washing, cleaning, cooking, renewing, supporting, preserving, etc." Ukeles continued, "I 'do' Art." I 'do' Art." I sometimes tried to visualize the hierarchies of my identity while Hannah smeared chocolate on me—to arrange who I was and the kinds of work I did, and wanted to do, into some less random order. It can be so hard for women to know who they are, what ranks where, with the world always telling us how to be. But sometimes I could almost see it: I thought perhaps I *could* make a life that way, turning domesticity into art.

BODY

I N THE EARLIEST DAYS OF MOTHERHOOD, I mouthed Hannah's cheeks, wanting to consume her. I studied her soft hands, thinking about how, for so many years and in so many contexts, I would hold them, until they became leathered and spotted, like mine. I found this a particularly miraculous thought: to consider the immeasurable stretch of time through which our bodies would continually come together, mine there to support hers as it grew—to console, to encourage, to keep safe. But over time, my child became an ocean of need. She consumed me.

Duras writes that in motherhood "a woman gives her body over to her child" until "they're on her as they might be on a hill, in a garden; they devour her, hit her, sleep on her." Hannah's touch began as something invited, but eventually every request, every tug, felt like a violation. "She lets herself be devoured," Duras writes. "Nothing like this happens with fathers."

I didn't want to be devoured. I tried very hard not to be devoured. I would not say I let it happen. If Jon had been able to spend more time with Hannah in her early life, had he not had to leave us to work long hours, perhaps I wouldn't have been so eaten up: perhaps he would have been more of a draw, emotionally and energetically, more of a comfort object for Hannah; perhaps he would have known the quirks for soothing her that I knew. In her book on the neurobiological effects of parenting, Chelsea Conaboy argues that sustained care work makes us more attentive parents by changing how our brains function—one reason policies like extended paid leave and flexible work schedules are important for de-gendering care work. But by the time we moved to California, Hannah, who was still breastfeeding, was completely dependent on me, and as Jon and my work arrangements grew increasingly traditional, Hannah's preference for me in times of crisis only grew. Jon became fixed in his role as provider, and I was fixed in mine as pacifier, peacemaker, soother.

The more the gendered division of labor in our home revealed itself, however—and the more it weighed on me—the more I found myself defaulting to the idea that I had asked for all of it. I hadn't managed my career or my relationship with my spouse or my child correctly. I hadn't pushed bottle feeding enough or pushed Jon and Hannah to find their way together. Maybe, actually, I had just married the wrong man or never should have been a mother at all. The mental acrobatics of parenting, the chaos of keeping track of what I should and shouldn't be doing, the fucking up or trying to convince myself, the constant internal and external policing I was doing, even in the most tender, intimate moments with Hannah, were a chorus of voices inhabiting my body. They told me how to feel, when to hold my tongue, what to say, and what my face should look like when I said it. Now firmly implanted under my skin, they told me who to be. I felt physically and psychically taken.

I was devoured, in other words, by a certain control I felt I needed to keep over my facial expressions, my thoughts, and my words, just as much as I was overrun by the physicality of caring for my child. When Hannah was two months old, I had my first taste of stinging maternal regret—the kind I would feel so many times in years to come—that made me wonder whether I had accidentally crossed some threshold, gone past a point of no return, done something to both me and Hannah that I could never take back. When, less than two months after I gave birth, I turned thirty, I organized a small get-together in Buffalo with friends at a nearby park. Determined to drink wine in the sun and "wear" my napping baby like an accessory, I brought with me something called a Moby—the longest piece of fabric I had ever seen. Hannah was tired and inconsolable, and I grew hot and red-faced, sweating while she yowled, as I tried to tie us both up in the wrap. Everyone pretended not to stare at me, and I was embarrassed by my inability to find each end of the lengthy piece of cloth. As I fumbled to pull up an instructional video, Jon fretted and held my plastic cup of wine, not knowing how to help. "What can I do?" was his new refrain as I juggled around. A mother-poet I hardly knew calmly and gently swooped in, took hold of the Moby, then tied and twisted the material around me as if by magic. In her faux womb, Hannah fell right to sleep.

I bounced around, patting Hannah's rounded back, and the mother-poet and I talked. The subject of Attachment Parenting, a philosophy I embraced at the time wholeheartedly, came up. In the early '90s, when I was coming of age, AP gurus Bill and Martha Sears had picked up on Dr. Benjamin Spock's popular emphasis on attachment theory, secularizing the Christian ideals of maternal suffering and sacrifice. Attachment theory, from which the parenting philosophy emerged, is broadly rooted in psychoanalytic approaches to child development that see an individual's sense of self as developed within the family unit. Such theories frequently rely on the image of the nuclear family, with the mother figured as a passive, primary caregiver and the father as a kind of stand-in for cultural and political ethics—the active authority in the house.

Psychoanlyst John Bowlby, considered the father of attachment theory, believed that attachment was an innate need—necessary within the first three years of life. Writing at midcentury, he emphasized the child's need for monotropy, or attachment to one primary caregiver, namely, the mother, above all else, and claimed that "maternal deprivation" could be blamed for later social, psychological, and cognitive difficulties. Bowlby was criticized later by feminists for his sexism, but also by many thinkers of his day, including the cultural anthropologist Margaret Mead, who noted that Bowlby's vision of the mother was particular to the Global North. But Bowlby—who likened the effect on the child of a full-time working mother to that of war and famine—was less interested in cultural, political, or institutional forces that shape children as they come of age, such as racism, capitalism, and white supremacy. Even if it were possible to de-gender his emphasis on the mother, many problems with his theories remain.

Dr. Benjamin Spock and, later, AP gurus William and Martha Sears, nevertheless popularized attachment theory further, claiming that good moms beget good children with secure attachment—gold stars all around. Decades later, attachment theories like the kind that undergird parenting advice still categorize people who did not receive attentive, loving parenting into a range of attachment styles, including "avoidant" and "anxious." Such theories, though, are a bit like a personality test: these categorizations mirror our internal realities back at us and give us a comforting set of classifications through which we might understand tendencies that previously felt confusing or deviant. They provide recognition, a way of making sense. But that doesn't mean they provide us with the original image of what they reflect. Theories of how human relationships evolve and take shape may give us language to describe our experiences, but they can also trap us in cultural attitudes that are neither fixed nor liberatory. What may be more valuable is recognizing how we turn to certain disciplines—for instance, psychology—to confirm the status quo rather than to offer us tools to challenge what we consider to be "normal."

In an essay for *Gawker* on how Americans grew so attached to attachment theory, Danielle Carr, a scholar who studies capitalism and neuroscience, writes that "attachment theory offers the consolations of the heuristic, a kind of rough-draft outline for a larger essay on our internal life. This is true of almost any Grand Theory of Everything that explains the unknowable—in this case, the interiority of the other—using a few rough-hewn concepts." Attachment theory is nevertheless used to explain both parenting (usually relying on the mother-child dyad) and romance (usually relying on the man-woman dyad), which furthers the theory's hetero-patriarchal feel and allows us to blame even our sexual and romantic relationship problems on our mothers.

At best, however, attachment theory is merely a tool for explaining how growing up in a hetero-patriarchal culture tends to create certain personality types, outcomes that are loosely linked to how our caregivers behaved when we were kids, or how we perceive them to have behaved years later, when we grow into adults and consult the attachment playbooks. At worst, attachment theory can be used to reify bad behavior that emerges from living in a sexist society, tracing it all back to Mom and Dad—but usually Mom. "What are the odds that the vast majority of heterosexuals would sort so neatly into what look like gender-coded slots—the women frantic for explanations for their romantic woes self-identifying as 'anxious' and slapping the 'avoidant' label on guys who seem to be just not that into them? Does this remind you of anything?" Carr asks. "The whole thing smacks of gender."

Not surprising, given that the theories we have available on how human development, psychology, and relationships both form and function are all inherited from white men. "I think a lot of that science is bad science," Kate Manne has said about the sexism that continues to plague contemporary studies on how men and women supposedly perceive the world differently because of biological difference. "There's no control group in a patriarchal culture," Manne points out. "There's no group of women raised such as not to have sexist theories and misogynistic enforcement mechanisms operating on them. Of course some differences will show up. But it doesn't lead to an enhanced kind of epistemic state, where we know something interesting and new about two different groups." The same is true for how we interpret the science that says secure attachments with our mothers makes us well-adjusted later in life. Who is to say this is not the result of growing up living in a family that felt "normal," judged by standards that relegate women to positions of inferiority in motherhood?

AP was nevertheless having a heyday in the mid-2010s, and I was fully on board. On the Searses' website, I had read about mothers metaphorized as emotional gas stations where children returned to "fill up." The Searses encouraged nursing mothers to know "when to say 'yes' and when to say 'no'" to the baby, but didn't offer much advice for how to tap into what they called "the wisdom to say 'yes' to yourself when you need help." At the same time they also told parents to set aside their needs to "raise babies the way nature intended" through the "5 B's": birth-bonding, breastfeeding, babywearing, bed sharing, and being responsive.

In our conversation at the park, the mother-poet mentioned her reservations about AP philosophy, which I had until then mostly treated as gospel. She took issue with how the Searses emphasized the mother as the primary figure for attachment, leaving no room for fathers or queer or adoptive or other non-nuclear family arrangements. I had always been firm in conversations with Jon about my goal to refuse a gendered division of labor in our house, but there were some elements of parenting, especially in the early days, that I felt belonged to my body—as the gestational parent—alone. Breastfeeding was one of them, but so was everything that came along with that labor: holding, calming, settling. The mother-poet's qualm, was one I had perhaps not wanted to consider, for how it might implicate me, and Jon, in our failure to reach a more equitable, more feminist arrangement: even in the earliest days of motherhood, others can provide the same care a gestational parent can.

I suppose I wanted to believe there was a reason why I always seemed to know what Jon didn't—a reason that wasn't entirely cultural, or personal. It made it easier not to blame him, to not hold him responsible for his inability to calm Hannah down when she cried or couldn't sleep. But we were also up against decades of our own very different socializations. Jon had been raised to be an empathetic man, but he had never tended to babies or kids as a line of work; I had. And I think I wanted, on some level, to buy into the idea of my own maternal instinct because it gave me special access to Hannah. The conversation with that mother-poet, however, flagged for me a question that was becoming hard to ignore: how many elements of my relationship with my child had already been written by the stories and ideas I had internalized passively all my life?

I was continually trying to slot myself into some version of parenting that seemed like it reflected the person I was or wanted to be, which often felt debilitating, as I feared I was always veering irreparably off course. Early 2000s parenting was "all about performance," Judith Warner writes in *Perfect Madness*. Motherhood became a religion, a theology, a devotional practice fueled by "living in an age of such incredible competition and insecurity—financial insecurity, job insecurity, *life* insecurity, generally." The next decade did not fare much better in terms of parental anxiety. In her own book about anxious mothering, Kim Brooks writes, "When I wasn't worrying about fevers and mucus, there were plenty of other uncertainties to keep the cortisol flowing." On top of all the sources of worry, there were also "at least a hundred different ways of responding, countless methods and approaches for nurturing these little people I loved so deeply," such that "every choice that needed making, every path not taken," Brooks said, gave her, too, "a tiny tinge of fear, a ripple of anxiety passing through" that came from "the infinite ways it seemed possible to mess up."

One of the narratives I had internalized without much thinking about it was that I should give my body over to my child at any cost. Yes, I owed my baby my professional ambitions—"They're only little once," the mothers of the world whispered whenever I doubted my overcommitment to motherhood—but I also owed my child my arms, legs, breasts, face, thoughts, and emotions. Motherhood, it seemed, required a complete surrendering of my body. But in reality, the idea that mothers should make their bodies and minds completely available to their children at all times is a culturally and historically specific one, emerging from the alienated and isolated conditions in which caregiving takes place in America.

When I started working at my sister's home-based daycare—the only job I could find where I could earn some money with Hannah by my side, therefore canceling out the expense of childcare—Hannah's and my bond grew stronger, but so did the physical and psychological strain of care. On my shifts, I had six or seven kids spread between the living room and patio of my sister's condo, while my sister was off running errands or carting her own kids about town. Caring for multiple children was not a line of work at which I excelled, but because I had nannied years earlier—a job for which, as for this one, my only qualification was my gender—I knew the routines. There were lots of needs to which I had to attend: toy disputes, diapers, potty training, separation anxiety, nap schedules, snacks, and meals. The cleaning and the caretaking were unremitting, and I struggled to stay on the schedule my sister had provided, which wasn't even rigid.

Every morning I lined the kids up by the door, then we all walked to the park down the street, me pushing a double stroller in which the two littlest children sat and beside which four others ambled, loosely holding on to colorful safety straps that were meant to keep them close, but just left them all jockeying for position. I carried Hannah by strapping her to my chest, which grew wet with a mixture of sweat and milk. Sometimes she scratched at me asking to nurse as we walked. If I declined, she cried the whole walk to the park.

When the kids got hurt or missed their moms or lost their shit for no discernable reason, I did my best to hold them, running back and forth from one climbing apparatus at the park to another, trying to avoid a call-the-parents fall. As I did, Hannah hung out on my leg, making her possession of my body known. After an hour of physical activity, I walked the kids back to the condo, then cooked lunch in a frenzy, wiping snot and breaking up arguments while lunch baked or boiled, tripping over toys and baby gates, Hannah distraught on my hip. I channeled scripts I had found on mommy blogs and parenting advice boards, which I had aggregated on Pinterest, and in time, they replaced my own voice.

After the kids picked through their macaroni, I cleaned up whatever did not stick to the floor and let the rest harden for later, then I walked the kids upstairs to my sister's bedroom, lined them up again, this time for fresh diapers, popped pacifiers and blankets in their hands, and sat among all the small bodies cuddled on mats, wishing the room were darker, clenching my fists, trying not to lose it. I was always trying not to lose it. The children tossed and turned and giggled and muttered, and I wondered if I had some deep-seated problem: I hated all the kids in those moments and wanted to shake them. "Go to sleep," I growled under my breath, pleading. I patted warm, damp, small-muscled backs with one hand until my arm was sore, feigning tenderness as best I could, so they would pass out.

Through it all I carted Hannah around with my other arm, keeping her quiet on my breast. She always took the longest to fall asleep, unnerved by all the jostling around. Once all the other kids were asleep, I bounced and patted her. Her eyes fluttered open, shut, open, shut; now she was awake again because I had foolishly tried to put her down on her mat. Finally, I tiptoed downstairs, in tears or rage— who knew anymore? I was so worried about making it to the next hour then, I could hardly breathe. My sister, seeing my struggle to find work with a one-year-old at home, had offered me the job as a favor, and I wanted to do right by her. But caring for so many children alone also felt profoundly high stakes. I sank onto my sister's couch, escaping into my phone, watching the minutes tick by. In less than an hour I would have to wake up the kids so they would sleep for their parents at bedtime.

During my shifts I rarely remembered to eat, and over time I starved myself almost as a matter of course—to lose the persistent baby weight, but also to keep to the day's schedule. By avoiding my own needs, I could be more attentive to the kids. So I made ignoring my body a habit. By the time parents came for their kids at pickup, my hair was wild, my stretched-out maternity clothes stained with equivocal substances, my disarray verging on the cinematic. I sat disheveled on my sister's couch, vibrating, Hannah on my lap. I let her smush my lips between her fingers, stuff her hands into my bra, pinch a nipple, tug it out, and bring it to her lips.

Working at the daycare, I came to see how difficult it is to work in childcare, and how unprepared and untrained I was for the highly skilled work. But there were small pleasures to be found along the way: drinking coffee while the kids sleepily stumbled around in pajamas on my sister's little patio in the morning fog, watching them sell ice cream to each other from behind a kitchen cupboard door. The work was more draining and taxing than any job I had ever had, but I enjoyed chitchatting with parents as they came and went, which helped me feel less alone in the fear and overwhelm that now characterized my life. Beyond those conversations with parents, I rarely spoke more than a few words to anyone over the age of four.

Childcare had its own special fury and madness, but there were elements of it that magnified the small issues I was coming up against parenting at home. When Hannah and I were in our apartment together, Jon away at work with our one car, we did toddler activities like learning how to hold a crayon or playing with water and a cup. If I was tired, I lay on the floor of her room and let her pat me to sleep, then tuck me in with a thin muslin baby blanket. She ferried each of her stuffed animals over to me one by one, her ponytail bobbing as she stroked my back and shushed me. "Nigh, nigh, mommy," she'd say. "Go sleepy." She ordered me to protest while she turned off the lights, tugged her blackout curtains closed, and left the room. I did as I was told, eyes closed, half awake, crying out for her: "Mommy, Mommy!" Sometimes I fell asleep, waking minutes later in a panic to check she was okay. I could hear her busying herself with inexplicit domestic work in the play kitchen we kept in the hallway, moving things around, muttering frustrations. When she tired of her game, she ascended me, requesting books on laps, face as car track, a ride about the apartment, more breast. I turned my body fully over to the labor of care.

I was spellbound by my child's presence, totally addicted to mulling over every part of her body as she lay in my arms—her fat legs and arms, which fit right in my closed palm; her pursed lips, always a little blistered from where she suckled me; her skin, which felt like silk. But the amount of time I spent caring for others now outnumbered the amount of time I spent caring for myself, and when it all felt like too much—too much touch, too much posturing, too much meeting demands, too much trying to say the right thing and be *nice nice nice*—I tried to gently push Hannah off, to distract her, to get her interested in something around the apartment other than me, so I could have a moment alone. She, however, had a willful spirit and never liked being told what to do. And I was noncommittal, because I still believed that I *should* put all her needs and desires before mine.

As a mother I felt the way I had felt as a young woman: if I just made myself into an object that was accommodating and agreeable, perhaps I could fill my role. In my twenties, I had found methods for dissociating during sex: I studied corners of the room while men got themselves off inside me; I listened to their heavy breathing, calculating how much longer, moaning here and there to help them along, moving my hips methodically or going limp. "Most of our sexual encounters are spent in calculations," Silvia Federici writes. "We sigh, sob, gasp, pant, jump up and down in bed, but in the meantime our mind keeps calculating 'how much': how much of ourselves can we give before we lose or undersell ourselves, how much will we get in return." How much longer.

Motherhood too was filled with an unbearable sense of calculation—of waiting, of pushing my body to the brink of what it could take, of counting down the minutes, of doing what I did not want to do, trying to get to the end of the day, just to do it all over again. It all stirred memories of sidelining my own desires, and of waiting for others to finish taking what they wanted from me. The first year we spent in California I gave my body over at the daycare, and when I went home, sitting to nurse or play or talk with Hannah, I let her too have her way with me, wondering whether life, for some women, was just a series of moments in which we grit our teeth and watch the clock.

Back then, my body was a curio, claimed and set aside by my child's request. I was utterly confused about how to set limits with my child in a way that wouldn't forever damage the unseeable outer reaches of her psyche. The parenting advice I located online, which confirmed that I was solely responsible for everything that might someday go wrong in my child's adult life, didn't help. But I tried to take a more active role in moderating the use of my body. Finding the language, however, proved difficult. During the day, I abided by other, more palatable advice found on the internet: I set *boundaries*, and I took up pointed refrains, ones I heard spoken by mothers at the daycare as they wrestled children off their backs at drop-off and pick-up. When I sat on the couch at home after a long day, and Hannah scaled me, I said, "Mommy is not a jungle gym." I was a mother, not a plaything.

But growing up in the '90s and early 2000s, I had received the message that my body *was* a plaything. And now, when I told Hannah I needed a break, it was hard to locate what exactly I needed a break from. I had read about feeling "touched out" in parenting forums online, but the material I found didn't fully explain what I was feeling or how to respond. At the time, the physical overstimulation some parents felt was usually linked to breastfeeding mothers. One 2016 article for La Leche League described the feeling as a mix of anxiety, claustrophobia, and "guilt over feeling irritated by your loved ones." I was still breastfeeding, so that tracked. But the definition didn't offer much of a solution.

I considered weaning Hannah and had been actively working with Jon for months on eliminating the last, lingering night feed. But I worried that any effort to cleave my breast from my one-year-old's mouth would be hard to execute, given the constant proximity of our bodies during the day—a problem related to the availability of affordable childcare. The La Leche League article, however, also implied that perhaps the problem was even more complex than that: the author traced touched-out-ness not only to breastfeeding but also to mothers' being "the vehicle baby goes everywhere with" and the parent who worries about giving her baby "secure attachment." Though I had grown skeptical of the attachment parenting movement's religious overtones and its emphasis on mothers as always the primary source of care, with no society or community to speak of in sight, I still felt that cultivating a strong attachment with my child was the goal above all else, the one to which all parents should aspire. But given my increasing isolation, it was also all I could think about.

Parenting philosophies that rely on the image of the nuclear family isolated from the culture at large place a heavy emotional burden on the behavior of parents, rather than on communities and governmental policy, and beg suspension of disbelief with respect to how networks of care, cultural imagery, gender relations, ideology, and social and economic systems also shape children, families, and adult relationships. Still, the advice drawn from this canon and widely circulated on the internet becomes, for many parents, an invasive series of earworms, especially for those who have grown up in a rape culture that urges them toward questioning their own voices and their own authority over their lives.

In the late 2010s, Attachment Parenting also fueled a broader movement toward so-called "gentle parenting." As Jessica Winter wrote in a piece for the *New Yorker* titled "The Harsh Realm of 'Gentle Parenting,'" gentle parenting is an umbrella term for any number of non-disciplinary approaches to raising kids. "In its broadest outlines," Winter writes, "gentle parenting centers on acknowledging a child's feelings and the motivations behind challenging behavior, as opposed to correcting the behavior itself." But the approach often gets disconnected from its sociopolitical and economic context. By 2022, when Winter penned that essay, "fatigue" was setting in for many parents concerning "the deference to a child's every mood, the strict maintenance of emotional affect."

Whether or not strict maintenance of affect is the real key to gentle parenting, the sheer volume of advice I consumed led me to feel that fatigue, long before I could articulate it. Motherhood was an abduction, like landing in front of some strange alien spectacle in which I was pushed constantly to report for duty, to *behave*. I wanted to tear all these hands and ideas off my body. The only thing that gave me comfort was finding, in my aimless scrolling online, that I was not alone in my exhaustion and bewilderment. I found mothers like me online who wanted to pull their own skin off, and when that feeling reemerged for me during the pandemic several years later, I dug around online again, finding the content had exploded. Everyday moms and parenting influencers—some clinically certified, others not—speculated that feeling "touched out" can come from consumerism, which contributes to overstimulation with toys that make noise and mess in the home, as well as from the general sensory overload of parenting alone in the home, especially for those with ADHD or sensory processing disorders. One mother described the urgent fleshiness of parenting in a caption to a touched-out Instagram meme: "[My baby's] small hands clawing at me. His legs kicking me as he writhed in pain and frustration with the wind stuck in his tummy. Every time I put him down, he screamed. His cries were so piercing at times and the sound went straight through me and really hit a nerve. I had no choice but to pick him up again."

In another popular TikTok, since taken down, one woman describes how motherhood changed her from "a hugger" who loved physical touch to someone who has not felt self-ownership over her body for six years. "All day my body belongs to another human being, and at the end of the day I am done being touched," she says. Considering whether she might just force herself to be intimate with her husband, she says, "To lose myself to one more person would take away any control I do have over [my body]." Numerous accounts posted by usually white and married women on social media and mom websites talked about these ambivalent feelings regarding their partners' sexual demands and their sense of losing control over their bodies. These anecdotes tended to follow a similar pattern: after describing the absurd physicality of caring for children in isolation in the domestic space, the narrative pivoted to the male partner returning from work who is shocked to find himself pushed away by his wife—a wife who has been home alone all day, alone, taking care of the home and children.

Not long after I started working at the daycare, though Jon and my shared intimacy had unraveled as soon as Hannah was born, I had for a time forced myself to give my body up to him, but like these women, I was becoming uncomfortable with any more claims to my body beyond what I was already experiencing with my child and at the daycare. There was clearly something amiss in men's expectations. Even so, at the height of the pandemic, one article would suggest that women who felt "too schlubby" to have sex should just force themselves to start touching their partners. The article accepted the basic premise that "fear, worry, loneliness and boredom" are "buzzkills," but ultimately proposed more touching to "get out of your head and let your body take over."

Like many elements of American motherhood, women's profound struggles with something as critical as touch to human intimacy and development have been mostly written off as par for the course—as a natural condition of biology, perhaps even of the feminine condition, but also as normal, a vague designation that sidesteps culture and politics. Nearly all reporting on the "touched out" phenomenon assures mothers it's "normal" to want to jump out of one's own skin, something I appreciated as I began frantically googling the term. The assurances kept me from spiraling into cycles of regret, confusion, and shame, knowing how American culture side-eyes negative emotions felt by mothers, especially rejections of closeness or tenderness. The "it's normal" content was destigmatizing. But women's tendencies to have overwhelming urges to push the world away in new motherhood also risked being misinterpreted as simply part of the process of becoming a parent, despite the clearly unreasonable expectations women were under to perform sexually in their marriages, renegotiate careers and identities, parent in isolation, and play nice no matter what their children did.

Despite the clearly complex social, cultural, economic, and political stressors that an aversion to touch indicates are at work in the body, articles on mothers' experiences of it mostly downplayed this complex, carnal, corporeal reaction to the often traumatic culture of white, middle-class motherhood, even claiming that women's not wanting to be touched by their kids and partners is caused by "nothing specifically," even though it's "a thing." I could not help but wonder why we let things go on this way. As a new mother, I felt completely touched out all the time by the knockabout nature of care work—the heaving, the scrambling, the rubbing, the sounds, the literal shit under my fingernails—and most strongly on days when it seemed I never stopped moving, too frenzied by the constant productivity of my body. But I was also complicit. Not only did I not see any feasible mode of escape at that time in my life, but I also still believed that laying myself down on the train tracks to be railroaded by my child—or on the floor *as* train tracks, so my daughter could run her caboose over my back—was the best way to parent. It hadn't yet occurred to me to consider what other lessons I was teaching my daughter in the process.

I was living still with a grander narrative of women's subservience, the one I had pieced together over the course of my life, from girlhood through motherhood. It would take several more years for me to see that the expectations we place on mothers in America are merely an extension of all the highly gendered cultural rites we pass through when we are young. We are taught as girls to service emotions, to self-objectify, to take pleasure in the pleasuring of others. "The duty to please is so built into our sexuality that we have learned to get pleasure out of giving pleasure," Federici writes in "On Sexuality as Work." In motherhood I felt the need to perform, to accept every caress, to smile constantly. To disappear myself. And when Hannah innocently followed me into the bathroom while I showered or shit, studying my naked body in awe, I saw men's eyes on me, scrutinizing with approval or reproach. That year, Hannah's nascent voice—so full of childish curiosity about the world—also began to drown out my own thoughts, and I was reminded of the many men, including my own father, who had spoken over me for as long as I could remember.

The beliefs we hold about children and families come from philosophies we hold about parenting as a social institution—for instance, that raising children is a private, not public, matter. Parenting under the resulting conditions, in turn, becomes its own process of forceful remaking—an ideological and physical assault on the body and mind of the parent that for women further molds us into the image of something called *mother*, who appears nearly indistinguishable from that thing we call *woman*. There are elements of this transformation that are—or can be—meaningful and liberatory. The way our bodies and brains bend to care is a gorgeous thing, maybe even more so when men get involved, as in how I witnessed my own husband move from clumsy idiot, inelegantly gripping our floppy infant and "What-can-I-do-ing?" to confident, adroit babywearer and, later, a man fluent in the language of parental love. That transformation can also be—as it eventually became for me, years later—an opening for women to reexamine their relationship with their bodies, as what's hidden there cracks open, bubbles to the surface, releases, and urges us toward new questions and understandings. But there are other elements of the conversion to that thing called *mother*—the feeling of being trapped, the professional immobility, the social alienation, the emotional repression, the many physical strains—that are entirely culturally and politically motivated. It's no wonder our bodies resist.

Eventually, I picked up some language online and at the daycare for affirming my own autonomy, trying to scribble an outline around myself, to regain some sense of control. I learned to recognize that sacrificing my emotional and physical needs was good for neither me nor my child, though implementing that belief remains a struggle, having been told since girlhood that my desires do not matter. When I was trying to find my footing as a new parent in a sea of recommendations, American parenthood also became inseparable from a wider culture of burnout. There was no amount of boundary setting parents could do verbally, with their children or partners, to create space for themselves in our increasingly siloed, isolated home lives, especially while still living under the cultural expectation that boundary setting, big or small, made us a little worse at raising our kids. Anne Helen Petersen writes of the general vibe of millennial parenting in the late 2010s in a chapter devoted to the subject in her book about burnout, *Can't Even*: "The 'best' parents are the ones who give until there's nothing left of themselves." Mothers especially felt the pressure "to be everything to everyone at all times, save herself."

Not wanting to be touched evokes a particular kind of burnout, one that is visceral, perplexing, often automatic. It comes in waves, when children meltdown, hitting and screaming, or when they demand to be held. It's the kind of feeling that leads parents to hide from their children, and it hits hard at the end of a long, manic day caring for children in the insular settings in which we raise kids in America. As Dr. Pooja Lakshmin, a board-certified psychiatrist and *New York Times* contributor specializing in women's mental health, wrote in response to the parenting crisis of the pandemic, society has turned its back on mothers, and what women feel when they find parenting full of impossible choices is better characterized as "betrayal" than burnout. "While burnout places the blame (and thus the responsibility) on the individual and tells working moms they aren't resilient enough," Lakshmin wrote, "betrayal points directly to the broken structures around them."

Feeling touched out is one way women's bodies sound the alarm bells on those broken structures that have betrayed them, and on a misogynistic culture that has told them how to comport their bodies, moderate their tone, and carry themselves in public and private spaces all their lives. It's also a feeling that indicates the body has reached its limit and doesn't quite know how to cope—understandably, because in such a culture, women are discouraged from articulating any feelings about what's not working for us. The pressure we place on mothers to perform constantly at the expense of their own physical and emotional health is to some degree a generational demand, but holding women responsible for everything that goes wrong in a child's life—or that might go wrong—is an American pastime, one that creates a lot of anxiety for mothers, keeping them busy worrying about what they have done wrong, rather than organizing against the betrayals.

Mothers have been blamed for everything from serial killings to combat PTSD. By the end of World War II, Freudian fears surrounding incest had spread to popular culture. Films began to depict women with a perverse closeness to their children—especially frightening when the mothers focused too much attention on their sons. These mothers apparently posed a danger to the purity of motherly love. In the early 1960s, the character Norman Bates became one famous victim of his mother's excessive devotion, and in the cultural zeitgeist, psychopathy in men remains frequently linked to the absolute control of a too-close mother-son love. Like our cultural narratives for women in pain, national discussions of the intense connections women sometimes experience loving their children—and our views of what counts as normal versus pathological—have often reflected political and social anxieties.

In his best-selling 1964 book *Generation of Vipers* Philip Wylie blamed "megaloid" mom worship, gotten "completely out of hand," for numerous forms of American national suffering, including both McCarthyism and the widespread PTSD experienced by those sent into combat. Wylie's theory of "momism" relied on homophobic logic, characterizing overattached sons as psychologically compromised—a popular take at midcentury. His writing was also, confusingly, anti–free enterprise, anti-Communist, and pro-Freud, whom he felt Americans misinterpreted because they foolishly thought that since they didn't have sex with their mothers, they weren't implicated by their obvious incestuous obsession with their mothers. Wylie's distaste for maternal desire, however, outlasted the book's momentary popularity. Helicopter moms, theories of overprotection, the meddler, mama's boys, Matthew McConaughey's pathetic character Tripp in the 2006 film *Failure to Launch*—all are reverberations of momism. In these narratives, intense connections between mother and child are understood to be a direct threat to the child's ability to flourish in a country that values rugged individualism and independence.

These examples are not hyperbolic nor even worst-case scenarios. They are part of the fabric of American psychology. In his 1967 book *The Empty Fortress: Infantile Autism and the Birth of the Self*, Bruno Bettelheim argued that autism is caused by mothers who withdraw from, rather than coddle, their children. Bettelheim's "refrigerator mother" is so cold and disaffected that her child psychically runs away into a prison of his own mind. At the time, autism was categorized as a mental illness (as well as incorrectly conflated with schizophrenia), and although autism spectrum disorder is now widely understood to be caused by brain chemistry, the tendency to lazily imply psychogenic causes for the vast diversity of human experience remains entrenched in popular psychology, implying not only that there is a hierarchy in brain function but also that mothers are to "blame" for human variation—as if the latter were true, and as if difference were a bad thing.

The field of child development and child psychology has in large part been an institutionalization of mother blame that considers only the white, productive, able-bodied, cis, hetero, male mind (always divorced from the body) to be free of pathology. This framework nevertheless continues to filter into public consciousness and shapes the parenting advice industry, which targets underwater parents—especially women—with philosophies that promise to help them not fuck up their children, or finger-wags at them when they say or do the wrong things. Is it any wonder mothers find themselves hiding out in bathrooms with their hands over their ears? In the late 2010s, as Hannah was moving into toddlerdom, my own little somatic rebellions would converge with #MeToo, urging me to reconsider what assumptions I was passing down to my daughter by sacrificing my body on the altar of American parenthood. But until then, I coped the only way I knew how, by numbing out—a method I perhaps inherited from my mother, or perhaps from America's hyperconsumerist culture of excess, which tells us all that we can indulge our way out of a fundamentally unequal world. Soon I was drinking every night to quell the relentless anxiety and the voices inside that said I was doing everything all wrong.

American motherhood has always reeked of misogyny—of the expectation that women give and never receive, and of the belief that whatever women do give, it will never be enough, or it will be too much. But what new parent can see anything straight? I had spent my whole life making my body do things it didn't want to do and so I continued doing what I knew best. Every evening, while Jon worked late at the tutoring center, it was more of the same: tugging and pulling, demands and tantrums, flying food, unconscionable mess. I cooked dinner between screams and upsets, tried to pull together one fruit, one veggie, one carb, and one protein, all on a colorful Ikea plate. I often fell short of completing the pattern, and of course in other ways. I slammed cupboards and raised my voice. Hannah burst into tears. I atoned, holding her, nursing her, apologizing.

"Mommy's just very tired," I said. And after we ate dinner I fell to my knees, scooping food with my hands from the floor onto the mat

I kept under her highchair. I let her cry as I mumbled about what I could and could not give her, what she could expect from me, who I was—as if I knew. Eventually she moved on, tearing apart the living room while I pulled the corners of the food waste mat together, took the pouch to the trash, and dumped most of what I had cooked into the waste bin, calculating the cost of all the uneaten food. Before bed I bathed with Hannah, her wet, naked body nursing mine in the tub. This was touch we both welcomed and wanted. I stroked her wet hair out of her face, her eyes looking into mine, as I listened to the clicking of her breath as she gulped and swallowed. We fell together into silence. Some days I repented more for my poor behavior. She melted me; I ached for her. And there was something heartbreakingly consensual in those moments, in how clearly we both said yes, a mutual consent that cleared away all the other muck that often stood between us.

After I packaged her up for sleep, I stood in the hallway outside her room, waiting for silence, all the lights in the apartment turned off. I propped my glass of two-dollar wine—now a nightly feature—on a shelf in the hall closet, and I ran through all the ways I had wronged her. When I could finally close the door without waking her up, I drank more, falling asleep on the couch to the glow of reality TV, sobbing women flickering on my face as I passed out in the wreckage of our day—a shit show of broken toys, dirty snack cups, kids' water bottles, puzzle pieces, crushed crackers, costume changes, ripped books, miscellaneous trash. Hours later I would awake on the couch to my own thirst, walking into the kitchen for water, eyes half closed, forgetting for a moment how the outside world moved inside our apartment at night. In my stupor I would step right into a trail of slick, wet slugs, which crawled in the through the open seals of the apartment at dark, dotting the kitchen floor as they hunted for the scraps of food I had neglected to clean up after dinner.

———

At night, when I was a little drunk, I went searching for answers in books, looking to fix some theory in my mind about what was happening to me, and how it connected to the larger landscape of parenting in America. I read Adrienne Rich's *Of Woman Born* for the first time one night not long after we moved back to California, gasping through my cloud of red wine. I felt that if I could just locate the line between what Rich called the *experience* of motherhood and the *institution* of motherhood—if I could pull apart the differences between the real and the unavoidable aspects of parenting—I could regain some agency. Rich argues, however, that the institution can be hard to locate. "When we think of the institution of motherhood, no symbolic architecture comes to mind," she writes, "no visible embodiment of authority, power, or of potential or actual violence." It is composed of art, law, punishment, medicine, even those "Marxist intellectuals arguing as to whether we produce surplus value in a day of washing clothes, cooking food, and caring for children, or the psychoanalysts who are certain that the work of motherhood suits us by nature." Motherhood is made of cultural images we carry in our bodies, which deny us power, and which we nevertheless try to uphold, or meet, or transcend.

But there seemed to be some existential truths hidden in the way my child's body needed mine, the way my insides boiled when she was upset, the way I could not help but rush in to save and soothe her, the way her smells enraptured me. It was love, but also a raw spell I was under that begged me to tend to her. I didn't want to resist those physical urges, the only bits of pleasure I had left. But I was also beginning to see that I was ensnared by cultural compulsions. I wanted so badly to parse out what I did because I felt the pressure to conform to some ideal and what I did for some other, unnamable reason that came from deep within. Only then, I thought, could I settle into my new role.

I wanted to locate some natural element of motherhood to help me separate my work from the patriarchal, sacrificial bullshit, to see my way out of the institution and into something like my *own* experience. But we cannot separate our bodies from the cultures in which they grow and love, or from history. And increasingly, my body was rising up all by itself, not just in the way it craved Hannah, but in the way it rejected her. When Hannah whined for a cup of water while I tried to finish the dishes, or for a yellow plate after I gave her a blue one, or for a cookie she saw high on a shelf, or about another long car ride around town, I roared at her. I couldn't always control my reactions. There is a limit to what all bodies can stand, and though those limits are certainly different for all parents, they are always related to our need to feel human, and to feel free.

Once, on a no-daycare day, I took Hannah to the local animal hospital. We watched owls rotating their heads as if to say, swiftly and with conviction, no to this or no to that. Hannah was tired and hungry by the time we left, and I found myself muscling her into the car seat while she smacked her arms and legs against me. "I cannot let you hit me," I said steadily, as I had been told to do by some internet-based advice. I made my voice higher and sweeter, because I didn't want her to feel as though her hatred of the car seat was unwarranted. She, like me, hated feeling trapped or forced into doing things. I related, and I knew that children also live their lives in a constant state of coercion. But I could only take so much. My arms pressed down on hers a little too firmly, and when she resisted, I shoved her into the seat and buckled her in anyway. She looked on at me with horror, the same way my mother did when I, as an adolescent girl, felt my life spinning out of control. I walked around to the driver's seat, my body shaking in the sun. I stood outside the car in the parking lot for a few long minutes, my hand on the door handle, trembling. I could hear Hannah wailing inside the car, but my body was also yelling, and I was trying to listen.

I often wondered whether I would benefit from a diagnosis, a pathology by which to catch all my discontent, or by which I might classify the experience I was having. According to the Motherhood

Center of New York, "Worldwide, as many as 1 in 5 women experience some type of perinatal mood and anxiety disorder (PMAD)." This rate is higher for Black women, who nevertheless receive reduced rates of treatment. The overall rate at which women suffer from depression, anxiety, rage, and other mood changes is also likely much higher overall, since plenty of mothers go undiagnosed or untreated. PMAD, after all, is an understudied, catchall diagnosis that refers to a range of symptoms people who give birth may feel long after childbirth. There is an incredible lack of nuance in both naming and treating the traumatic experience of becoming a parent in a misogynistic culture, even though there is plenty of evidence to suggest that when mothers are not cared for, it hampers their ability to be present with their children. Studies show that mothers with chronic anxiety and depression are more disengaged in parent-child interactions. Depressed mothers also tend toward less interactive touch with their children and are more irritable.

Touch is an essential component of care work. As the first sense to develop, touch is unique in that it provides the scaffold for all other forms of perception. Infants' awareness of their bodies emerges from physical interactions with caregivers, and haptic feedback dominates social, psychological, emotional, and intellectual development. Caregivers themselves engage in many kinds of caring touch— one study catalogued nine forms of maternal touch, from loving to playful, though there are likely many more. The importance of touch to caregiving, in other words, is clear, but like most issues related to women's health, research devoted to parental touch aversion is minimal. Despite America's longstanding cultural legacy of blaming mothers for all manner of social and societal ills, postpartum care and psychology continue to fall short on helping mothers understand their own experiences.

Some of the most compelling studies show that, perhaps like an aversion to touch, postpartum depression can be a coping mechanism that causes mothers to turn on those they love. Rather than follow the tradition of viewing postpartum "disorders" as aberrant psychological states that should be treated and "cured," some explorations of the range of symptoms that fall under the PMAD umbrella consider these mental states as indicative of mothers bargaining for power and more support from others. This dynamic is something feminists have understood in detail for decades. "The power-relations between mother and child are often simply a reflection of power-relations in patriarchal society," Rich writes in *Of Woman Born*. In motherhood, as women are made to feel powerless, many of them retaliate. "Powerless women have always used mothering as a channel—narrow but deep—for their own human will to power, their need to return upon the world what it has visited on them."

Often this retaliation is misdirected, especially given that most new mothers find themselves trapped for a time alone with their children. I certainly took my frustrations out on Hannah. She became for a time that "piece of reality, of the world, which can be acted on, even modified, by a woman restricted from acting on anything else except inert materials like dust and food," as Rich writes. But I was not alone. Rich writes of how women's powerlessness often morphs into an expression of dominance over their child, citing in a footnote the psychologist Alice Miller's book *The Drama of the Gifted Child*. Miller argues that the idealization of the mother—and women's resulting preoccupations with trying to be a "good mother"—destroys empathy in the mother-child relationship. This insecurity often causes mothers to turn to authoritarian power models in the home. Again, clinical studies corroborate what feminists have been saying for decades, with findings that are too often divorced from their political context: maternal sadness can also endanger empathy between mother and child.

I wanted to be a "good mother." Desperately. But that wanting became as all-consuming as it was impossible to quench. And the more I studied the shape of motherhood, the further I got into it, the more I began to see the unreasonable expectations we place on mothers as a mechanism of control. Andrea Dworkin wrote that misogynistic culture teaches people to see good women as inert and passive. Good women look like good mothers—like dutiful, invisible housewives. And so it's no surprise that nowhere have I felt more compelled to evacuate myself than in motherhood. This is what a good mother is made of: largely nothing. No needs, no desires, no inadequacies, no hunger, no complaints, no body to speak of.

As I began to see my own disempowerment playing out in my relationship with the only person I felt I had ever loved completely unconditionally—my child—I also came to see that the struggle that emerges between mother and child, especially mother and daughter, is perhaps the grandest trick of the institution: motherhood, as it's been imagined, turns us against each other. In her analysis of maternal feelings, Federici writes that the unpaid nature of work performed in the home stokes resentment in mothers and a generalized animosity that manifests in our relationships. It's a cleave, however, that she claims could be alleviated by monetary compensation for our vital labor. Federici supposes that if "our mothers had had a financial reward, they would have been less bitter, less dependent, less blackmailed, and less blackmailing to their children who were constantly reminded of their mothers' sacrifices."

There are many reasons for mothers to be blackmailing and bitter, but they experience no small amount of culturally induced shame when they make such feelings known. "Instead of recognizing the institutional violence of patriarchal motherhood," Rich writes, "society labels those women who finally erupt in violence as psychopathological." And the punitive effects are of course much higher for women of color, even though these "expectations" laid on women are "insane" ones, and as Rich writes, "Motherhood without autonomy, without choice is one of the quickest roads to a sense of having lost control."

Angry parenting is obviously not a sound ethos. Domination, moving from parent to child, replicates a patriarchal understanding of power, which, Rich points out, "insists on a dichotomy: for one person to have power, others—another—must be powerless." And yet, while the story goes that mothers who love too much or not enough cause boys to become men who do bad things, the domineering anger of violent white masculinity—responsible for no shortage of brutality, mass murder, war, incarceration, ecological destruction, and other everyday forms of abuse and violation—is rarely met with the charge that it is not only unproductive but literally fatal. As Audre Lorde writes in her essay on the misdirected anger white women often hurl at women of color, and on the freedom men have to express their anger in public spaces, "It is not my anger that launches rockets, spends over sixty thousand dollars a second on missiles and other agents of war and death, slaughters children in cities, stockpiles nerve gas and chemical bombs, sodomizes our daughters and our earth." Though women's anger remains culturally taboo, for men, losing your shit is just part of the job.

In the era during which I became a parent, white male anger was an American political ethos. That brand of rankled masculinity rapidly gained ground the first year I spent in California, which would only further complicate my work as a mother—and my ability to *not* take my powerlessness out on my around-town companion. After the 2016 presidential election, I was increasingly enraged by what was happening beyond the walls of my home, but I felt helpless to respond. During the pandemic several years later, rage would have a revival with mothers as women called in to the *New York Times* to primal-scream and, later, to organize public expressions of rage under the hashtag #MomScream. As Minna Dubin, author of *Mom Rage*, wrote in an essay on maternal anger that went viral: it's the feeling that one might "physically explode." That era would do much to de-stigmatize the anger so many women feel when they find motherhood is not what they were promised, but in early 2017, alone in my apartment, nothing made me feel less motherly—and less like a woman—than my own anger at my child.

"A mother cannot articulate anger *as a mother*," Marianne Hirsch observes. "To do so she must step out of a culturally circumscribed role which commands mothers to be caring and nurturing to others, even at the expense of themselves." Too bad for me, because my own anger became unshakable after the election. The scope of male power in America felt salient; the path forward hazy. I wanted to resist, to collectivize my rage, even move beyond a politics of resentment, but I was exhausted. "Two jobs have only meant for women even less time and energy to struggle against both," Federici writes. The design is flawless. Dejected, using my government-subsidized healthcare, I went to talk therapy for the first time since I was a teenage girl living in my mother's home. I hinted that I thought I might—still, almost two years after giving birth—have postpartum depression. My concerns didn't gain any traction. Instead my therapist told me it was "scary" how much my internal dialogue sounded like an argument I was having with my mother. I felt so frustrated with this trope of trotting my mother out, reproaching her for everything, when I was so clearly being bullied by other forces: by men, by the world in which we lived, by all the voices that told me how a mother should be.

Women who are full of rage—or just sad and falling apart—are rarely seen as responding with reason to America's uniquely isolating, intensive parenthood models, or to the historical depreciation of their round-the-clock work in the home, much less to the misogynistic culture in which they grew up, only to find their bodies used and abused further in work that goes unrecognized as work, with little free time to agitate for better working conditions without risking being called unfit or in need of psychotropic drugs. "We are seen as nagging bitches," Federici writes, "not workers in a struggle." Bad mothers, frigid wives, hysterics—all are more cultural images that police women's latent rebellions and their burgeoning desires for rejecting what's piled on them all their lives. Rarely are such women understood to be intelligently tapping into a wise internal voice, an intuition, and a clamoring inside their bodies for change.

I grew up with hardly any language with which to assert my own autonomy, only to find myself absorbing the widespread cultural belief that women should martyr themselves for motherhood. But I knew somewhere inside, even in the early years, that it didn't have to be this way—that it wasn't supposed to be this way. That there was some other set of terms—beyond dominance versus "gentleness," powerlessness versus power, passivity versus anger, self-erasure versus running, normalcy versus madness—another, altogether different approach to the way we were doing this work of raising children, which in its current state felt like such a ruse. What Adrienne Rich had written in *Of Woman Born* was true: if sexual violence felt like a form of patriarchal "terrorism," motherhood felt like "penal servitude." But her statement following this analogy was also true: "It need not be."

REFUSAL

I'M NOT SURE when I started watching *The Bachelor*—it's as if that magnetic display of heteronormative attraction was always there, beckoning me to shed my shell and throw myself into marriage and motherhood full tilt. The franchise debuted in 2002, the year before I finished high school, but I had little interest in any season before the thirteenth, which aired in 2009, a few years before I met Jon. That season culminated with Jason Mesnick dramatically jilting Melissa Rycroft, to whom Jason had previously proposed, then reconciling with Molly Malaney, his one-time runner-up. I loved all the drama and surprise of that season: the way Molly took her time accepting Jason's late revelation of love but was ultimately wooed; the way Melissa put Jason in his place publicly on "After the Final Rose." Of course, I also watched *The Bachelorette*, which I found particularly refreshing for the way it portrayed men fighting over a woman, rather than women vying for the attention of one unimpressive man.

I lived with my mother during my early trysts with the franchise. I had moved back to Los Angeles halfway through college in part because my mother's drinking was spiralling, and I wanted to care for her, though I also moved back to be with a boyfriend who had already cheated on me during our long-distance relationship. My mother had spent years refusing the boredom and lack of fulfillment she found in motherhood by drinking, getting high, and sleeping with men who betrayed or used her. In a few months I would drive her to an inpatient rehab facility in Santa Monica, where she would refuse to go inside. Several weeks later she would join an outpatient, 12-step program. But when I was lazing around watching *The Bachelor* she chided me, huffing out of the room with a sploshy glass of wine during my weekly dates with ABC, appalled by the disorderly, unkempt women on the screen. She too was agonizing over unavailable men and excess alcohol in her life, her plight not unlike that of the women on the show, but she would have adamantly refused such a comparison.

I, however, liked the looking-glass quality of the women on the show. In my early twenties, I related to how much the women wanted marriage and to how haphazard their efforts in that direction were. Years later, in Buffalo, I would incorporate *The Bachelor* into one of my classes, after assigning the introduction to Lauren Berlant's *The Female Complaint*. Berlant claims in their book that women's culture has been central to American life in its containment of a common grievance shared by women, which is that "women live for love, and love is the gift that keeps on taking." Women's culture, Berlant argues, in this way provides a sense of belonging—a feeling of being connected to that shifty category called woman. These "complaint genres" also "foreground a view of power that blames flawed men and flawed ideologies for women's intimate suffering, all while maintaining some fidelity to the world." In my notes for a lecture on Berlant's writing—which I probably presented next to clips of Sean Lowe's 2013 journey to find his wife Catherine née Giudici, who would later describe her televised wedding aesthetic as "grown sexy"—I wrote: "In what ways is emotion both internal & external, where do we locate feeling." A nascent provocation for my students—and for me—about how we find ourselves.

Berlant's book is concerned with twentieth-century narratives, but their writing on sentimentality in media speaks to contemporary guilty pleasures and the hook of popular art forms that feel at odds with our politics, even as they also feel like a necessary affirmation of our lives. *The Bachelor* represented what I wanted so badly growing up—a happy ending—but the show also allowed me to mock my desires, to pretend that such a dream was foolish and uninformed. The prospect of finding a husband on TV, however, was not just a dramatization of the quest for heteronormative love; the "journey" to "break down walls" and "open up" was also wrapped up in the desire for family. For as long as I could remember, I wanted what I never had when I was young: an untroubled, unbroken nuclear family with a stable and committed mother and father. In July of 2014, *The Bachelor* aired the first live ultrasound of the fetus of cast members J.P. Rosenbaum and Ashley Hebert, and I watched the televised procedure with rapt attention in our Buffalo apartment, convincing myself I was doing it for research. But the erudition I brought to that "After the Final Rose" episode didn't just stem from my scholarly interests. By then, I had a fully formed ache for a baby.

It was a desire I didn't quite understand. J.P. and Ashley had married two years before their ultrasound, the same year I had, and they would be divorced by 2020—a year when I, too, would be questioning what the institution of marriage had made of me. In the early months of the pandemic, I binged the first season of Fox's short-lived reality show *Labor of Love*, which featured a forty-year-old single woman named Kristy vetting multiple potential fathers. In the first episode, male contestants were asked to provide sperm samples to determine whether they could deliver as baby makers, and subsequent episodes revolved around challenges that test the male competitors' fluency in the work of care. But Kristy was not just looking for a sperm donor, she wanted it all, and she envisioned "it all" as I once had—love, marriage, baby, and career.

Kristy already had professional success outside the home. She was ready for the rest. And the show was presented by its creators as revolutionary, even feminist, in its direct, no-nonsense approach to marriage and reproduction. I burned through the whole season in a few nights, wondering whether I should have put Jon through a similar parental gauntlet before we married. By then we had spent years arguing over the division of labor in our home, a wedge steadily increasing the distance between us. When it came to parenting, his only tools were shouting and permissiveness—complete dominance or its absence—while I was still trying to find some third term. He had an unflappable ability to ignore crying, but also a level of anxiety around potential injury that was at times debilitating (he wanted to buy Hannah a helmet when she was learning to walk). Things were very on or off for him. And while I tried to get him to see that parenting was more nuanced than that, I was tired of leading him around.

Which is why I was so captivated by Kristy's measurement of her suitors' skill at care work. She often gently threatened the men, assuring them she could go it alone as a single mother if need be. She didn't want a boy, she said; she wanted a *man*. *Labor of Love* was not dissimilar in that sense from *The Bachelor*, which would face its own identity crisis later that year as the long-term racism and misogyny on the show came to a head. But the unreality of these sorts of reality shows was what gave them their charm, even if it was also what made them so horrible. When we watch people fall in love on TV, we often do so to pursue the fantasy that love can exist outside the world in which we live. *Labor of Love*, however, implied a realm of work within marriage and parenthood, even if it also poked fun at that labor. But in the end, Kristy picked a mediocre man who didn't quite excel at anything, to whom she was clearly attracted, and remained decisive about her commitment to becoming a wife and mother—which was for me perhaps the most hypnotizing element of the show. Watching Kristy's resolve in my domestic isolation in 2020, her certainty about what she wanted amid the emerging childcare crisis, I really could not remember what it felt like to have such clarity.

I once bought into the fairy tale of marriage, but I had always been skeptical about the institution. A few months before my wedding, I flew up to Northern California alone to meet my sister and mother at a discount dress shop in the East Bay, where I bought a poofy cupcake of a wedding gown—which I tore off in the dressing room the moment I was alone, after the salesperson fitted me. I had doubts, but I loved Jon, so I pushed on, outfitting my bridesmaids in pink, despite their complaints. In the weeks leading up to the event, in our small studio apartment, Jon and I wrapped mason jars in burlap and lace and hand-bound wedding programs that were peppered with lines of poetry. I became so invested in the planning and Pinterest-ing of the event—a way to distract myself from the inner turmoil I felt about our commitment—that when we drove to taste slices of cake at a bakery on LA's Westside, I had to clutch the side of the car to root myself back into my body and remind myself how to breathe.

To cope with my anxiety I ate less and walked two miles round-trip to hot yoga on days I wasn't nannying, sweating out as much as I could. Days before the wedding, I let a stranger airbrush bronze skin onto me in her garage in the Hollywood Hills after locating a Groupon for the service. My vows were about how Jon hated ketchup, which I found unexplainable. He sobbed through his. Our siblings officiated. My father had RSVP'd that he was bringing two girlfriends, one of whom was still married to a well-known music producer imprisoned for killing his first wife, but I had fought with him on the phone until he promised to bring only the long-term girlfriend I had known since childhood, whom I thought of as my stepmother. One of the kids I nannied for threw up near the oversized balloons I had selected to decorate the altar, then nearly took down the dessert table trying to grab a cupcake. Jon and I got too drunk, danced, ripped our wedding uniforms. After the reception, Jon temporarily lost his ring in the hotel bathroom while embracing the toilet. We both blacked out before we could consummate the marriage.

Two days later we moved to western New York to start a new life. Before we left Los Angeles, we unmethodically shoved clothes and kitchen utensils into our shared white hatchback. Weeks earlier we had mailed boxes of books ahead, our only treasures, hoping the media mail travel would rid them of the bed bugs we had been battling for months in our Echo Park apartment. We had sold whatever we couldn't fit in the car to fund our move. It took us seven days to drive to New York, and we honeymooned at campsites and motels along the way. I took selfies at the Grand Canyon, where we awoke to an elk outside our tent; at the red rocks of Arches National Park in Utah, hungover one morning, I found a picture I could barely remember taking on my phone of a rat that had visited our campsite after dark; at a sulfur-smelling commercial hot springs in Colorado, we were disappointed to find a therapy pool that disallowed alcohol, but we swam and snapped shots of each other anyway; and at a famous gas-station barbecue joint in St. Louis, which took so long to find we ended up fighting in the car, took no pictures, and were later rendered immobile in our hotel room by heartburn.

By the time we got to Erie, Pennsylvania, my tan was flaking off. We drank Yuengling beer in a little dive bar because Jon had grown up in the state drinking it with his father and he was nostalgic for the taste. He peeled the labels; I peeled my skin. To him, the whole week had been a romantic adventure, an intentional snub of normative marital consumerism. "Look at us, making our own way through the institution!" I too wanted to feel that our marriage was a form of refusal—to believe our love was different, untouched by the history of what marriage had always been for women. At the same time I wanted our relationship to fulfill the romantic fantasies I had. But that night, the last of our honeymoon, we parked under the glow of the Bayfront Sheraton, did not have sex, and slept sitting upright. When the sun came up, we crossed the state line, stopping at the first Dunkin Donuts in New York for breakfast. I tried to pretend that as a girl I had not dreamed of more.

Of course I had. Jon and I had met only a few years after the night in Santa Monica when I had felt so shaken up by the man who guided my drunken body up to the loft bed. I was seduced by marriage and the prospect of motherhood, seeing in each a vague promise of feminine completion, an identity in which I might find some ease. It was not that I thought marriage was *every* woman's next step, but I had become convinced it was mine. Our once sensual love, however, was quickly complicated by two opposing desires: my eternal pining for something *normal*—tied to the mythological story of family I had witnessed at a distance since I was a girl—and both my and Jon's aspirations for something like rebellion in our everyday lives.

The idea that marriage was *work* became a battleground between us. I harangued Jon about the lack of effort he put into us, as a couple, but he took a laissez-faire approach to love. He had once dotted our apartment in LA with Post-its that told of his love for me, tucking sweet nothings into the medicine cabinet and my dresser drawers, but he was generally put off by grand gestures and the consumerism of love. He believed we didn't need much to bring us together, an optimism and confidence I didn't really get. When I was a girl, my life had only ever felt real in the big moments I spent with my mother: birthdays, holidays, surprise vacations she couldn't afford but that we took anyway, when she wanted to leave her adult life behind. These were the moments when she turned her attention fully toward me—when she felt like my mother. But my desire for romance, and my belief that buying stuff and being wooed meant "love," had also been part of my gendered upbringing as a girl.

Jon's upbringing, as a boy, had taught him something different. Not long after we married, we fought in the parking lot of a dollar movie theater in Buffalo before we even got inside, initiating a chorus that would follow us for years. "If you want me to want you, I need you to work for it," I said, pressing my thumbs hard into my eyes, as if to gouge them out. It had been my idea to go to the discount cinema. I was always the one arranging joy, breaking us out of monotony. And now I was telling him what I needed if he wanted me to give him what he wanted—which was always, it seemed, my body.

I had for years accommodated men and tried to quench what I had been told was their insatiable hunger for sex, but in marriage, I wanted to hand my body over only when I felt full of desire. Jon never demanded anything, but he didn't have to say it, or even think it, for it to be there: wives were supposed to please their husbands, even when they would rather not. And as this thing called a *wife*, I felt duty bound to please him, which only made me reject him more forcefully. He made it known, whenever we argued, that my demands for romance were, to him, unreasonable, but I still felt then that his desire for my body was natural, or at least normal, a component of love and monogamy, while my longings were somehow more culturally inscribed, and gendered. "Maybe you should stop watching *The Bachelor*," he said during one frigid Buffalo winter. And I hated us for playing out such a predictably gendered division of love languages: man wants sex, woman wants *more*. It felt like it might go on for us forever this way: a chicken-or-egg debate over how love worked. What came first, touch or all the rest of it?

Part of what I enjoyed about *The Bachelor* was the dumbly transparent performance of desire. Contestants admitted to love as it was: a big show. Helicopter dates, awkward kissing, staged run-hugs. Usually, in film and TV, Katherine Angel writes, "Desire is simply there; then follows some quick groping, the insertion of a penis, some breathless moaning, and grateful, giddy mutual orgasm." In *The Bachelor*, everyone is working for it. Women in the show are courted tediously by nonsexual—often material—incentives: fancy dinners, nice clothing, and promise of finding TV love, which will only bring more money. With its growing attachment to celebrity, the show underlines how the quest for love can also be a quest for financial security.

Sexual economics theorists have supposed that the mythology of love helps make invisible how sex *is* linked to work. Marital sex, of course, isn't the equivalent to sex work, Kristen Ghodsee writes; rather "Love and romance are mere cognitive veils humans used to occlude the transactional nature of our personal relationships." There are obvious flaws and challenges to embracing sexual economics theory full stop, not least of which is that it "commodifies all human interaction and reduces women to chattel," just as patriarchal capitalism does. It's also depressing, to say the least, to suppose there is no such thing as love or intimacy beyond their economic function. There is little room for personal agency under such a theory.

But marriage has always been an economic institution. And in America, it has become rather common to talk about marriage as a form of labor, without questioning not only how gender plays out in the work married couples usually divide between themselves—such as childcare and housework responsibilities—but also in the division of sexual responsibility. When we talk about sex and desire, it's often argued that women are more cerebral and calculating when it comes to sex, whereas men are pure drive—a story of desire that implies sexuality is naturally external to women. But this perspective also naturalizes men's entitlement to sex, making it seem as though they are constantly and unavoidably in need sexually, and that it is a woman's natural role to lodge men's ravenous desires.

Research on female desire, especially in motherhood, has been predictably underfunded, but in a study on women's sexual health conducted during the pandemic, researchers found that gender inequalities contribute to low sex drive and exacerbate the pleasure gap between men and women, which is hardly surprising. "Sexual health refers to a state of physical, emotional, mental, and social well-being in relation to sexuality," the authors of the study write, "which requires respect for everyone's sexual rights and the possibility of pleasurable sexual activity." Sexual rights and other "overlapping systems of oppression," including "race, ethnicity, and socioeconomic status," were all found to affect sexual desire. And anyway, as the philosopher Michel Foucault famously argued, "The history of sexuality" is inseparable from "a history of discourses." Sexual drive, for anyone, is not some natural beam of physical energy coursing through the body that governments must work to constrain or repress. Sex and sexuality are shaped by a complex nexus of many systems of power, and by the ways we talk about them.

My feeling of powerlessness in early motherhood blunted my erotic life, as did all the forced disembodiment I felt in my entrance into the role of mother. Jon and I now barely touched, even though I felt the pressure to hold my marriage together by giving my body over to my husband, whether I wanted to or not. By our second year in California, I was regularly pushing off Jon's advances but scheduling sex every few weeks to keep him happy. This was how I put "work" into my marriage, but I was also disturbed by my lack of desire, constantly wondering whether it meant I didn't love my husband, whether I was neurotic, whether I had become completely alienated from my own sexuality since becoming a mother, whether I should try masturbating more to see if there was anything left down there, whether I had deadened my body because I was becoming an alcoholic, whether I had married too young, whether I had been too drunk at my wedding to know what I was signing up for. I bought into the idea that motherhood was inherently desexualizing rather than radicalizing, but also that my husband's easy relationship with sex, which had been largely untroubled all his life, was a baseline for comparison. I couldn't yet see that my sexual refusal was a way of taking my body back in a time when I had so little control over it. Instead, I googled marital sex statistics, trying to locate some criterion by which I could judge my marriage and my sexual health.

Where my husband and I agreed, perhaps, though we couldn't see it then, was that we both wanted our marriage to feel uncomplicated and unburdened by the stories of love we had inherited. It just wasn't that easy. When Jon came home late from the tutoring center, if Hannah was sleeping soundly, I sometimes texted him begging him to pick up wine on the days I couldn't stomach dropping into the store to purchase only alcohol with my daughter by my side. Drinking remained my primary form of rebellion. It helped keep the discomfort of modern parenthood at bay, at least at night, when I receded into a version of my body that felt giddy and light. So if Jon missed my desperate texts, when he came home I pleaded with him further to please go back out to the store, too tired to peel myself off the couch. Sometimes I offered sex in return for the errand, an arrangement in which we both seemed to get what we wanted. He usually agreed, returning from the store with Pinot and ice cream and potato chips and a little energy of conspiracy. We had sex efficiently in the dim bedroom before returning to the couch, where we laughed and drank and shared salt and sugar before falling asleep. It felt like a small act of resistance, this staying up too late and trashing our bodies together, even if it was tainted by the politics of exchange.

Increasingly, though, I was troubled by the presumption that women should force themselves into unwanted sex with their husbands. In 2018, one anonymous writer published a piece for *Vox* in which she admitted that in marriage, sex often felt unavoidable. "At the time, it didn't feel like a choice; it felt inevitable," she wrote. "I lived every evening dreading the signals of my husband's desire. I bargained my way out of sex as often as I could." I too began to dread Jon's need, knowing how his anger or sadness at my pushing him off would make me feel—like there was something wrong with me. Kate Manne argues that most husbands carry a deep sense of sexual entitlement over their wives, and women come to internalize this entitlement.

I had certainly adopted the idea that Jon had some right to my body, that I owed myself to him, even if I never could have said so out loud. Some of this perception of entitlement came directly from him: Jon had made me feel, over the years, through this disappointment, that we *should* still be touching, that I should force myself to want it, to want him, until I did, because otherwise, our marriage would fall apart. "You never even touch me," he would say suddenly in anger, an unexpected swerve in some argument about the dishes.

For a while he took to encouraging us to hug for five minutes every day because he had read online that this would stimulate oxytocin. I could barely make it thirty seconds without thinking of all the other things I could be doing.

It never occurred to me then that one thing I could be doing was exploring what brought *me* pleasure—what *I* actually wanted. "Sex can become obligatory—a chore undertaken to keep a partner happy," Angel writes. "And so a woman's own pleasure can become less and less important, which in turn affects her desire to have sex at all, since the sex itself may not be worth having." I was pretty sure sex was not what I wanted at that time in my life because I was so physically run-down from caregiving, but it seemed this was the time—the early years of marriage and motherhood—when my marital life should be thriving. Federici notes that women are discouraged from being too sexual when they are young *and* when they are past their childbearing years, which means "the years in which we are allowed to be sexually active are the years in which we are most burdened with work"—the work of caring for the home and for the kids.

Marriage and the mythology of love that upholds it compel women not only toward the unpaid material and emotional labors that come from mothering and housework, but also toward the emotional and sexual labor that comes with marriage. Men, meanwhile, grow up used to having women care for them in a society in which most primary caregivers and care workers are women. In marriage, sex becomes a natural quick fix to the day's troubles, the wife a kind of affective trash can into which a man can dump all his shit when he gets home from work—shit he collects, it should be noted, as an alienated worker who is exploited in his own right. In this way, capitalism and its attendant exploitation of women's labor in the home turns not only mothers and children against each other but also men and women against each other.

My feminist husband didn't consciously expect me to service his feelings when he came home wrecked and deflated from targeting parents' "points of pain" at work, but unconsciously he did. This was what he thought marriage was for. And this was what I resented so much about Jon's resentment of me. Increasingly it seemed my physical availability had become the exclusive source of his happiness. "We have been set up to be the providers of sexual satisfaction," Federici writes, "the safety valves for everything that goes wrong in a man's life." Jon's acting crushed and hurt by my lack of desire only created more labor for me, as I tried to explain to him tediously the phenomenon of women feeling touched out, identifying every visceral sensation I felt at night after working at the daycare and caring for Hannah all day. I was regurgitating analyses I had read online—more labor. And while I could see that he wanted to understand, that he was trying to be patient with me, I could also tell, in the way he held his tongue, that he remained unconvinced.

In a section of her provocative book-length essay *I Hate Men* titled "Shacking Up with a Man," Pauline Harmange writes about her own "beloved," for whom she finds she must offer up "pre-digested concepts and reflections on masculinity" to help him be a little less mediocre, and a little less implicated in patriarchy. Women often end up shouldering "the entire emotional burden of the relationship," Harmange writes, because "in a heterosexual relationship it's always the woman who's learned to do that." Men could learn to take on this role, to speak the language of feelings the way women have been taught to do. But men have been raised to speak the language of sex, not feelings. And, as Harmange writes, there's often little incentive for them to change: "If there's already someone there prepared to make the effort to speak the other person's language, why bother?"

In heteronormative marital sex, there is also always an imbalance of power to contend with, something rarely discussed in marriage books and popular advice for heterosexual couples. That power gap alone can bring with it a sense of violation. The radical feminist writer Andrea Dworkin, whose ideas were often sidelined in favor of characterizing her as an angry, ugly, fat feminist, articulated this throughout her career. Dworkin has been misquoted as saying that "all sex is rape" and "all men are rapists," but she didn't argue for the categorical dismissal of men or sex, nor did she argue that women aren't strong enough to consent to sex. Her writing instead considered how sex and intimacy tend to rely on misogynistic tropes and principles, and how patterns of intimacy and desire are entwined with violence against women. For Dworkin, penetrative intercourse especially had a violent element to it. She felt sex shouldn't be an "act of aggression from a man looking to satisfy himself." Which was not to say pleasure couldn't be restructured in some other way. Rather, the subjugation of women dominates sexual fantasy, and we have to remain vigilant. "Nothing is one's own, nothing, certainly not oneself," she wrote in *Intercourse*, "because the imagination is atrophied, like some limb, dead and hanging useless, and the dull repetition of preprogrammed sexual fantasy has replaced it."

After we moved back to California, arguments came up around the shape of Jon's desire—the way he talked about my body or looked me up and down. These were advances I had welcomed when we first met. They made me feel desired. But I was beginning to reevaluate my past, and I couldn't comfortably welcome this plain objectification anymore. I told him this talk felt boyish, adolescent, which hurt him. But the stakes felt high for me now: in bed, Jon's touch also sometimes triggered memories of being coerced or forced into sexual acts. "When you touch the back of my head when I'm going down on you," Angela Garbes writes in *Essential Labor*—quoting a friend who also fell with her husband into a routine of her turning his sexual advances down—"what I feel isn't you—it's every person who's ever pushed me to do it when I really didn't want to."

Rather than pursue some shared sexual awakening in which we both excavated our trauma and bonded over how gender had led us apart, it was easier to push all these uncomfortable power relations between us away. Like many married couples we got into appointment television, nights when we could count on poking fun at people on

TV while eating and drinking together. When we were living in New York, I had roped Jon into my love affair with *The Bachelor*, and in those days we often stayed in on weekends, splayed on our wobbly couch. We read and wrote, then recycled cans at the grocery store down the street, using the quarters we got to buy frozen pizza, soy-based Buffalo wings, and tallboys of Molson. We ate while catching up on *The Bachelor*, our bodies flanking the computer screen, not touching.

In California, Jon settled into my general lack of desire, and we returned to hedonistic shared pleasures. "Sex is just one part of how we stay connected," Garbes writes of her own relationship with her husband, just as "parenting, cooking, bingeing *Survivor*, and nursing each other through illness have been." Jon didn't always see it that way. His dissatisfaction still came up whenever we found ourselves in long spinning arguments. He told me he had a fantasy that we would soon move out of whatever phase we were in and start having sex every single day. I tried not to laugh. But what seemed funny or absurd also, at times, made me livid. I was hopelessly wrecked by the fairy-tale romances on which I'd grown up, and I knew I wanted to be courted, again and again, infinitely. But I also wanted to say no, and to not feel as though my refusal might ruin me, and the relationships I had with those I loved. I was coming to recognize my desires, though now I was tasked with a whole new complicated endeavor: the question of what to do with them.

"Sometimes I feel as if, these days, for women, the love language should be getting whatever you want," Lisa Taddeo writes in an essay on the pop psychology topic of "love languages," a term coined by the marriage expert Gary Chapman. "In heterosexual relationships, women have performed acts of service for hundreds of years. It is time for men to listen." I remain convinced that if we want women's bodies to heal from what patriarchy has done to us at every phase of our lives, this is exactly what we need—for men to just listen for a while. But in the early years of marriage, I didn't know what I wanted. I only knew what I did not want. My love language was refusal.

"We need men to be exemplary in their behavior," Harmange writes in her essay on misandry, "because when we women speak, no one listens. We simply can't afford to let them get away with doing things half-heartedly." Long before I could name my troubles around autonomy and the division of labor in my home, I felt this in my marriage: I was no longer interested in putting up with men who acted like . . . men. There was an air of punishment there, in what I did not want, but more earnestly there was a request for penance, for someone to repair the damage that had been done. Over the years of sorting through the best relationship I have ever had with a man, however, I have often stumbled on the fear that if I were to remove everything that had touched me, there might not be anything left. "I think I'm really just very angry," Taddeo writes. "About the years of no suffrage, the rapes and beatings and the come-ons." I was so angry about so much back then. I am still so angry.

Besides pushing my husband away, there were other ways in which I tried to extricate myself from the institutions that now seemed to rule my sensual life. Sometimes Jon and I even resisted together. When we first made plans to move to the Bay Area, we pictured a fulfilling life of art making, teaching, and political activism, but we landed east of Oakland, in the suburbs, and never met up with the few child-free radicals we knew who lived in the city. After the 2016 election I loaded Hannah into the car for the Women's March, desperate to express defiance. The night before, knowing he would have to work the next day, Jon made Hannah a poster that said "Elmo Says Hell No," with the character's big red face frowning. I made for her favorite stuffed kitty a little sign that hung around its neck and read "Pussy Power." Pushing Hannah in her stroller, I marched alongside my mother, who had knitted her own magenta hat. Hannah fell asleep, both of us half listening to my mother tell stories about the '60s. When Hannah woke up, I stopped along the route to nurse, posing for a photo. In the big, invigorated crowd of vaginal bonnets, it did not feel like enough, but it felt good to get out, to be among people as mad as I was, and to feed off their hope.

We sent a long confrontational email to Jon's conservative family that winter, hunching over our computers, banging out our rage. All our efforts brought little relief. But Jon and I kept getting into the streets, taking Hannah with us, trying to explain protest to her in toddler-speak. "We're using our voices," we said, then returned to the isolation of our apartment. Outside these moments of resistance, my moods conspired with the dull ache of depression—a sadness that spread through my muscles each evening, which I could only soothe with drunkenness and TV. The December after the election, the Ghost Ship fire consumed a warehouse in Oakland's Fruitvale neighborhood that had been converted to an artists' live-work space. It had been poorly maintained by the building owners, and the fire killed thirty-six people who lived there. I was consumed with mourning. We had an apartment that was safe and well kept, and though we were barely getting by between Jon's modest salary from the tutoring center and my work at the daycare, we *were* getting by. The Ghost Ship fire had occurred just a half hour from our apartment, and I didn't know anyone who lived there, but the tragedy made me feel foolish for how often I had wished we lived in some imagined utopian commune of artists who shared caregiving and shirked traditional work. The fire felt like a harsh reminder that there was nowhere to which we might escape. And I couldn't see how to resolve such a sad revelation.

Love, especially marital and familial love, is often sold as an antidote to such times, and because I wanted Jon to stay, I continued trying to make room for him. "Usually we imagine that true love will be intensely pleasurable and romantic, full of love and light," bell hooks writes. "In truth, love is all about work." hooks often refers to love in her analysis as labor, but elsewhere in her writing she calls love an "art." "Our culture may make much of love as compelling fantasy or myth," hooks writes, "but it does not make much of the art of loving." Jon and I always wanted the same thing, even though we spoke different languages: for being together to feel creative and freeing, for it to feel like art. But we struggled to find the right genre, the right medium, for what we were making together, constrained as we were by forms we had inherited.

The burden of work outside and inside the home also weighed heavily on us. And I, especially, resisted giving my husband too much of myself. I had already spent too many years on the other side of unequal wants, and I no longer wanted to "surrender the will to power," which hooks writes is necessary for knowing love. Sometimes Jon and I could momentarily set aside our differences and achieve something like temporary autonomy, but even those moments reared their head, reminding me that the repercussions of giving into marriage and family life weighed more heavily for me. One afternoon, after a long hike, we eagerly jumped into bed while Hannah napped in the other room, our bodies hot and blooded from walking and talking all morning. Sunshine poured through the small bedroom window in our otherwise cave-like apartment, and we laughed and made love, sticky and alive. A few weeks later, just a few months before Hannah's second birthday, I took a pregnancy test alone in our apartment. I was set to start a new part-time job at a local arts center in three days—the position was supposed to be my big return to public life. I had pulled together a plan: I would do the arts center work and shifts at the daycare, try to get some teaching jobs; my sister would let me have some free daycare for a while in exchange for my working when she needed me. The pregnancy test was positive.

My second pregnancy was not *not* part of the plan—it was not *un*planned. The potential for conceiving had brought Jon and me together that afternoon, after the hike, both of us searching for—something. And we had turned to the one place we had found it: caring for Hannah was taxing, but full of joy and discovery. She was a lesson in love, and though we were rattled and broken trying to find our way as new parents, she enchanted us, and was the closest thing to magic—or art—we had ever known. We wanted her to have a sibling, mostly conceptually, someone with which she could take on the world. But pregnancy is always a surprise, even when it's not, and when I told Jon about the test, he assured me I didn't have to keep the baby, seeing how the volume of the work two kids would require now panicked me. We both knew this was the plan, however mislaid, but he was trying to restore some sense of agency in my life.

As I again presented as a pregnant woman, I was assured by mothers I bumped into at the daycare that any skepticism I had about my ability to make room for this child in my life was unwarranted. "You won't believe how big your heart grows!" they said. I think I saw my second pregnancy, however, as a kind of rebellion—a refusal to return to the world of capitalist work, a "choice," or, at the very least, an ineffectual attempt to take back some control in my life—to make a decision and just fucking go with it. There I was, in this world. I may as well make something of it. But to accommodate the love I would develop for this second child, many other paths in my life would narrow or get blocked off completely.

In pregnancy I would fall in love all over again with my body's ability to create something from nothing, but in the postpartum period I would hate my body in new and old ways, as I pumped breast milk in a storage closet at the arts center, surrounded by stage props and clay busts that looked on as I huffed impatiently and poked at the new stretch marks and folds in my stomach. I would begin taking medication that I would need for the rest of my life for a thyroid condition spurred by my two pregnancies, and I would be repeatedly diagnosed with adjustment disorder, leaving me to wonder whether my problem, as a mother and woman, was just my stubborn inability to exist in the world, rather than the world's inability to let me exist as is. I would refuse, however, to take any psychopharmaceuticals—antidepressants, anti-anxiety medications—even as it became increasingly obvious I would benefit from them—not because I thought it made me good or strong, but because I had watched my own mother struggle, going on and off different pills and diagnoses, reaching unsustainable highs and lows, during which I never knew how to reach her, then supplementing with alcohol and pot and coke. I knew too that my grandmother had spent much of her adult life shut in her home, a housewife in a housecoat addicted to tranquilizers, and though in the coming years I would find myself given to fits of utter hopelessness, I didn't want to give into the idea that I could not fix my own circumstances except by medicating myself.

I would soon meet more precarity in my work, juggling numerous part-time positions, literally running to and from my car every day for years to get to the kids, the jobs, the responsibilities; to make enough money and do enough things. I would become more dependent on Jon, for his income, and not surprisingly, my disdain for the intentional economic disempowerment of women and caregivers would grow as well, a special rage I would mostly fire at my husband, who had much to learn, but whom I also turned repeatedly into a straw man for all the maleness in the world. I would recoil from his touch again, my skin stunned not just by the physical contact two children would require but by every sense memory of how my body had been used by men previously.

So, yes, I would go on to love that second baby. My heart would grow, I guess, in the metaphorical sense. But I would also have to reshape my entire life to make room for the love—and the labor—that my second baby would require. There would be so much loss in making room.

My second baby, however, would also inspire in me a new wave of resistance. Motherhood the second time around was more triggering than ever, but it was also an awakening for which I hadn't planned, one sparked by the larger cultural shifts I witnessed, mostly from a distance, as I learned how to make my way as a mother of two. When I was seven months pregnant, throngs of brave women began sharing stories of sexual violence online. Even my mother shared a post on her

Facebook page about what she called "the 'Me Too' conversation" in which she claimed she had been raped by two family members. Most of my mother's post was about how much she regretted working so hard to attract men—about the money she spent on lingerie, makeup, and the general performance of gender—only to find herself degraded on "all fours," but she also wrote about the inequality she felt in her marriage, claims I had mostly written off, when I was young, as tiresome hostility. But by 2017, like my mother, I was rethinking all my relationships with men, and I began to see how, as a girl, I had spent so much time disbelieving my mother's pain. I shared none of my sexual experiences online that fall, though I posted something on Facebook about how not all women wanted or felt ready to share their traumas on social media, a post I later deleted. I suppose, though, that it was true—I was not yet ready. As an isolated mother on the verge of giving birth, I was terrified to relive more of my old pain, to face it fully.

Elliott was born on what I think was a rainy night, though I had little awareness of the weather outside the hospital while I was in labor. It was December, the last day of the fall semester. I was teaching that semester at a community college in the Bay Area, but my second baby, just like Hannah, must have felt I had put my work down. Hannah was born just days after the close of the spring semester, which meant the annual celebrations of both of my children's births and my own bodily cycles had been forever patterned to the academic calendar. My second labor and birth was, as is often the case, more rapid and therefore more painful. Jon held me in a tub in the hospital room, and I alternated between that position, throwing up in the bathroom, and squatting deep to coax contractions, hoping to speed things along. The birth brought Jon and me together. I let him care for me, and he let his limbs go numb, trying to hold me up.

That winter I had given myself over to the nostalgia of the season, buying into the wistful futurity of the event: my littlest gift. I had decorated Elliott's nursery with cacti because I imagined his arrival much the same way I had imagined Hannah's: as a sign of life in a fruitless desert. Many women in America, especially those like me who had been sheltered by a certain kind of racial and economic privilege, were absorbing the centrality of inequality and violence in American life. We could no longer listen to the news without crying or exploding. By the time Elliott was born, I knew Jon was poor at many aspects of parenting young kids, but he continued carrying the work in ways he knew how. He *tried*. But by then I had stayed home with Hannah and worked odd part-time jobs for nearly three years. I had come to need Jon in ways that made me feel weak and unfeminist, including financially, and I resented him even for the ways he supported me.

In my second postpartum period, Jon's work at home transitioned from changing to diapers to removing one child when the physical contact of two became too much for me. During his nine weeks of partially paid leave (funded by his private employer, since the school at which he worked had too few employees to qualify him for state leave), Jon took Hannah to the parks, and they developed the relationship they'd never had—united by my sending them away. Elliott and I spent days alone, getting to know each other. And then Jon went back to work and everything at home fell on me again.

On the first trip to the park with my two kids alone, one an infant, the other not yet three years old, I was overcome by terror that I could not manage both babies' needs, or remember all the stuff I had to bring with me to keep both of them alive and happy. I missed Jon; I missed not being around another adult. But at night we resumed arguing about how we had gotten where we were, who made what choice, what choice even was. Jon, ever the optimist, believed then that he and I had hardly changed in ten years; that we had made good choices, even if we had sometimes "made it hard on ourselves," as he put it, by trying to do so much. But to me, we had only ever done what we grew up thinking we should do: get educations, get married, have children, be good parents, work to support ourselves.

I tried to convince him that we had been *destroyed* by the work of caring for children, because that was how the whole thing had been designed, but he never wanted to see it this way. He defined our love by exceptionalism, when all I could see was how preprogrammed it all felt. "I am not the enemy," he would say. But all the men I knew *had* become the enemy, especially when they could not *see* what I saw, just as every oblivious man in the street or driving around town had become a stand-in for the men in power I now regularly saw on the news—the ones who assaulted women, raped them, beat them, rose to power anyway. And really, was blaming all men for all of it so bad, in comparison? "All that time they spend sniveling about how hard it is to be a poor persecuted man nowadays," Harmange writes, "is just a way of adroitly shirking their responsibility to make themselves a little less pure products of the patriarchy."

Sometimes it seemed Jon was saying men could not be blamed for carrying power within them, but women could be blamed for carrying a rage against it. And yet nothing felt more warranted than my own discontent with how things had ended up. "We aren't hurting anyone when we hate men," Harmange writes. "And, for that matter, we don't really hate them, because we've all got boyfriends, brothers, fathers, sons, colleagues, and friends whom we like and love." After #MeToo, it felt much clearer to me how ignorant most men are of how it feels to be tasked from girlhood with the work of taking care of everyone— with the labor of speaking happiness into being as evidence of one's capacity for womanhood, while at the same time privately wishing so much of the world away. And now, with two children, the question of how, if ever, I would get my life back loomed again.

Jon often offered to "trade places" with me, a sneaky trick he used to try to soothe my anger and sadness, by encouraging me to quit my piecemeal work and just write—to make a life of what I really wanted. All I had to do was say the word, he said, and we would find a way. I wanted to shake him, to make him see how impossible it would be to flip our lives that way. But Hannah tugged at my leg and Elliott cried out from his crib and I fled these bedroom conversations, stomping around the house, yelling about the tiny shit objects I found everywhere around the house. It had become a fixation of mine lately—the odd unmatched sock, the stray Lego, the arm from a lost doll, a full bag of useless plastic toys brought home from a birthday party—all of which I would find piled on the kitchen counter or strewn in forgotten, cobwebbed corners of the apartment. There was a lot be upset about, but it all seemed to come back to one thing: men never attended to these kinds of tasks—to the everyday sorting of the details.

In 2019, Jon and I took the kids on a winding drive in the North Bay. Months earlier, I had finally completed my dissertation and landed a lectureship at a local university. Four years after becoming a mother, I was finally working nearly full-time, and though that life had its own troubles related to the impossibility of doing it all—the hunger I now felt for the bodies of my children during my four-hour round-trip commute and the guilt that came with putting my second child in full-time daycare so young—I enjoyed feeling part of a larger community beyond my home again. It was what I had needed for so long.

On our drive, Jon and I argued as we rounded the cliff on which our little car seemed to teeter, looking out at the bluffs and the ongoingness of the ocean, which threatened to devour us. That afternoon, we staged for the kids a nice middle-class afternoon: we bought them ice cream sandwiches that made streaks down their forearms and chins; we drank rosé out of little glass bottles. Jon was so good at the art of loving them, carrying them on his shoulders, making fun of himself to get them to laugh. In the sun I could see he had a kind of loyalty, a devotion, that I wasn't sure I had. He was bumbling at times, but a very good father, wiping up the kids' messy faces, swinging them around in the grass. He looked at me while trying to hug me that afternoon, and I could only compare that look to the way I looked at my children—to how I pulled them close, huffed their hair, studied them, craving in those moments only them, forever. Popular marital advice may discourage mothers from letting the love for their children replace their love for their partner—but what a ridiculous ask. My children were my great love story; they always will be. And I had to pull away from my husband, to love my kids the way I wanted to *and* the way I was told to.

That year we moved into a rental home with a yard and an extra room in which I could occasionally write. We had space and security, and this was so much more, I knew, than many in America had. But when the pandemic hit in 2020, I was again inundated with domestic and maternal work. I felt physically constricted and crushed by all the labor that had previously been spread among a community of daycares, schools, and social worlds. It felt like I was falling back into the early days of motherhood. Jon was working another tough job, teaching students at a high school, which required that he lock himself in a room for hours every day to teach. I became responsible for endless feeding, servicing feelings, playing, entertaining, cleaning, teaching, socializing. Jon tried to help me as best he could on his lunch breaks, but for most of every day I was spread between my computer and my children. I lost some work and tried to hold on to the work I still had.

In the spring I insisted we start a garden, where we all tinkered. The kids and I planted tomato plants that smelled like earth and pumpkins that went wild; sunflowers eventually towered over the kids' heads. I wanted to give them something during this time, which I assumed would be uncanny and disorienting, but brief. Jon tilled the soil on weekends, sometimes cheerily, other times begrudgingly. He hated the garden, the labor of it, but he did it for me and for the kids.

We spent afternoons outside, he and I drunk with sun and blush wine with ice and berries inside, all four of us piling into a hammock we had ordered online, until one of us toppled out, laughing. For a few months, the wine in the yard made me forget the career and identity losses I was enduring. But when the sun went down, I kept drinking, hiding under a thick cloak of self-effacement—in the timelessness and spaciousness of drunkenness, just as I always had. Jon drank with me, then we had sex or watched TV. The weeks dragged on; he went to bed early without me. I watched television and drank more, leaving housework for another time. Here was time for me, earned and necessary. The more I drank, the more I felt that to be true. I saw my body as I saw my house: pure atmosphere, a landscape through which my children moved during the day, which went dim at night.

Spring turned to summer, the world unchanged, still a place where we could not venture safely. I struggled to get out of bed. I spent every day cranky and rageful, watching the clock, counting down the minutes until I could give it all up and start drinking again. Underneath it all was that question again, that feeling: *Did I ask for this?* An echo, perhaps, of Betty Friedan's famous question: *Is this all?*

Jon tried to carry more of the workload around the home. I convinced myself that the afternoons, rarely relaxing or undisturbed, provided the pleasure and autonomy that was missing from my life. Drunkenness was a way to leave the trap of domesticity when I had no clear exit. But by June, leaving my body no longer brought the comfort I was seeking. Collapsing into cold glasses of pink wine at the end of the day and reclining in my cheap plastic outdoor chair— one of the blue ones my mother had bought when we first moved to California—all while holding my glass just so, was more than a part I was playing. It had become a tacit agreement I made with myself to transmute from woman into backcloth. Like the hidden mothers who in the nineteenth century draped themselves in black fabric to disappear themselves while they held their babies still for photographs, I was vanishing myself.

In anger, and in anguish, I quit drinking. I had spent so long trying to shape myself around the needs of others. I no longer wanted to live in the background of my own story. I wanted to be the protagonist. As Duras writes in the final lines of her essay on alcohol, which she penned after getting sober, "After a time you have the choice— whether to keep drinking until you're senseless and lose your identity, or to go no further than the beginnings of happiness. To die, so to speak, every day, or to go on living." I reject the characterization of sobriety as a choice because it's simply not that easy for most who struggle with addiction. But for me, it was the ultimate form of refusal, of throwing the heavy world off me and beginning to take my body back from a culture that told me women fared best when they blended into the walls.

Jon quit drinking with me, in solidarity, and a few months later we had sex sober for the first time in years, sun peeking through the blackout curtains in our room as we sweat and pushed into each other. After that though, I kept my body mostly to myself, for that first year of sobriety, and we separated in our own home, trying to make sense of who we had become. At first, I saw this withholding of sex as a sign of neurosis—as what Freud would have called frigidity. But I was eventually able to see it for what it was: I had simply issued my resignation, freeing myself for more important work.

CONSENT

I CAME TO MOTHERHOOD for the fantasy of family, but I stayed, at least in part, for the scientific and spiritual mysteries that shrouded my body, thanks to the sex education I had—and had not—received when I was young. Though most of what I knew about women's bodies came from the cultural narratives I consumed growing up, my formal schooling around sex began in fifth grade, when my class was divided into rooms based on gender. Each group was forced to watch their own traumatizing videos on the terror of puberty. Girls went home with pads; boys, as far as I could tell, went home with permission to masturbate.

I saw then that boys lived in their own world, cordoned off from the one shared by girls, which was filled with fears of passive-voice diseases like herpes and pregnancy. This gendered separation, though, only made boys more interesting to me. While all my first sexual experiences had been with girls, fooling around during parentless playdates, playing "massage parlor," once the school system separated us out and introduced the subject of our looming reproductive capabilities, I craved what I thought of then as a *real* first kiss, the kind that would count. My attraction to girls felt deviant and dirty, so I found new ways to connect with them—talking about boys. Eventually we scrawled volumes of handwritten notes to each other in high school, lamenting boys who used us or led us on, leaving us brokenhearted and depressed. We put our agony in writing to try to get it out, and we had conversations after school about swallowing cum and shared insecurities, wondering over whether we were too slutty, too prude, too ugly, too fat.

We sometimes got what we wanted, only to realize it was not what we wanted, and then we whispered and wrote to each other about the tacky residue of boys' fluids, the taste, the way sperm swam back up our throats after we barely managed to gulp it down, the dark bedrooms we had gone into at parties, what had happened there, leaving us wondering if we should have said no and if what boys had taken from us meant they liked us or hated us. I can't recall discussing with friends how, every time I jerked a guy off, he insisted on pulling up my shirt and leaving his mark over my bellybutton, never cleaning up his mess. We spilled secrets, but we also wanted to appear sexually mature and experienced. I did, however, write a note to a best friend in high school, after I felt duped into sleeping with the virgin football player. In it, my penmanship burst with indignation and hurt: *Why did he sleep with me if he didn't like me! Why am I crying over him!* That act of using girls was of the era: boys' unsympathetic hands shoved into us, the talk about girls' smells heard later on the blacktop at lunch, each boy laughing with two fingers up—female desire appreciated only as trophy, as proof of a boy's manhood.

Despite all the sex off campus, in the late '90s, at school, a lot of abstinence talk was put on the table. There was only one banana demonstration to my memory, slipped into a broadly conceptualized "Health" class that took place in a hot, second-story room filled with giggles—whose source was less our own pubescent embarrassment than our disbelief at the incompleteness of the information presented. "Health" class at least helped me revise my early childhood belief that babies were born from women's assholes—a belief itself born from the reasoning that my body could not possibly stretch *that much*. Beyond the condom lesson, though, pregnancy, our teachers warned, was just something girls had to look out for, something we could "catch" if we were not careful. Even in California, sex education in the late '90s and early 2000s was all about the maintenance of authority, and the job of educators was to navigate us away from our bodies, not actually teach us anything about them.

Not much has changed in California since, although sex education has become increasingly politicized, and increasingly seen as an arena in which the American right can attempt to exert power over the bodies of children by policing discourses on gender, sexuality, and the family. Across the country, as I write, a growing body of legislation stipulates what educators cannot say about sex and sexuality. The way we talk to our children about their bodies has become a political frontline—though of course, it always was. Though the conservative rhetoric around sex education is frequently couched in narratives about "protecting" children, attacks on gender-affirming healthcare for transgender youth and on non-heteronormative families through the public school system have the same ideological goal as attacks on women's reproductive freedom: they seek to groom children for the gender binary and the nuclear family, two primary sources of male power.

Most of what I learned about sex, however, did not come from school. It came from my early sexual encounters, during which young boys taught me, without words, not only what sex was for, but what my body was for. My first real boyfriend, Kevin, was two years older than me, a junior who didn't wash his long dark hair often—he had a stable Christian family, but he was actively rebelling. He showed me pictures he had taken of graffiti he'd spray-painted in alleys and on buildings, and I daydreamed that he might one day tag our names inside a heart, on a train, but he never did. The boys' crew name was FSU, Fuck Shit Up. I envied the way Kevin cared so little about everything, even me.

Kevin was frank with me about how bad I was at jerking him off—how I chafed his dick when I went to work in his best friend's hot tub—and he coached me, albeit impatiently, until I improved. The logistics of friction, however, remained confusing. Kevin was uncircumcised, and he often put his hand over mine, hurrying me, trying to demonstrate how not to strip his foreskin, moving my hand at an unsustainable pace. I tried to keep up after he let go, moaning and sticking my boobs and butt out to coax his orgasm, but my triceps throbbed. I switched arms, irritating him more. Everything I did was not quite right. He redirected me, and just when I thought I had him, he would carp about my dry palms, as if my hands—and the rest of my body—were just getting in the way. Sometimes he just took over and finished himself.

My presence seemed both incidental and integral to something boys wanted, though I also suspected that Kevin pined over an older girl with big boobs and a round butt, someone womanlier that me. My body was shapeless and bony, stringy like my hair. When my hand job skills failed, eventually Kevin began pushing my head down, but grievances and teasing about my teeth followed. I should have bitten down.

"The loss of innocence," Andrea Dworkin writes in *Intercourse*, "for a man already socialized to exploit—is a real and irreversible corruption of his capacity to love a woman as a human being." I can't say how Kevin knew to exploit me for his own sexual gains—how he lost his own innocence or why he didn't love me or ever quite see me as a human being. He was an adolescent, and an otherwise kind boy. I think he's a father and a husband now. But there was a barrier between us then, something I read as a direct result of my un-desirousness, my relative unattractiveness, my inability to please *and* my sexual over-availability. The FSU crew watched porn together after school. It was 1999. And even though porn was becoming more accessible on the internet, they had tapes and magazines that they circulated, just as my husband did with his friends when he was a teenage boy. Dworkin, frequently criticized for her polemics against porn as "sex negative," would likely trace at least some of Kevin's willingness to make use of my body to images of women he was consuming—representations of women that linked sex to violation. But she also would have noted that most heterosexual intercourse is laced with contempt for women and "a sexed hierarchy"—a phenomenology about which "we are inarticulate."

It's undeniable that Kevin saw me as a means to an end, a set of limbs and holes through which he might live out his fantasies. But outside our sexual encounters, his interest in me was unsteady. In front of his friends at lunchtime, laughing and tossing his dirty hair aside, he sometimes bit the knobby bun I wore atop my head when my arm ached too much to take up a blow-dryer and curling iron—an expression of how much he disliked my hair that way. So perhaps it was just that Kevin didn't like *me* that much, even though I wanted him so badly, I would have followed his sexual teachings anywhere. The year 1999 may have been a good one for teenage-boy porn, but it was also a big year for outsider girls metamorphosing alongside angsty, popular boys. I watched *10 Things I Hate About You* and *She's All That* in movie theaters with girlfriends, sucking down Diet Coke and buttered popcorn, dreaming about making myself over through love. I wanted to believe I could reform Kevin, but the night I entered a shipping container used to store sports equipment on the dark athletic field of a Christian high school in Sun Valley, he taught me much more about sex than love.

While I'm sure the boys had all been drinking forties of malt liquor that night, as they often did, taping glass bottles to their hands, trying to see who could finish eighty ounces before pissing himself, another girl and I had shared a bottle of Boone's Farm, our drinking preferences already gendered. Kevin found a thick gymnastics landing pad in the shipping container and we set ourselves up there in the dark. I put my hands in his pants, and soon he was jamming my head down over his cock, skipping right over the burden of kissing and my poorly executed "hand stuff," his head pitching up, his hand on my bun for leverage. I gagged, strawberry flavor coming up. He fumbled under my shirt for a nipple—the way I would learn, years later, babies do as they nurse. On the opposite side of the shipping container, the other girl and her boyfriend were having sex. Our closeness was erotic and embarrassing. The two boys grunted and laughed—sonic high-fives. And I stared off into the abyss of Kevin's long, unwashed pubic hair. I tried not to throw up. I moaned again. I swallowed. I learned.

Consent was not a concept I ever heard of growing up. It wasn't common discourse among girlfriends, it wasn't foregrounded in sex ed, and it wasn't discussed at home. I read my mother's *Cosmo* for tips on how to get men off, but it didn't occur to me—or to my mother—to pursue an education around my own pleasure, much less to question why I found early sex acts painful, nauseating, and disorienting. I knew much more as a teenager about the differences between holding and mouthing dicks depending on their circumcision status than I knew about where my clitoris was or how my vulva connected to my labia—much less about how much better it felt to rub myself than to be penetrated. Sometimes, at drunk parties, I kissed girls, which I had always enjoyed, but it was usually staged for the male gaze. My sexualization moved me further and further from my own desire.

My mother told stories about the women in our family, but her chronicles were rarely cautionary tales, and they didn't provide any kind of concrete template for pushing back against a sexual world that placed male desire at the center. The stories she told were simply about what women did; what women knew. When there were stories about violation—about men in positions of power who had thrown her against walls, threatened her, shoved their tongues down her throat, or about men who kept up relationships with her because they didn't have money of their own, men who tied her up, who coked her up, who wouldn't leave their wives for her—she didn't offer any morals I could use as a guide for my own life.

She did see clearly, though, that the world was set against women. When I was in elementary school, a man parked his car beside the school playground where I was climbing with my friends, all girls. We squinted in the sunlight, noted something twitching and sparkling in the man's lap, and ran. That was when I learned the term "jerking off." The whole incident was bewildering. I wanted someone to tell me how to make sense of this man's half-nakedness, his eyes on us, his barely perceptible movements. No one really did. We told teachers and parents what we saw, but I had no revelatory debrief with my mother. She just scoffed at *men*, upset but unsurprised, and her reaction confirmed an idea that was already blooming inside me, which was that men did want they wanted, while women and girls picked up the pieces. Later, I learned the word "rape" when a friend was absent from school—she had been attacked one afternoon while walking home.

My mother passed down to me a generalized disappointment with men. Very young, I saw resentment written on her body, which was, however confusingly, a map on which I located my own flesh and my own frustration. It seemed she was blackmailing and bitter toward me not only because being a single mother taxed her but also because she was still looking for love, finding only cruelty in its place. Any connection—between the violence and violation she experienced in her sex life and the challenges of motherhood—was murky for us both. But I sensed in her, always, a repudiation of the roles of both mother and woman, even when, at times, the closeness the two of us shared felt stifling. When I was in the third grade, she had an abortion and told me about it on the night of the procedure as we bathed together. The water that night, like all her stories and like all her baths, was scorching yet therapeutic, and I must have begun to understand then the impossible task women face, which my mother taught me through her storytelling, but also night after night as we burned off the day together in the bath. To survive as a woman in this world, she seemed to say, we must regularly destroy the shit we have collected inside our bodies.

There was not, to my knowledge, any alternative. But I knew that some women in our family had resisted motherhood, for reasons I didn't quite understand. They did away with unwanted pregnancies in clinics, or in bedrooms, or tried. My great-grandmother, Jean, gave herself multiple abortions at home. My mother told me Jean used hangers repeatedly, disfiguring her reproductive system over time, but it's possible Jean used other abortive methods, and that these were simply cultural images of abortion my mother patterned on to what she knew. Jean was white and came from money, and although her father forbade her from going to the women's college she wanted, she was educated at a finishing school meant to prepare her for marriage. Safe abortion may have been possible for Jean, living just outside of Chicago at the turn of the century, because of her race, class, and marital status. It's also possible that Jean was raped in her marriage and then suffered through abortions alone, though it's hard to say how Jean herself would have categorized the way her body fit into her marriage—whether she endorsed a kind of marital duty. But given how many times my great-grandmother had to do away with unwanted pregnancies, I have always assumed she simply couldn't say no to the man she lived with, who was known to be an angry alcoholic who drove a Duesenberg and threw big parties.

Jean died before menopause due to complications caused by a final at-home abortion, never getting the chance to know her body as something other than a maker of children. The details of those complications are lost to time and the haziness of generational memory. But I know Jean's life was altered by legal and medical institutions that endorsed a husband's ownership over his wife, and that didn't see women as capable of making choices about their bodies. Even so, whenever my mother spoke of Jean, she spoke only of my great-grandmother's sadness. My mother was ashamed of Jean's depressive tendencies, as though they issued from some flaw within— something perhaps we carried in ourselves, too. Jean's feminine melancholy was, for my mother, just another thing Jean could not rid herself of, however she tried—and it was, perhaps, the thing my mother, too, was always trying to overcome. Ultimately, my mother came to see her own dark periods the ways she saw Jean's. My mother's alcoholism, her trouble with men, her imperfect motherhood—these she would come to see as indications that there was something broken in her, rather than in the world.

In her book on the logic of misogyny, *Down Girl*, Kate Manne writes that boys and girls receive two very different educations in a misogynistic culture, both leading to the same beliefs about women's sexual roles. By age six, Manne notes, girls begin to doubt female intelligence. As they grow older, they are assailed daily by male expressions of desire: verbal harassment and catcalling, for instance, continually remove girls from their own thoughts, giving them information about their social value. Young boys, on the other hand, grow up with a sense of entitlement to women's bodies and emotional work, a claim that resounded in 2014, the year I got pregnant with Hannah, when Elliot Rodger killed six people and wounded fourteen in Isla Vista, California, a few hours from where I had grown up. Rodger killed three Asian men before heading to a sorority house with a Starbucks latte and three semiautomatic weapons, where he shot three women, killing two. Later, he killed a man at a deli, wounding others as he drove wildly, before crashing and killing himself.

Some commentators claimed that Rodger didn't hate women but loved them too much, given how much he wanted to have sex with them. In his own manifesto, however, Rodger blamed women for all his "suffering," even as his text reveals his racism and a history of being bullied by young boys. Amia Srinivasan argues that Rodger neglected to explore the interconnectedness of the ideologies that allowed him to objectify women and feel entitled to their sex and those that made him unfuckable. But "these were the rules of Elliot Rodger's universe," Chanel Miller writes in her analysis of the massacre, one of which she framed as "'*I desired girls, but girls never desired me back. . . . It is an injustice that cannot go unpunished.*'" Rodger's case has been much debated by feminists: for the extent to which his violence demonstrates male entitlement not just to sex but also to violence; for the role Rodger's racial hierarchies played in his own disenfranchisement. The incel movement, however—incel is short for "involuntary celibate"—demonstrates what Dworkin observed decades earlier, which is that "hatred of women is a sexual pleasure for men in its own right."

Though any understanding of consent would have been helpful to me growing up in the '90s, the idea that affirmative consent can act as a cure-all for such a culture neglects how misogyny structures and polices men's and women's sexual relations from a young age. Enthusiastic and ongoing consent is a wonderful vision to which we should all aspire, but many cultural and interpersonal forms of power rear their head in intimate encounters between bodies, and in relationships. Overemphasizing affirmative consent elides how misogyny works—by taking root in us and teaching, among other things, that the burden is on girls and women to protect themselves from the unchecked violence of men, while at the same time claiming that women, by nature, cannot be trusted to know what they want.

I kissed and often desired the boys I had sex with in high school, at least before the sex acts began—before they pushed me down and told me how to behave. But I felt entirely forlorn, deserted, puzzled, and emptied when my relationships ended as quickly as they—and those boys—had come. Skateboarder Kevin eventually broke up with me on the phone right after I told him I loved him. I cried alone in my bedroom, slowly peeling off my wall photos of him I had printed at the drugstore and taped up, including one of him biting my bun, and then I moved on, looking for someone else to want me. My life ran together into a string of nights riding around in cars driven drunkenly by older boys, me drunk and high in the backseat, watching streetlights blur to a loud base pulse. My adolescence was ruled by a desire to be desired, but mostly I lusted after boys who discarded me. "It has never been expected that a man ask a woman's consent before using her emotionally," Melissa Febos writes. The same was often true, as I experienced it, with men who used me, and the girls I knew, physically.

After #MeToo, memories of these aspects of my sexual life before marriage rematerialized. I felt used, emotionally and physically, if not by my child, then by whatever forces were shaping my role in my home. Parenthood also forced me to look more closely at what I expected of other people, and what other people had always expected of me. I had to consider what exactly I believed about giving and taking, consent and assault—at what behavior I had excused on behalf of others, at how I blamed myself—because I was now tasked with structuring, for my daughter, daily lessons on touch, autonomy, violation, and care.

One memory that resurfaced in pieces in the early years of motherhood was of an afternoon I had spent with a coworker at my apartment in San Francisco, when I was in college. I had invited this guy, whom I worked with at a grocery store, over, and he got me drunk on high-proof banana schnapps before he started kissing me. At first, I did what I had done since I was a teenager at parties, then later at bars—and what I would eventually do as a nursing mother, when my children asked me for more of my body and I did not know how to refuse them: I snickered playfully and, as kindly as I could, I cooed *no*. I didn't know how to mean it. The coworker and I were sitting on my couch, alone in my apartment, which I shared with an ex-boyfriend with whom I had recently broken up. My ex was away for the rest of the night, working at a restaurant, and I felt suddenly terrifyingly alone and vulnerable. I had flirted with this coworker during shifts at the grocery store, and I had invited him over, so I felt responsible for his advances, obligated to see them through. "Women know that their sexual desire can remove protection from them," Katherine Angel writes. Even the performance of desire—I had never really wanted this guy; I just wanted someone to get high and talk with—I assumed gave this man a right to my body.

Doubt was white noise in my pursuit of recognition then. Sex had for me mostly been defined by pushing through my own discomfort, waiting for men to cum. Years later I can see what was happening that afternoon: my coworker was getting me drunk, expecting either for me to give him sex, or for him to take it. But at that time in my life, protection from male desire wasn't something to which I thought I had any right. I felt I deserved whatever I got unless it was the image of back-alley rape I had held in my mind since I was a girl. Just by virtue of being alone with men, getting drunk with them, inviting them over, flirting with them at work from time to time, I had set something in motion I could not stop. "Once a woman is thought to have said yes to something," Angel writes, "she can say no to nothing." But had I ever said yes? The coworker was older than me, strong and overpowering, and he kissed me aggressively, his tongue poking the back of my throat. I pushed him off coyly, suggesting we smoke some pot, which bought me time. We lit up a little pipe and shared it on my couch, then he kissed me again and kneeled on the floor below me and pulled my pants off.

I can't remember whether I was scared or just disgusted, or whether in these situations I even had access to my feelings. I was more concerned about staving off what felt like an inevitability. I felt what was happening incriminated me, not these men. So I said no, or maybe just "I can't," without conviction, not wanting to make myself undesirable, even though all I wanted was for him to stop desiring me. As he unhooked his belt and pulled his pants down and tried to enter me, I think I held his dick in my hands while he kissed me, buying time. But something in me prevailed, and I told him I didn't feel well, which was not a lie. He revolted me. I felt sick, I said, and cupping my mouth I ran naked to the bathroom, puking, forcing myself to throw up more, fingers down my throat, trying to sound loud and long gone.

That man, like many others, robbed me of a sense of security, of dignity, but also of self-trust. I had to render myself completely abject just to get him to leave my home, to stop pushing himself on me, and I stayed in the bathroom a long time, emptying out, pretending as though I didn't feel his presence lingering in the hallway, committed to making myself as unattractive as possible, hoping he would leave. Eventually, he stood at the bathroom door to say he was going home. I lay on the cold bathroom floor and buried the moment, but his presence never left me. I was so used to casting off my own shock, revising it as flaw.

I moved back to Los Angeles a year later, halfway through college. By then, sex with men I hung out with alone felt even more obligatory, perhaps because I had lived through moments like that one with my coworker. Girls and women often have sex "stolen" from them in their transition from girlhood to womanhood, Manne writes, then are left to sort out these confusing sexual experiences alone. She references a line from J. M. Coetzee's *Disgrace*, a novel about a rape that feels ambiguous to the characters in the book, but not to the reader: "Not rape, not quite that, but undesired nevertheless, undesired to the core." In the novel, Melanie, a student, reluctantly helps David, her older professor, undress her before going slack, as though dying within herself. She finds herself "cast into a cultural script in which such a man's sexual desire has outsized ethical importance." Melanie dissociates after running through what might happen if she did resist. David, reflecting on the encounter afterward, acknowledges that had Melanie fought him, had she had "a sense of entitlement to deny him," their encounter might have been rape.

The scene highlights how legal definitions of rape, which include force but not other forms of coercion, fall short of articulating the complex movement of power between bodies, but also how men and women come to know our sexuality. It also illustrates some of the internal mechanisms at play that lead girls and women not to fight unwanted sex, because it feels like something they are just "meant to do." They worry about repercussions, about force being leveled against them, about rape, but they also "do not want to hurt him or let him down; we want to be a good girl." As a result, many women grow up to expect violation in their sexual lives, and find themselves constantly navigating around it. None of the boys or men I had sex with demonstrated an awareness of this, not until I was married and had plainly laid it all out to my husband in a series of conversations. This disconnect made girlhood isolating and utterly desolate. "To be alone in a one-way exchange of intimacy is sometimes a devastatingly lonely place," Melissa Febos writes.

Coming of age in a culture of assault before the revelations of #MeToo, I saw loneliness and a certain level of regret as a given in a woman's sexual life—a characteristic of longing for love, which would one day be soothed by the arrival of some modern prince. But I also assumed my own internal weakness, like the way my mother had seen the women in our family tree. The feminine sadness that runs through my blood appears to me now, many years later, to be the clear result of men using and abusing women, and of women feeling disempowered in their roles as keepers of the domestic facade. But when I was young, my intuition was subsumed by male desire. Like many women, I assumed whatever hurt was my fault—the result of something I had said or done, or something I should not have said or should not have done. I didn't have the language, as a young woman, to hold men accountable, or to name what was happening—the experience of men exploiting me, of them making me feel my desire was secondary, of them using my body when I was barely conscious. I had no words to name forms of sexual assault that didn't fit inadequate definitions of the term "rape" or even "assault"— such as the times when I gave up or gave in, because it was easier than fighting, or when I hated what I was doing, but had no tools to reverse course. Instead, I carried with me a feeling that had I been more forceful—the way I intuited I should have been—the story might only have turned out worse.

Had I not run to the bathroom that afternoon spent with my coworker, for instance, had I fought back somehow instead, would he have raped me in a manner that was more culturally discernible? Had I not worked with that man many days a week, or had he been smaller and weaker, would I have been more willing to kick him out of my apartment? I can't imagine what I could have said or done back then. I had been conditioned to view my own violation as inevitable. Perhaps if I had been raised in a culture that told me I had the right to make a man leave, to withdraw consent whenever I wanted—and had that man had also understood this—that afternoon would have gone differently. As the prominent feminist Ellen Willis puts it: "What would we choose if we had a real choice?" But I had grown up in America. The choices were simple. I made excuses for the violence of men, for their active mishandling of and disrespect for my body, and I took back ownership of my body the way I knew how: by desexualizing myself, making myself as ugly as possible with my head in the toilet, desperately trying to yank the lever of male desire into the off position.

The terms available to us to describe the ongoing sexual violence and betrayal girls and women experience—harassment, unwanted sex, coercion, assault, rape—are not sufficient to explain what it feels like to grow up in a culture that grooms women from a young age for a life of sexual and emotional sacrifice, while simultaneously measuring our experiences against the cruelest traumas imaginable. This cocktail alone is an assault on the psyche, on the possibility of women knowing and believing themselves. Growing up, it seemed every girl and woman I knew, even those in my family, had more striking stories than mine, about men who had violated them. In the introduction to the anthology *Not That Bad: Dispatches from Rape Culture*, Roxane Gay writes that she once thought of her own rape as "not that bad," but came to see how that thinking gave her an "unrealistic measure for what was acceptable in how I was treated in relationships" and eroded her empathy for others' experiences of sexual violence. "Buying into this notion made me numb to bad experiences that weren't as bad as the worst experiences I heard," Gay writes. "For years, I fostered wildly unrealistic expectations of the kinds of experiences worthy of suffering until very little was worthy of suffering."

Beyond measuring myself against the worst crimes men had committed against women, that voice that said I brought all this violence and violation upon myself never let up, perhaps because my young "sex positive" lifestyle was shrouded in drunkenness and in flecks of what sometimes felt like real desire. I backed down, for instance, from saying "That was rape" of the night I cannot remember with the man in the loft in Santa Monica, and with the man in New York who I knew from high school, because I blamed myself for not knowing what I wanted (did I have some attraction to those men?), for what I did want (to get drunk and flirt and feel wanted), and for what I saw as my own hand in making myself a vulnerable woman (I must have left my friends or told them it was okay to leave me). But if something like this ever happened to my child, there would never be a question: without the capacity to walk or remember, one cannot consent.

When I became a mother, the physical intimacy of caring for children—and the everyday navigation of questions about autonomy and consent—brought up a slew of unprocessed memories. I began thinking more about my experiences growing up in what Gay calls "a culture where it often seems like it is a question of when, not if, a woman will encounter some kind of sexual violence," because I once again felt the need to qualify my unhappiness by downplaying it. Didn't that feel familiar. I hadn't had a very traumatic birth, the postpartum months weren't extraordinarily fraught, I had breastfed mostly with ease and even enjoyed it, I had a partner who tried to help, we got by financially, and I had found a job where I could care for my child and make a little money at the same time. My family enjoyed immense privilege. Sure, I was deeply depressed and lost and angry, but my troubles just weren't *that bad*.

Thinking this way, however, compromised my ability to consider how other women around me were suffering—and, maybe more important, how everything was connected. I found myself scowling at mothers in parks who spoke to their children or disciplined them in ways I perceived as wrong. As Gay writes, "The surfaces of my empathy became calloused." But I needed that empathy for other parents, and for the children I was raising. I now had to consider how I would prepare my children for a culture in which the issues of routine violence against women, the politics of sex, and the gendered division of labor are far from settled, a responsibility that felt heavier in my relationship to my daughter. My greatest fear for her has always been that I might have to hold her someday while she cries, telling me she has been raped or assaulted, but there are many peripheral fears around the big terror: fears that she will hold herself responsible for men violating her; that she won't come to me for help because she feels guilt or shame; that she won't be able to access her own sense of pleasure, seeing sex and sexuality and care as burdens or sources of confusion, as I often have. Most simply, I fear for her happiness.

Parents can't let themselves go too far down that road; I know. We must nurture some other vantage point, one not of this world, so that when we talk to our children we aren't passing on all the junk we *have* collected in our bodies. I have to maintain in my mind the idea that no matter what happens, my daughter, like me, will survive, she will not be shattered, she will not be torn apart. To provide that path, though, I have had to relive painful truths about myself, my childhood, and the trauma that was passed down my family line. "Being female in this world is having been robbed of the potential for human choice by men who love to hate us," Dworkin writes in *Intercourse.* I believe this to be true, however painful it is to admit. But one can't parent from such a perspective. We have to imagine something more.

When I gave birth to Hannah, whom the doctors marked *girl,* I had no idea how complex the work of passing on a sense of bodily autonomy would become, in part because I failed to account for how much the world would intervene. As our isolated domestic world cracked open more and more over time, our relationship was filled in with ideas from the outside. Not long after Hannah was born, my sister turned me on to Magda Gerber, a specialist in infant development who claimed that one of the best ways to respect children's autonomy is to engage in "sportscasting," the verbal narration of a child's behaviors, interactions, and feelings. The primary argument for this approach is that it helps children attach language—rather than moral judgments—to whatever is going on with their bodies. Gerber's odd evocation of our national obsession with athletics aside, the practice is supposed to offer caregivers a method for nurturing children without imposing or projecting our own beliefs on to the child. The best sportscasting is coolly detached, loving in its objectivity.

Early on, I was a zealot of this approach. Jon and I tried not to gasp or laugh at the diapered explosions—out of deference, as the Gerber-inspired advice suggested—but we still found ourselves laughing uncontrollably the day I looked on while Jon changed a diaper, streams of greenish goo squirting from our baby's butthole all over his hands, which flailed wildly, tossing wipes in all directions. Hannah's wide unknowing eyes looked up at us, wondering what she had done to make us smile, wanting more. After we moved back to California, when Hannah began speaking and asking questions, sportscasting became even more confounding. I struggled with the notion of objectively conveying the world to my child, because all language is morally and symbolically loaded. Observing my child aloud felt like a kind world building, and the power of the work intimidated me. I could say anything to her, and I would make it true.

Telling the story of the world, I eventually decided, is the most important, most creative, work of parenting, and neutralizing my voice felt like giving up the only corner of political struggle I had left in those years. My attention to detail and the process of interpretation, each of which I had been trained to labor over as a writer and academic, became my daily out-loud work. I abandoned objectivity, and instead I spoke to Hannah about everything around us, telling stories about how we live—and how we might live better. I abandoned objectivity, and instead I spoke to her about her body, calling attention to it in ways I sometimes I regretted, and sometimes felt proud of. Over the years, especially as I began reevaluating my early sexual life after #MeToo, I worked hard to use the time I spent alone with Hannah to teach her a language of consent. "I don't like it when you tug on my nipple and hit my face while you suck on me" or "stop licking my arm and laughing," I would say, the limits I had to set as absurd as they were necessary. About what Ashley Simpo called "the rough rough road to gentle parenting," she writes, "As we attempt a more gentle reality for our children, our own childhood trauma resurfaces."

I wanted Hannah to have the education I never had, and in many ways, doing this work taught me about my own body—a resurrection of experience I didn't always welcome or want, but which led me to understand my own coming of age. The language that passed between me and my daughter has, from the beginning, been filled with urgent lessons about gender. But like my mother, I have not always known exactly what lessons I am trying to pass on. When I was pregnant with Elliott and back at work, Hannah began observing the way I navigated labor in and outside the home, trying my methods on for size, as she sometimes did with my too-big-for-her clothes. "Oh gosh," she said one afternoon at the apartment, in the middle of her newly favored game of "I'm the mom." She looked down at her doll sternly; then, with a heavy sigh of feigned exhaustion, hoisted the doll high up on her shoulder, as she mimicked the disciplined, reluctant labor of motherhood. She gathered herself up for more. "All right, baby," she said. "Let's go."

Sometimes she loaded many bags up with knickknacks she found around the house. She piled them all on her two tiny shoulders, lugging them around. She was imitating the slog, the depressive's heavy body. She was imitating me. Watching these little performances unfold, I felt embarrassed, shaken, responsible, misrepresented. I hadn't controlled the narrative the way I wanted to, because my own life remained a reflection of that culture that beats women down until they are wearied, frayed. And now there she was, performing submission. I couldn't help but follow her around, correcting the archive. "Mommies sure do work a lot!" I'd say. "Do you think they should be paid for their work?" Trying desperately to introduce some structural critique into her game. I read the scene as evidence of my own failures at refusal and consent reflected, a mother's own fun-house mirror of shame.

Hannah absorbed messages from me young about the work of motherhood, but the times when I had to sit with her fury, and her pain, taught us more about how daughters learn to make sense of their bodies from their mothers. Hannah's anxiety about blood and the breaking open of skin often overtook her when she was a toddler. She refused to look at her wounds and didn't want to know, when she got hurt, what had happened to her, even when she couldn't stop thinking—and crying—about her injury. If I asked whether she wanted to see a scrape, to know that her body was okay, she wept and shouted and shut her eyes, screaming "*No!*" at me as though I were offering torture. Sometimes the crying went on for hours; she refused food or rest. I begged her to stop, to pull it together. Her unrestrained loss of the world undid me.

And so it went with every bloody hangnail, every deep cut, and with the skinned knee she reopened three times that summer I was pregnant, as she learned to run. Over time she learned to gather the strength to say, "Mommy, I want you to look. Tell me if it's big." And I took this new way of dealing for what it was: an unexplainable trust that had developed despite how I had wronged her with my impatience over her distress. "It's teeny tiny," I would say. "Not even a boo-boo. More of a boo."

I continued to narrate her pain, to measure the volume of her suffering, unsettled by the knowledge that sometimes I diminished it. Just before Elliott was born, Hannah slipped on a step at the park.

Back at home, when I unfastened her from her car seat and put her down to stand, her leg buckled under the weight of her little body, so I hurried her to the ER, where a tall male doctor asked her about her pain. She sat on my lap as the man moved her foot and leg, and I stroked her hair while she buried her face in my chest. She sobbed, looking up at me, fearful of his touch, and I fumbled for words, unsure how to explain that this man we did not know had to touch her despite her wishes to the contrary, but that no other man does—not ever—not unless she offers them an invitation.

The doctor ordered an X-ray, which was inconclusive. There was no way for us to know what sort of pain she was really in, or to what extent her noncompliance with the doctor's requests was rooted in fear or injury. This kind of not knowing, in the early years, maddened me. What could she have said at that age to take part in her own story? She had said, "Ankle still hurt," but I had asked her if her "ankle still hurt" on the drive to the ER. Eventually she said, "Hurt all over," sweeping her little hand up and down her shin and foot, but this was soon after I had asked her if it "hurt all over." I worried that maybe my language, and the limited terms I was able to offer her, had not been enough. Maybe they would never be enough.

The doctor advised putting a cast on her leg up to the knee, just in case, and I called it the "super magic boot" to help Hannah understand why she could not remove it for fourteen days. She asked me to retell the story of the doctor touching her legs many times, interested less in what had happened than in the dynamic exchange of emotions that had passed between us during the event—my repetition of the story the only way for her to make sense of what she had felt. I worked in vague lessons about bodies and consent, but I could not shake the feeling that I had been complicit in a violation, even though the ER doctor's touch had been gentle, clinical, and quick.

When the nurse removed the cast two weeks later, Hannah sat in my lap again, and I held her as she cried. We took the cast home as a souvenir, smelled it together, sticking our tongues out, then tucked it into a box of keepsakes. I told her she was brave because I wanted her to believe it, but I was unsure of what bravery meant in that context, other than an active repression of her own emotions, a going along. I no longer felt that defusing my voice was any kind of answer—that I could or should be an objective force in her life—but I was still finding my footing in the story I wanted to tell. Perhaps I always will be.

During my first days at the hospital after Hannah's birth, we were ordered to stay for two days while her little red feet were repeatedly pricked for glucose tests. She was so small she had to be monitored constantly, per hospital policy, and the wails she let out as they squeezed blood from her heels made me sweat. I wanted to tell the nurses to stop, but instead I just said, "How much more?" I desired, even then, resolute autonomy for her, but I have not always known how to give it to her in a world that doesn't want her to have it. When she was an infant, as I bathed her, made decisions for her, all the tiny, trivial moments of control felt to me like harrowing, irreversible swerves in her budding story. I was confounded by the potent dance of consent that took place between mother and daughter—by how often I continually had to revise my approaches to caring for her.

Parenthood, in other words, isn't just a tool for passing on our beliefs about bodies, but for learning about them. The ever-shifting nuances I had to embrace as I taught my children about needs and wants, and as they challenged me, made me realize how little I had been taught young about how to give and receive, how to account for power imbalances between friends and loved ones. It all demonstrated so clearly that care requires consent, and consent requires great care.

In the process, I felt jerked around by the lessons I *had* been taught and was still receiving about parenting. I was constantly doing damage control, struggling against my own impulses. When Hannah entered grade school in the middle of the pandemic, I began fussing with her hair unconsciously, following her around with hairbrushes in the morning, asking if she wanted to comb out her bed head, seeing she did not, but sometimes still insisting. Eventually I stopped telling her how to present her body to the world. She likes to leave her hair wild. I let her. I know that untamed hair and a sense of self-possession won't be enough to protect her—to secure the basic rights she deserves to make decisions about her body or to keep her from harm—but they are an element of her feeling the right to her self. My anxieties about the future remain though, even as Hannah has become so self-assured, so confident in naming what she wants.

I try to remember, too, that the demand for women's self-knowledge is a common way in which we police female desires and place blame on girls and women when boys and men wrong them. I used to buy into this thinking in my parenting too—this idea that if I could just teach Hannah to speak for herself, to stand up for herself, to know herself completely, she would be safe. When little boys hit her or pushed her around on the playground, I used to rush in to tell her to hold up her little hand and yell, "Stop!" Sometimes, it turned into an odd victim-blaming moment, in which I'd scold her, "You have to stand up for yourself!" But asking anyone to know themselves unfalteringly as a means for avoiding violence against them discounts that "self-knowledge is not a reliable feature of female sexuality, nor of sexuality in general," nor even of being a person. And self-protection is not the same as feeling safe. I want my daughter to be okay not knowing what she wants just as much as I want her to know what she does want. I want her to know she is allowed to be uncertain without opening herself up to violence or assuming that uncertainty is a condition of her gender or sexuality.

But this demand still follows me. In America, mothers are also supposed to know themselves—to be intentional about falling in love, getting married, and having children. Women are told to wait until they're "ready" for all the work and disempowerment having children will entail, as though one could ever prepare. We consent or we do not. It's on us. Women especially are expected to have a deep understanding about what they're getting themselves into with motherhood, even though everything changes once we arrive at what we've been told is the final destination. The truth is, we rarely know what we are getting ourselves into with motherhood, because parenting is secreted away as a private experience, while we grow up hearing that marriage and motherhood are positions of status and self-actualization that we *should* desire, above all else. Though Jon and I built much of our love on the dream of family life, we came to realize, as most parents do, that we had no idea what we wanted, even if we thought did.

Even so, the accusation that mothers should have known better before having children is a common retort to calls for for paid leave and affordable childcare. In 2022, Senator Ron Johnson of Wisconsin remarked that it's not "society's responsibility to take care of other people's children," emphasizing that "people decide to have families and become parents." Comments like this suggest that a woman's decision to have children isn't encumbered by years of social pressure, gendered expectations, misogyny-laden sexualization, and ordinary human indecision. They also occlude American history: mothering in America has never been entirely consensual. Choice and agency around reproduction have always been limited along the lines of gender, class, and race, and while fetuses and embryos enjoy a kind of "super" citizenship, pregnant people, under the law, are legally regarded as parital subjects. As Silvia Federici writes, "Free will is a liberal myth." When a woman does not efface her subjectivity in the name of fulfilling her alleged biological function, she is seen not as fighting for her own personhood, but "as excessive, wicked."

Even though informed consent is supposed to be a condition of American democratic citizenship, America's history of forced sterilization of Black, Native American, Asian, Latina, and incarcerated women is also stark, as is the history of rape and forced impregnation as mechanisms of enslavement and colonialism. One American Civil Liberties Union summary of cases catalogues a clear history of nonconsensual medical interference in the lives of pregnant people, from coerced prenatal care regimens, to forced cesareans, to compelled blood transfusions, to prosecutions for drug and alcohol use during pregnancy. At the time of writing, following the fall of *Roe v. Wade*, the medical community is in legal and ethical chaos, as they try to sort out the rights of pregnant people and children. But even before that ruling came down, further endangering the lives of those seeking abortions and those with a range of medical conditions, people seeking abortions were being coerced by pregnancy crisis centers and turned away when they did seek abortions—even though women denied an abortion have almost four times greater odds of having a household income below the federal poverty level. Pregnancy was also already being criminalized across America, with "more than 1,200 documented cases of women, disproportionately Black and working-class women," arrested between 1973 and 2020 because of "pregnancy outcomes." In such cases the historical effacement of women interlocks with the historical removal of the personhood of people of color, feminist philosopher Susan Bordo writes, showing how "in this culture the pregnant, poor woman (especially if she is of non-European descent) comes as close as a human being can get to being regarded, medically and legally, as mere body."

There is a subplot in my great-grandmother Jean's story that reveals still more about the false premise that one has ever been completely free in America to choose whether to become a parent or not. Jean's second child was born deaf, something for which Jean held herself responsible. She not only saw her daughter's deafness as a kind of defect, but also saw her own body as defective for producing a child who could not hear. One reason, my mother has always presumed, that my great-grandmother was so set on aborting the children she didn't want was because she feared she might have another child with a disability. But it was Jean's husband, the drunken party man with the fancy car, who had their daughter sterilized when she was an adult, because the law still gave him control over his grown daughter's reproductive life.

Even with all this early knowledge of how abortion and reproductive control played a central role in the lives of the women in my family—there were others: aunts, cousins, friends who were raped, assaulted, violated in other ways, or who had abortions simply as a healthcare matter—when I was sixteen, my older sister came home from college for the holidays, and we fought about the topic of abortion. I have no memory of the argument, but my sister tells me I ended up in tears, arguing for the protection of the unborn, shaming women who had taken control of their reproductive lives. I guess I lived in two worlds as a girl: one rooted in an intergenerational, embodied experience of sexual trauma and self-protection, and another, shaped by the stories I had heard about who gets to make choices in America. If there is anything I want most for both of my children, it is for them to never feel riven this way, caught between one world, in which they know something is wrong, and another, which tells them to doubt the truth that is so plainly set out before them.

Raising a girl in a world that wants to control her body has been a mind fuck, but the work is no less complex with children of any other gender. By the time Elliott was born, I had accepted the ways in which I did and did not gender my love for my daughter. Having a boy in my arms felt immediately different, a sentiment for which I scolded myself, knowing my second baby certainly did not yet have the capacity to endorse his own gender identification—he did not even know he had hands!—but that I nevertheless could not shake. Hannah identified early with her femininity, but when I parented her as *girl*, it was with the knowledge of how I had lived my life perceived as *woman*, and with an understanding of what she might be up against if she and others perceived her similarly.

Jessica Valenti writes of hoping for a boy when she was pregnant with her daughter, a feeling I experienced in both of my pregnancies. Valenti at first reasoned, as I did, that her fear of having a daughter had something to do with the intractability of female adolescence. "A baby girl would turn into a teenage girl, and I remember the young asshole I was to my mother," Valenti writes. My mother had always gone on about how difficult I was as a teenager, even though those were the years when she woke up too hungover to take me to school, when I wrote notes to girls at school from whom I was drifting, telling them what a mess my life was at home—I had reasons to be a teenage asshole. But my worry about having a girl years later was much bigger than any trepidation I felt around the prospects of teenage angst, and even greater than the hurt and anger that still pass between my mother and me, our relationship a cipher for our resentments toward a culture that demands so much of women and gives them so little. Valenti writes, "This is closer to the truth: having a girl means passing this thing on to her, this violence and violations without end."

When I learned that my second baby would be designated "boy," I googled the term "gender disappointment," but my search didn't turn up anything that tracked with how I was feeling. My love already felt endangered by the breadth of its demand: now there would be two kids to care for, and now I understood the comprehensive nature of that work. And in any case, hadn't I always been disappointed by gender? Once he was born, I even felt for a time less pressure. He would be endowed with many layers of privilege; the kind I had as a white person and also the kind his father had, as a man. Jon and I joked uneasily that our jobs would be easier this time around. This baby would be fine. He would grow up to be a white man in a white man's world.

In other words, at first I saw my second baby not as a victim of power, but more as an inevitable foe. As if here, in front of me, was someone who would benefit from all the power structures I hated, from everything that had troubled me and the women in my life. At the very least, I saw my new baby as someone who did not need my emotional protection in the same way my daughter would, and my rage took a different form with him in the first two years of his life, as it always had with rowdy little boys who seemed to take up all the space. As he brought his baby wrath to bear on my body every night at the witching hour, mouthing my breasts and tearing into me with his impossible-to-trim nails, I projected masculine violence onto his healthy infantile aggression. When he began to walk, I was harder on him when he bumped into other kids carelessly, just as I had always been with the boys at the daycare. I knew his right to take up space would always be greater than my daughter's, and when he acted out in frustration, threw his body into it, I scolded him harder, trying to block off some path on which I felt he was already walking a little too firmly.

Parenting a son with patriarchy in mind meant I had to be extra attentive to the ways in which my best efforts at making him a good person would be thwarted by a culture of masculinity that would teach him to *take take take*. But by the time he turned two, I felt like I had been conned into reproducing the exact gender roles I was trying to avoid. I had positioned my daughter as a victim of the patriarchy, my son as an aggressor. I had left no room for anything in between. I had, despite my best efforts, developed a pattern of reinforcing the gender binary, even if the way I was doing it wasn't quite in line with how I saw others projecting gender on to my children.

Trying to keep up with his big busy sister, Elliott became quite the bruiser. Whatever I did, however I hovered, I could not keep him from injuring himself. Those around us often linked his gaucheness with his perceived gender identity, which frustrated me, because I saw in him the confusion I felt as the younger sibling, carrying around a body so full of energy, without any clear understanding of where to direct that vitality, or how to get anyone in the family to pay attention to me. But Elliott also grew to be so tender, thoughtful in a way I never expected. Like all children, he became a multifaceted little creature. In the years I have watched my children become themselves, I have thought often of *Post-Partum Document*, a six-year art project in which Mary Kelly recorded in scientific detail the growth of her infant son and her role in each stage of his development: the weaning process, the introduction of solid foods, the early utterances, the socializing force of nursery school, her son's first comments about gender, emerging from his observations of his mother's body. The project serves as a reminder that safeguarding our children against their entry into the world is an impossible task. No matter how many stories we tell, children are of this world.

Kelly's is a project of mourning, as she prepares her son to enter that world, one that disempowers her as a woman and mother. In one series she creates triptychs that include objects collected by her son in nature, transcriptions of intimate conversations with her son about her body, and diagrams of women's bodies that are editorialized by medical vocabulary. What emerges is a collage of her child's budding world, filled with competing voices: those of masculine scientific reason, the indifference of nature, and the voice of the mother. In my collage I might include clippings of parenting advice found on the internet, alongside the little treasures my son pockets at school and brings home to tell me about himself: a stray sequin, a wrecked toy car, a rock, a curled silver ribbon.

Over the years my children have also picked up and brought home their own stories about gender. They have studied each other's bodies and my own, as well as the differences they perceive there. I have tried to make room for them to be curious without imposing my own vocabulary. They joke about tying penises into ponytails and run around the house singing songs about vaginas because they like the sound of the word. I have tried to help them find joy in their bodies and to resist the urge to shut it all down for fear they aren't approaching the subject the right way. I have many times messed up, quieted them down because of my own past. After I got sober we started "listening to our bodies" together, putting our ears on a hand or an elbow or a leg, tapping our parts like a hot mic to see if they were on, giggling through the literalization of the metaphor. We tried to hear what our bodies were telling us, what they were talking about, what they needed. We couldn't always be sure.

I want my children to know themselves, their own bodies, but this can only be one arm of protection, one limb in a larger system. I also want them to see themselves as implicated in institutions, their desire as both coerced and liberated, limited and privileged, because with that comes the power to refuse what's pushed upon them, and to understand how consent functions as a practice of caring for others. I do the obvious things around the subject: I teach them that a friend saying no once is enough, but also that, sometimes, bodies tell us what they want or don't want without words—with facial expressions, with grunts or noises, or by tensing up. Giving my children the tools to affirm their own autonomy and the autonomy of others feels undeniably important, like the path from which all others diverge, even if the work also feels impossible, all-consuming, and never enough. I worry that the world beyond our home will undo my efforts, because children aren't made or molded; they are dynamic subjectivities, pulp, taking it all in and trying to make themselves out of what they find.

Because the home and the family are sites of social reproduction, however, they can also be a place where we teach expansive understandings of bodies, autonomy, and a nuanced ethics of care and consent. Adrienne Rich writes that power under patriarchy is defined by "ownership of human beings." We often reproduce these one-sided power systems in the home, whether deliberately or unthinkingly. "To hold power over others means the powerful is permitted a kind of short-cut through the complexity of human personality," Rich writes. Sometimes we take the easy route. "Do it because I said so," as my mother used to say. But love is not compatible with control or one body having ownership over the other. As hooks writes, love can only occur in a process of mutual recognition, and "when we love children we acknowledge by our every action that they are not property, that they have rights—that we respect and uphold their rights."

My powerlessness as a woman in America—where my rights are continually under threat, and where I often feel willed to submit to my children as though serving them alone should make me whole—still plays out in how I mother. I am also of the world, and sometimes I parent reactively, trying to flip whatever dynamic I feel forced upon me. Even when I overcome the drive to exert control over my children because power is lacking elsewhere in my life, I am often lost with where to go next. "In the move from powerlessness, toward what are we moving?" Rich asks. It's a question we must continually pose. When I tell my kids stories about inequality, about the world burning around us, I sometimes rush in with abstract gestures of resolution. But my imposition of logic and optimism often come too soon, as I fail to allow them, and me, to sit with the hard questions on which we stumble. I parent the future, making sense of what has happened, what could happen, before it has happened.

I am trying not to do that here. Manipulating temporality like this—acting as though the ending has already been written—is a bad habit I am trying to break.

Like my mother, though, I am still endlessly telling stories. But I know that in the end, it doesn't matter what I give my children, so long as they know they are not mine, but their very own, no matter what anyone says. Already, they are finding their own way. Elliott has very little interest in narrow conceptions of gender, and as I have come to know and love each part of his personality, I worry less that he will absorb a sense of masculine entitlement over others, and more that the culture of masculinity bearing down on him will make him feel as though he must shut away his genderless parts, the ones he identifies with now.

Hannah, for her part, still likes narratives about bodies in pain— about the worst possible cuts and breaks, about illness and distress, about people getting hurt with no one around to help them—not because of some childish morbidity or voyeuristic interest in the suffering of others. She just cares. She wants to understand how bodies come back together after they are wounded. And she wants to know how we help each other when we are hurt. We are alike in that way. I know that wanting an answer. That desire to braid the threads together into one solution for all the pressing problems that afflict our bodies—to tame the mess and locate some language that will once and for all ensure we will all be fine. But being with children every day teaches you that any story we tell inevitably becomes what it must be: a wild unspooling.

Hannah reads to herself now—chapter books about fantasy and relationships, bratty girls and brave boys. I let her read whatever she wants. I cannot keep the world out, but I can sit with her and talk. As I was writing this book, I cuddled up in bed with her while she read aloud to me from a book about little girls who go to Neverland—that place with no rules, no grownups to spoil the fun, no society at all. "Would you like to live there?" I asked.

"No," she said, without hesitating.

"Oh?" I asked. "Why not?" My mind filled in, assumed she was afraid of something, some apprehension I had instilled in her. But all at once she tilted her head toward mine, tucking it for a moment into the space between my hunched shoulder and chest, where she had rested many times before, for more than seven years of pain and happiness. She folded there briefly, into that spot of my body that was still, after all this time, part hers, part mine, and as I took her in, she said, "Because you wouldn't be there."

And I wished then for nothing but the late and ugly world in which we sat together, on that bed, in that house, as the sun went down.

BEGINNING AGAIN

I N THE SLIDING-DOORS version of my life, I might have given up writing, kept working at the daycare. There is nothing less worthy or valuable about choosing such a path. Arguably, it's a nobler path than the one I took. But for me, it would have also meant unhappiness, regret, anger, a disavowal of what made me me. Some will say that this reveals a lack of character: poor work ethic, entitlement, and most especially, a pathological lack of feminine instinct. But that logic—the kind that says whatever chaos, whatever pain, emerges in a woman's life after she has children, she had better shut up, buck up, and take it—is exactly the kind of logic leveraged on women about sex from a young age. It is exactly the kind of logic that supports the removal of women's reproductive choices. It is exactly the kind of logic used to support domination and an culture of endless violation.

My babies *would* only be little once, and I would have to learn not only to let them go but also to let the image I had of myself as a mother go as well. I would have to give up my impossible quest to locate a line between nature and nurture, and to be a good mother, whatever that meant, to turn my focus elsewhere, beyond my home, to the way the world was, for better or for worse, and to the question of how I could prepare my kids to enter that world, to participate in it meaningfully, and how I could not. Mothers often cry on their children's birthdays because we tell the story of time in a particular way, counting the years our children grow older as years we have lost them. No matter what we do, our children move away, take in the world. They need us less. Sometimes not at all. We follow them around, trying to hang on, hoping not to lose them.

All children wade into the world, and when it happens, if they don't take us under completely, they take us out with them. We are sucked out by the tidal force, by the gravitational pull, by interweaving orbits. We hold on tight to whatever we can grab: a warm hand, a little finger. We cling to them, however we can, until we can no longer feel any skin against our own. It can be hard to know who is left on the shore, much less whether anyone will come for us—a terror only worsened by the fact that, in America, it is rare that anyone does. The current strengthens, pulling the little bodies who once lived in us, once *were* us, farther and farther out. We try not to get separated; parent and child tossed all around, bodies battered by the tides. We do our best to swim, and to teach them how to paddle alongside us.

Through it all, our bodies are irrevocably changed. How could they not be? Care rewires brains, alters skeletal structures, destroys lower backs, jumbles emotions, digs out memories. The work teaches us about ourselves, asking us to explore old wounds and preconceptions as we try to make something new with and for our children. In the common narrative, childbirth marks a woman's entrance into motherhood, but the finite quality of this story obscures, intentionally, the long socialization that leads women to motherhood. In truth, becoming a parent is a protracted journey that continues long after a baby is born. The anthropologist Dana Raphael called for further study of this transformation, a period she called "matrescence," when women find their place within the institution, or try. When I first learned of the concept I bristled—how can one ever become a "mother"? Those who have studied motherhood from this perspective acknowledge that the process can take years, that quite possibly it's an endless learning, and their terms, I think, are different from mine—the goal may not be to become a "mother," an impossibly shifty role, but to learn to mother, to care for one's self while caring for another.

Much of that learning involves our bodies. Dr. Aurélie Athan, a clinical psychologist specializing in reproductive identity and matrescence, says that motherhood can cause a woman to view "her body as only something functional, a resource that is to be taken from, even damaged, but rarely given back to or healed," an assault Athan feels is paralleled not only by how we treat women in other phases of life, but by how we abuse the earth and its resources. Most parents are not prepared for the psychical and psychological changes that come with parenthood. "The touched body, the degree and frequency it is touched—how much and how often—is not even imagined as a potential stressor until it happens or reaches a crisis," Athan says. "Nor is the physical labor of bending and lifting, the wear and tear on the body."

But in discovering the touched body there is possibility. For women, there is the possibility of taking the body back—not "getting" it back, but taking ownership, in a culture that wants women to do anything but. "At some point the issue of touch—if, when, and how to approach it with more intentionality—is waiting in the wings. It is a deep and important learning for all parties," Athan says. "One could argue it is at the heart of learning what is truly meant by consent." Rather than simply run us ragged, the work of parenting and all the memories it can arouse, "this very basic, foundational feeling of needing space" can lead us to reclaim boundaries and even bodies on our own terms, maybe even for the first time in our lives. As the author Rebecca Woolf writes in a piece on rediscovering one's sexuality after feeling touched out—and after experiencing sex as filtered through the male gaze, as sexualization, and as taking care of men—rather than "reclaiming the parts of you that feel lost," we should be telling women to "let those parts of you go and build a new paradigm in their place."

Becoming a parent can be transformational, radicalizing even, in its invitation to see the world differently than we ever saw it before.

But so much of what causes these shifts is pain we never should have had to endure in the first place. I am glad for the marks my children left on me, the impressions they made, the gutting that came with it, and the healing becoming a parent inspired. But I am not glad for all the marks men left on me—all the shit I was always trying to get off my back, the scores left on my skin, marks of a culture that sees women's suffering at every age as inevitable. And I am not glad for the way the institutions of marriage and motherhood continued this exploitation, and how they contaminated so much of my own experience.

When we first moved back to California, before Elliott was born, I entertained the idea that motherhood could be a nudge toward reimagining my life. Toward starting over, trying again, but in a manner that meant giving up what I had once thought mattered— art, women, bodies, thinking, writing. When Hannah and I needed some escape from the walls of the apartment, I dressed myself in athleisure, readying myself for the mission of motherhood, packing up snacks and water, driving around town, looking for a new local park. Hannah played on jungle gyms in the harsh summer sun while I hopped around, arms out, making an emergency basket for her little stumbly frame, which I pictured falling from big-kid heights. She knew her body well, what it could handle, and was cautious from a young age, but I was still learning to trust that. Her self-knowledge felt foreign to me.

My attentiveness to her was also how I clocked in for the job. It was that role I played, without thinking, and a show I put on for other mothers. I learned to usher my body and my voice into the images of womanhood I had consumed, and my hypervigilance was an effort to show other women that I could rise to the challenges of this thing called motherhood—that I could survive. But other mothers always seemed to be doing it better than I was. Breaking from play, while Hannah munched on Goldfish crackers in the stroller, we observed those women together. One afternoon we stumbled on a group of moms doing a high-intensity workout together under the summer sun, on a grassy field adjacent to the park near our apartment. The mothers' strollers rested under a shaded tree, and Hannah stood nearby, surveilling instead of playing, as she often did, swaying on her unsteady legs, mouth agape, head cocked to one side. The women bounced and cheered each other on and pushed air out of their chests with force, like they were trying to get something out of their lungs. Hannah scrutinized the jumps and burpees, then looked up at me, opening her hands flat. "Dat?" she asked.

I steered her bony shoulders toward the slide, asking loudly what she was staring at, even though I understood her interest in the spectacle of plyometrics before us. This was another tack I had picked up—this subtle mocking of my kid's lack of social graces to prevent my own embarrassment. We were midflight, nearly free, when the mom-instructor jogged over to us, sweat gracefully disappearing into her tight skin. She offered me her card. She was a personal trainer. Another day, another mother chatted me up on the play structure while our kids looked each other up and down. She fooled me into thinking she wanted to be my friend before handing me a flyer for a belly-flattening wrap. "Maybe I do need this crazy wrap thing!" the flyer said. I declined, felt self-conscious about my body (maybe I did need that crazy wrap thing?), then watched her swoop in on her next victim: an unsuspecting mother pushing her baby on the swings.

Most of the mothers I met or eavesdropped on at the parks were reinventing themselves through some direct sales hustle. If they weren't selling products yet, they debated selling shakes, leggings, supplements, and oils. I knew a bit about what these women were selling because in New York I had joined an "expecting couples" group when I was pregnant. The fathers fell away from the group after the babies were born, but the mothers stayed in touch, and we had a few fun play dates during which we drank champagne and dished on partners and babies, nursing freely and talking about loving breastfeeding or giving it up for good, and ways to get our babies to sleep or to let them cry it out. One mother in the Buffalo group was a self-proclaimed entrepreneur of the essential oils MLM (multi-level marketing) company Young Living. She would later start a YouTube channel documenting her third pregnancy and her use of oils at home. She was kind and never pushy, bringing up the oils in conversation so naturally she convinced several moms in the group to buy into the trend and become new Young Living distributors. My "oily" friend—she used the term "oily" to define many aspects of her life—shared my frustrations with toxicity, excess, and work. Her products seemed like a tempting extension of a progressive life.

But around that time, old friends from high school and college also started peddling bags, makeup lines, and clothing in my Facebook feed. They were part of a whole "find what you love and you'll never work a day in your life" mood—a seamless integration between the domestic and the commercial that I found both alarming and alluring. Their products became their lifestyle became their work became their brand, and I wondered, hovering over the sign-up buttons for their online seminars, what of their new lives and relationships did they plan, and what simply unfolded. In New York I was tempted to switch over to Thieves, a Young Living household cleaner made of a blend of essential oils, but Jon thought the $200 cost for the starter kit was outrageous, despite my hounding him about the benefits of the oily life. I took the free samples from my oily friend instead, frantically trying to shake one more drop out of a miniature amber bottle of clove oil each night whenever Hannah, teething, couldn't sleep, rubbing what was left on her bulging gums.

By the time we moved back to California, everywhere I looked moms were building lives and relationships around new products and services as their babies napped and their toddlers toddled. MLMs like Young Living found new footing online in the 2010s, but their lure was largely the same as it had always been. Since their midcentury inception, direct sales companies such as Avon and Mary Kay had promised women who felt disempowered and alone at home—always part of the plan of capitalist American motherhood—a way to stay busy and to feel like they belonged again, to turn domestic life into a kind of public life. Twenty-first-century MLMs continue to offer up readymade online communities where new moms can connect and build a life around common interests and goals.

The resurgence of MLMs using predatory practices to target mothers in the late 2010s, however, was also fueled by the empowerment discourse of that era. In 2016, a former Ralph Lauren executive, Nicole Feliciano, articulated the underlying promise of digital saleswomanship for new mothers in her book *Mom Boss*. In the age of social media, she claimed, any woman can "learn how to be a super mom." The internet became a living, breathing friend to mothers on the quest to have it all. A new commons, and a way for mothers to monetize their unpaid labor at home, or so it seemed. Feliciano's direct sales company's chummy website, momtrends.com—the self-described "girlfriend you always look forward to bumping into at yoga class" (yes, the website is the girlfriend)—promised "solutions for the challenges of modern motherhood," tailor-made for women who want to "live with purpose and passion." But what these companies really offered new mothers was something that had become central to the story of American motherhood—the potential for personal reinvention. "Wasn't it easy before the kids came along?" the website girlfriend said. "We all managed to look pulled together, travel, stay fit and even entertain on occasion. Well, we don't believe motherhood is an ending. We think of it as a beginning. A time to edit what you bring into your life."

The notion that the ostensibly natural destruction of women by American motherhood is not an ending, but an opportunity for an edit—a chance for a trimmed-down new beginning usually tied to the consumption of products or services—still dominates the story of American motherhood. Many in America fail to question the deeply engrained assumption that mothers' lives will be devastated by motherhood, and that women should restructure their social, economic, and financial lives accordingly. As journalist Katherine Goldstein, creator of *The Double Shift*, put it, "The baseline narrative about being a mother in America is that every individual mother is fundamentally flawed in some way and the way to get out of it is through life hacks and products." Failures of American economic and political policy, and the unsustainable working conditions they engender for caregivers, are refashioned as market opportunities in this classic blame-the-victim plot, in which women are encouraged to buy stuff to "solve" not only infant sleep and eating but also kids' tantrums and meltdowns, along with their own continual personal breakdowns. The larger premise is that we can solve the problems of the sexual division of labor, the unfinished feminist revolution, and the lack of social services in America simply by turning to individualism and the market.

As Naomi Klein writes in *The Shock Doctrine*, capitalism feeds on periods of shock by "exploiting the window of opportunity" created by "a gap between fast-moving events and the information that exists to explain them." Motherhood in America has perhaps always been a prolonged period of disorientation susceptible to niche forms of disaster capitalism—a period in a woman's life many have struggled to explain. During the pandemic, caregivers lived acutely within this dark hole—what Klein calls "pure event, raw reality, unprocessed by story, narrative or anything that could bridge the gap between reality and understanding." The story of motherhood, and parenthood, and care more broadly, was suspended in time. We all held on. And as Klein writes, "Without a story we are, as many of us were after September 11, intensely vulnerable to those people who are ready to take advantage of the chaos for their own ends."

New parents, especially if they are women, usually find themselves within this narrative-less hole, as what we experience looks nothing like what we've been promised. But isolation, emotional and physical devastation, and economic precarity—just some of the struggles that people experience when they become parents, each compounded by intersections of class, race, and gender identity—are not inherent conditions of parenthood. They are the conditions of the ongoing and premeditated disaster of care in patriarchal capitalist America. The disempowerment of caregivers, and the suffering that lack of power brings with it, is foundational to capitalist economics. And the modern-day devaluation of sectors like health care and education in America only provides further evidence that, culturally and economically, we value industry, considered men's work, not care, considered women's work.

In aspirations to reinvent ourselves through careerism and consumer products, we lose sight of what Federici calls "one of the most important contributions of feminist theory and struggle," which is "the recognition of women's unpaid reproductive labor as a key source of capitalist accumulation." But by the mid-2010s, feminism had become "an unstoppable force of female agency and independence," Jessica Valenti writes, an era in which even women's "sad stories" were filled with "takeaway moral lessons or silver lining that allows us to buck up, move on, keep working." As one meme created by Young Living MLM superstar Lindsay Teague Moreno phrased it: "Suffer the pain of discipline or suffer the pain of regret." Rainbow-colored empowerment memes like these helped cover over the mess of American parenthood that would come to a head during the pandemic: an absence of meaningful postpartum care, the rising cost of childcare, the lack of a social safety net, women's unequal workforce participation. Women had plastered smiles over their longing for more, but over time, as Federici wrote in 1975, "Our faces have become distorted from so much smiling, our feelings got lost from so much loving, our oversexualization has left us completely desexualized."

In those early years of motherhood when I felt so distorted, I considered joining several MLMs, but mostly distanced myself from women who turned to the market to reinvent themselves. It hadn't yet occurred to me that many of the mothers I met at parks and playdates were also dissatisfied with their lives—that we could have formed some collective struggle. I felt that solving the total collapse of identity I was experiencing was something I had to do alone. Mothers I met at the daycare who worked outside the home had other ways of coping: poking fun at themselves, their failures, their bodies, the material conditions of their lives. There was something more appealing about this culture of disaster, about shirking the possibility of "having it all." About *not* smiling, grumbling a lot, laughing at the messes we had become. I had always identified with disarray, growing up in an imperfect family with an imperfect mother, becoming an imperfect woman. But soon this too—this portrayal of women's confusion and sadness with irony and levity—felt just as hollow as the hustle. Once again, we were acting as though the situation in which we found ourselves were an inevitable fact of women's lives.

Federici writes, in her essay "Putting Feminism Back on Its Feet," that the women's movement has "continually shifted between a utopian dimension posing the need for a total change and a day-to-day practice that assumed the unchangeability of the institutional system." As she points out, the day-to-day approach has only ever worked for women who have enough power to edit their lives accordingly, "so that changing their lives could actually appear as an act of will." And this limited approach emerges from the idea that there is no broader feminist movement that has the power to fundamentally change the cultural, political, and economic forces that govern our lives.

When my inability to bridge the gap between reality and understanding threatened to take me down in early motherhood, I often stood in my apartment looking for something with which to busy myself. All I saw was the same domestic scene: a dark apartment, dishes to do, toys to clean up, a litany of tasks in which I found no pleasure and that seemed forever; my daughter on the floor, chasing after me, howling, wanting. I felt cut out of my old life, unable to imagine how I would ever afford to send Hannah away so that I could do what I wanted to do—show her that being a mother who belonged to herself was possible. But we eventually learned to take long walks to distract her from my body, passing a big bush of lavender that sat outside a large house up the street. There we often saw a young woman, caring for an elderly man, whom she unloaded from a car, pushing his wheelchair up the walk into his house.

The woman always looked patient and wearied, and we waved at the pair when we saw them. As we did, trash trucks passed— another one of Hannah's favorite sights—and I thought about the artist Mierle Laderman Ukeles's project "Touch Sanitation," for which she shook hands with the New York "san men" for eleven months. The project was in some ways an answer to a question Ukeles had posed in her 1969 manifesto: "After the revolution, who's going to pick up the garbage on Monday morning?" Ukeles's lifelong artistic project was to consider how art institutions, supposed beacons of the avant-garde and progressive thinking, rely on hidden labor—indeed, how we all do. "Touch Sanitation" was an effort to make visible the work of those who pick up the garbage—who keep society moving. Her work also set maternal and domestic labor, which Ukeles explored in other projects, in relation to maintenance work, the labors that hum under everyday life.

On walks I studied the hidden work of care all around us, while from the safety of her stroller Hannah studied the lavender bush she both loved and feared—home to dozens of bees that buzzed around, toiling. In a few years, in 2020, Hannah would endure her first bee sting, setting off months of anxiety during which she avoided playing outside unless I was right next to her. I would have countless conversations with her about not letting fear control her, or keep her trapped inside our home, often breathlessly trying to hold back my desire to push her off and away from me, as she batted at bugs in the air that were not there. All of this—my child's distress, her need for my body, my own feeling of being trapped—would return me to the early days of motherhood. But by then I could see, acutely, that the struggles I was having, that so many parents were facing, were part of something bigger.

Mending what's been broken by the intentional erasure of care work, reproductive labor, and all maintenance work is necessary for achieving what the feminist philosopher Nancy Fraser calls, in *Fortunes of Feminism*, "gender justice." In terms of caregiving, Fraser believes that neither the models followed in America nor by Western European feminists and social democrats go far enough. In America, caregivers are expected to support themselves through waged work outside the home—considered the most important work in society—while childcare and elder care are contracted out. Women remain associated with what is perceived to be this lower-level labor and end up taking many hits. In some European countries, Fraser writes, informal, domestic-care work is either compensated on par with work outside the home or there are policies meant to relieve the stigma of splitting part-time work in the home with part-time work outside the home. These approaches don't aim to make women's lives look more like men's but rather try to elevate and de-gender the labor of care economically and culturally. Paid leave, mandated flex time, professional retraining and work reentry programs for parents, and continuous social services such as unemployment and healthcare are crucial to making this model successful.

For Fraser, however, the most revolutionary models "induce men to become more like women are now," that is, to become "people who do more primary carework." Bringing men into caregiving is perhaps the most radical step we can take toward gender justice. After all, as Fraser points out, the real abusers of our current systems are not single mothers on welfare, but men who don't contribute their fair share at home, as well as the corporations that rely on domestic and reproductive labor to sustain their labor force. Much more is needed for this model to succeed than getting men to pitch in in heterosexual marriages. Real gender equity requires dismantling the concept of gender and what Fraser calls the "gender-coding" of care, which divides work into tracks (domestic versus public). And everyone needs access to employment policies that offer time for care work and reproductive labor, as well as to continuous social services, so citizens without kids or "kin-based responsibilities" can also join in on communal care work.

Recognizing the work we do at home—whether care or cleaning—not as a choice but as what Federici calls a "social responsibility," is one way we can take the struggle out of the home and collectivize it. Reducing or reorganizing the work of social reproduction often feels like a personal battle, like the kind undertaken between a husband and wife, but the struggle is a collective one. So far, bringing housework and childcare into the market has mostly helped only well-off white women, who can afford to outsource their labor, usually to women of color for poor pay. "In the future society free from exploitation," Federici writes, we will need to "decide how the social responsibility is best absolved and shared among us." To unhook care from centuries of violence against women, however, at the center of such decisions must be the understanding that women's bodies are not destined to be the providers of satisfaction to men and children, and that "what we need is more time, more money, not more work." As Federici points out, we need childcare not just so we can do more work outside the home, but "to be able to take a walk, talk to our friends, or go to a women's meeting."

My professional life has been characterized by fits and starts, as perhaps all writers' lives are, but I was able to begin again not because I found great hacks online but because I had time, money, and a community of support—including people who watched my children while I wrote or just recouped. During the pandemic, when I began receiving unemployment and direct payments through the child tax credit, I did what Jon had always encouraged me to do: I let everything else fall apart, and I wrote this book. That financial freedom, though short-lived, allowed me to work and care at the same time—to afford childcare once daycare and school reopened. Contrary to the myth that social services breed entitlement and dependency, a bit of economic autonomy allowed me to do more meaningful work.

In her book *Silences*, Tillie Olsen expands on Woolf's concept of the Angel in the House, claiming there is also "another angel, so lowly as to be invisible, although without her no art, or any human endeavor, could be carried on for even one day—the essential angel . . . who must assume the physical responsibilities for daily living, for the maintenance of life." Olsen knew that no public work, including intellectual and creative work, can proceed without someone doing the labor at home that we all must do to survive. "*Someone* has to do it," Olsen wrote, "and that someone has, almost without exception, been the wife or mother in the house. In such situations, women become 'mediocre caretakers of their talent.'" Those who do the caring often fall into what Olsen called those silences of those who cannot access their creative life—an unimaginable hit to our shared culture.

My essential angels were the home daycare provider who watched Elliott before he turned one; my sister, who gave me deep childcare discounts; the immigrant women she employs, who have loved my children like their own; along with elementary school teachers, grandparents, and friends. When my husband, who was by then teaching high school, began his regular summer break in 2020, I pushed the kids toward him and shut myself in the little room where I kept my desk, resolved to locate what I had been looking for for so long: a way to connect all the threads. At night, after tucking the kids into their beds, Jon delivered blank notebooks to me in the bath, which I filled so frantically that the wet pages tore under the pressure of my bleeding pen, and tall glass cups of cold water— gestures of devotion. I retreated to the low-lit bedroom, red and sweaty, to read and write more; when Jon came to bed, he made no demands of my body. He wrote his own one-word poems or edited my printed-out pages quietly beside me. He, too, became my essential angel, a historical reversal we both welcomed.

When wildfire season started in the fall of 2020, we stopped watering the plants in our small garden, hiding inside to protect our lungs and refreshing air-quality maps each hour, hoping for some relief. Tomatoes fell from their vines and soured; zucchinis grew too massive; two pumpkins rotted from the inside out. When we did go outside, we held our breath. We waited for the season to change. In many ways we are still waiting. But we also trying to do our part to cultivate something altogether different.

Getting sober for me that year felt like choosing life over death, creation over pain, as Duras describes her decision to quit drinking. But returning to writing felt like gasping for air, and like returning to myself. It brought me the kind of pleasure I've always sought—a way to make sense, if fleetingly, of the pain. At night, I rubbed my kids' bellies, heat passing between us as they fell asleep, conjuring possibility. I think of creativity like that—as a practice of magic, of connection. But art alone, or one woman's access to a room where she can write, cannot remake the world. "At its best, one of the most creative activities is being involved in a struggle with other people, breaking out of our isolation, seeing our relations with others change, discovering new dimensions in our lives," Federici writes.

Mary Kelly writes that *Post-Partum Document* was an effort to "articulate the mother's fantasies, her desires, her stake in that project called 'motherhood.'" But in that representation of her labor as a mother, "there is only a replay of moments of separation and loss." A piece of art can never be a complete representation of the experience it records—it can never fully close the gap between reality and understanding, and *Post-Partum Document* could never fully account for all the work Kelly did as a mother in the six years she recorded in detail. Too much had to be left out; too much was lost in translation.

In the same way, something always feels lost in the movement of life from parent to child. Children suffer, and we argue with them, and they argue with us, and we wound them with our voices, our used-up and tired bodies, and then their wounds wound us, and then we really say the wrong thing, and so do they, and then we resent them, and we worry that they will come to resent us, too, blame us for all of it, as they will no doubt be encouraged to do by the culture in which they grow up. As my children have gotten older, it has become harder to repent, to feel like I will ever be the kind of mother I once imagined I would be, and I don't always know what to do with that loss. "I cannot help but feel the death of possibility," Carole Maso writes in *The Room Lit by Roses*, about the moment when a piece of writing takes "shape and becomes a stable, definitive text." Maso is talking about the creative process, but in a book about motherhood.

Parenting, too, walks us through this—this longing for of all the "books that now would never be." Motherhood is the ultimate recursive elegy. We are always mourning what could have been, how we might have written the story differently, or better, had we only known better, done better, been treated better, had more options, had *known*. As Maso writes, "With every major decision there is regret, for the very act involves choosing a certain sorrow." I'm not sure whether self-doubt is an essential condition of parenting, or a mark of the institution. It's likely a bit of both. There is evidence that the source of human sociality may have been maternal ambivalence, and the negotiation of needs that mothers faced as they began relying on kinship systems to help with childcare. But the abandonment of mothers and parents in America has undoubtedly deepened our self-doubt, our longing for something better, and our grief for what we wish we had been able to give.

I know the sorrow Maso writes about well. The regret is happening here, as I write and rewrite these lines, in an era of so much fear and uncertainty, as I see my own inability to offer that singular solution, and to fully account for my own experience. As what could have been becomes no longer possible. I also know the sorrow of feeling as though I have wronged my children too much—feeling that I have failed them with what I cannot undo, cannot take back, never should have said. With the inadequate story I have offered them. But the world comes inside our homes, our bodies, our minds, makes a mess, makes us a mess. We are left to sort it all out, clean it up. As a result, we often turn on those closest to us. How could we not? They're right there. And we wonder whether too much time has passed too quickly, too much has gone untended, too much life lived without intention. We wonder whether we have missed our chance to do away with pain, and to give our children a plot, a body, just a little freer than our own has been.

When Hannah suffered during the pandemic with anxiety, and I suffered with my worry, yet again, that we might never find our way out of the mess in which we found ourselves, I again held myself responsible, assuming I had left her feeling deserted, unattached, in need, one too many times. But I also thought of our walks, the ones we took years earlier, about that network of care that buzzed under everything, and about how she had once loved the busy insects she now feared. I thought about the stories I had told her, as desperate mothers do, about how the male bees worked to serve their queen.

I still long for those days, to have them again, to take a different approach, to try again. But what would or could I have done differently? In the poem "Night-Pieces: For a Child," Rich writes of hovering over the baby's crib, crying while her baby cries. It's the inescapable volume of need, always for the mother's body, that many mothers lament—the feeling of there being no way out, no one around to help or care for us, who feel ensnared by the lonely cries of children, piled on the need we have felt all our lives: from men, from everyone. But the final lines of Rich's poem express a particular kind of desire, one that may not be universal but that gives me comfort no less. Rich longs for the sensuality of early motherhood, to feel it once more, and to try again: "If milk flowed from my breast again . . . ," she yearns, leaving us on the precipice of the question. If, then what? However hard it has been, some untainted encounter with the pleasure of care, which we only ever catch in snatches, beckons us. But in the end we are who we become, not who we intended to be.

It seemed for a while possible during the pandemic that everything might change: that a collective struggle might emerge; that we might collectively learn to value the radical power of caregiving and throw the weight of our cultural and political institutions behind those doing that work. A cataclysmic shift seemed possible. But policymakers and political leaders continually failed to show up for parents, including the 3.5 million mothers who had been pushed out of the workforce. We kept telling our stories. No one seemed to be listening. The collective distribution and consumption of women's suffering, all to no avail, felt recognizable. The burden appeared again to fall on women's speech. Were we not telling our stories loudly enough, or in the right way?

In *Regarding the Pain of Others*, Susan Sontag asks, "What does it mean to protest suffering, as distinct from acknowledging it?" Sontag saw protest as involving some moral response to a representation of suffering—something not necessarily located in the representation itself, but in what we do with the depictions of pain that we consume. Sometimes this question seems to me a bit like the question of whether a tree falling in the forest makes any sound if no one is there to hear it: maybe the only difference between acknowledging and protesting suffering is whether anyone is listening.

Those of us who seek an end to the violence of our present moment often long for the creation of a completely new world. Power has marked everything. Burn it down. Start again. Hit the reset button. It's not the "new" of capitalist production we're after, which is just a repackaging of the same old shit. What we want is nothing short of a loss that leads us out of this world and into another. A completely new beginning. In *The Human Condition*, Hannah Arendt argues that the ability to create something truly new like this, something truly revolutionary, is only possible because of our understanding of human creation. Natality, Arendt argues, or the simple fact that people are born and emerge from nothing, is the template that makes change possible. Nations are birthed; democracies are, too. Not incidentally, Arendt articulated this theory in 1958, as Europe jostled to begin again in the wake of fascism. Arendt did not believe that only mothers, or only women, or only those with wombs, have access to the practice of imagination required to birth new worlds. All of us have encountered real novelty simply by coming into being, by emerging from nothing, by entering into the world.

Such genuine novelty has little to do with the story of personal reinvention that has become so central to the narratives used by capitalism to sell us the promise of another life, while keeping us firmly planted in situations that disempower us. Corporations are always hawking the idea of starting again, getting free through commodity consumption. Women are so often sold the idea they can start over. But I don't believe in the market of optimization. It's not real novelty. Beginning again—not with the same materials, but as if for the first time—that is the work of creativity, and that kind of novelty is much harder to come by.

It is also a kind of novelty that requires us to connect not through false discourses of empowerment but in networks of care and hope—the kind that keep us going, pushing on, when it seems like change won't ever come. One truth that is simplified by the myths of motherhood and the myths of America, a young and foolish country: beginnings are a fucking mess, and beginnings last a very long time. Real change is slow and boring and nonlinear. When change doesn't seem to come, even after we have wrenched the truth from ourselves, splayed our testimony out for all to see, it's hard to keep going. Telling our stories, especially, can feel like useless acts with impossibly slow results. In *Essential Labor*, Angela Garbes writes that parenting is fundamentally inefficient, inherently at odds with a culture obsessed with productivity and quick fixes. This is true for all care work, and all political change. The results of our everyday labors may be slow and steady, but they will come eventually. Care takes time.

But care also teaches us that body to body is where our best work happens. After all, in the earliest human cultures, believed by some to be pre-patriarchal, power was rooted in the spirit of daily survival and in transformation rather than in dominance or division. As Federici writes, the women's movement, too, must keep in mind this definition of power as a kind of collective creativity—"not power over others but against those who oppress us." Otherwise, feminism, too, "risks becoming an institution."

During my time working at the daycare, I learned a lot about slow transformations. My sister often lamented how some early childhood educators teach art by telling kids exactly what to make and how to make it. Deviating from the rules of the popsicle stick Mother's Day frame is in some cases a punishable offense; other times, the teacher just finishes gluing everything together for the kid so there is something to take home at the end of the day. This is one way that children are taught, from a very young age, that the quick production of objects for consumption is the most valuable kind of making. But my sister refused to follow this model, so the kids at the daycare had sprawling definitions of what it meant to make something, both alone and together. To them, art could be a handprint or a few pokes with a paint-wetted brush. It could be some faint scribbles made with a dried-out yellow marker that had long ago lost its cap, or it could be a simple green crayon circle, because it was the first circle that child had ever drawn. It could be an idea stolen from a friend, or, really, it could be a ripped piece of paper, cut up and glued to another piece of paper, balled up and tossed back and forth with a friend, because in that effort the child learned something that I could never quite identify.

Every time we all sat down to make things together, the kids emerged to find their world changed—a little clearer, closer, more nuanced.

I embraced art time at the daycare with zeal, trying to finally put my Pinterest-ing to use. When rain came, I searched for stormy-day crafts, gathered cotton balls for clouds and cut teardrops into construction paper to mark the downpour. Mostly, we used household items like Q-tips, coffee filters, crumpled butcher paper pulled from shipping boxes, lids of old peanut butter jars, cereal box tops or bottoms or sides, torn fabric, bottle caps, whatever we could find—basically trash—as paintbrushes and canvases. I put the materials out and let the kids create whatever they wanted, looking on as their minds went to work. I had been taught by my sister not to praise the work. I was to say, simply, "Tell me about this." It was a gesture of neutrality I could get behind, because it opened space for the kids to tell me about their worlds. They always had a story. It was my favorite time of day.

"Tell me everything," I would say, sitting in a too-small kids chair next to them, two kids vibrating on my lap, another jumping around behind my back, all talking over one another, with yet another pushing their way in to see what their friends had made. I watched their little faces erupt with pride as they spun a yarn about the nothing they had made. I saw landscapes, bodies, eyes looking back at me, emotions. "This is a monster?" I would ask. And they would say, disappointed or laughing, "*No!*" Without skipping a beat, they would explain: It was a frog, of course! Duh.

Sometimes I did praise too much. But I wasn't admiring their figurative drawing skills, or even their knack for the abstract. I was thrilled by the worlds they were making, hodgepodges of what they had absorbed from adults, TV, at the store, from other kids; what they knew and didn't, what their creations told me about who they were. Their artworks, which appeared to me as confusing mixes of color and shape, were for them a way of understanding themselves, their bodies, and the world in which they lived. Nothing ever fully came together. But they didn't care. They kept on making things, day after day.

Children have their own special relationship with reason: they outright reject it. In the toddler and preschool years, children are best at refusing the kind of sense that governs adult life. As Jean Piaget noted, in this "preoperational" stage children are only just learning the concept of time, and of history. Not surprisingly, the preoperational stage is the time of tantrums—a time of tears and fury, of unruly bodies. What children create during the time, however, is always new, something not of this world, something transformational from which they will never return, because at this age, small children also cannot understand the *reversal* of time, the idea that an action can be undone, or that anything, once shaped, might return to the state from which it came.

My own children have mostly moved out of that stage now, but they are still piecing together the world. Sometimes, when explaining his experiences to me, Elliott loses his words, as has been my own pattern all my life when speaking—part of what drove me to write. On the page I can fix the world in place, hold it there, exactly as I want it to be. I watch as others witness my child's temporary aphasia, his stuttering an idea into being. He skips ahead and around, pursuing and unraveling every connection he's made that day, not quite knowing where he wants to land, but also, wanting it all. Some seem to view the slowness of his articulation as a mark of unintelligence, but I know his mind to be a deep reservoir of knowledge, curiosity, and insight—as do the caregivers who teach him every day, who listen to him, who let him find himself, in his body, in his thoughts, however long it takes. The whole world is crashing through him. He is on the verge of a revelation.

It seems no accident of humanity that it happens this way: for their bodies to grow, children must learn to lose the world as they know it, not once but repeatedly. It's a process that cannot be forced, and one that takes many different shapes. The question before the rest of us is how we might learn to stand, as children do, in front of our own world, one that seems so hell-bent on reproducing itself, on keeping itself the way it is, and refuse to let it coalesce into something familiar, into a story we have read so many times before.

ACKNOWLEDGMENTS

I AM IMMENSELY GRATEFUL for all the time and attention so many people put into this book. To my agent, Martha Wydysh, thank you for your unwavering support. Your steady hand kept me going, and you know I'll never stop thanking you. To my editor, Haley Lynch, thank you for your thoughtfulness, urgency, praise, trust, and deep care for this book. To Caitlin Meyer, I could not have imagined a better champion for this book. I am forever grateful for your wisdom and expertise. To everyone else at Beacon Press, especially Gayatri Patnaik, Kate Scott, Susan Lumenello, Marcy Barnes, Emily Powers, Priyanka Ray, Frankie Karnedy, and Sanj Kharbanda, thank you for your enthusiasm and labor. I hit the jackpot finding a home for this book.

To the editors who gave early pieces of this book a chance to reach their readers—Meredith Haggerty, Rebecca Onion, Emily McCombs, Melissa Goldstein and Natalia Rachlin, Marisa Siegel, and Meg Lemke—thank you for answering my emails and for making my writing and thinking better. To my students over the years, for all you taught me, and for all you pushed me to teach myself. To my students in the mother lab especially, thank you for your vulnerability and community—we all needed it, and I am forever changed by the time we spent together. Thank you also to Macy Chadwick for the gift of solitude, and to the whole crew at In Cahoots for rooting me on as I completed final edits.

To the small number of early readers I trusted with this book in its rawest form: Allie Rowbottom, Elizabeth Hall, Christina Rivera Cogswell, Oksana Marafioti, and Maureen McCourt, you each helped me push this book where it needed to go. To the mommune—Minna Dubin, Patti Maciesz, Kaitlin Solimine, and Cindy DiTiberio—and all the ARIM mothers, for cheering me on when the way forward felt uncertain. And to all my fellow travelers—the mothers, parents, writers, and readers I met or corresponded with while writing this book, and while we all tried to make sense of what was happening to us during the pandemic, of which there are too many to name—thank you for reading, talking, sharing, and supporting.

Thank you also to the writers and thinkers I have not met or only met briefly, who have been instrumental to my thinking in this book, including Silvia Federici, bell hooks, Audre Lorde, Adrienne Rich, Mierle Laderman Ukeles, Mary Kelly, and all the feminist thinkers and writers who appear in this book. Thank you for treading the path. I'll keep pacing on it until we find the end.

This book would also not exist were it not for the labor of the many caregivers who have provided childcare for me over the years. Thank you especially to Ms. Marci, Ms. Haley, "Kaferin," Ms. Mary, Ms. Ez, and all the teachers at The Garden. To Melissa Cady, for always making the space and time, and for giving me that job when I needed it, even though I wasn't very good at it. To Elizabeth Loveton, for always playing the patient. I know things didn't go the way you wanted for us, but through it all you taught me the most important part of mothering, which is love. And to Jon Rutzmoser, my essential angel, thank you for your patience and support, for all the hours getting lost, and for always trying.

Most of all, to Hannah and Elliott, loves of my life. Thank you for teaching me the art of love. Being a mother in this world is complicated but loving you makes my life immeasurably fuller, stronger, clearer, and brighter. I am lucky to be yours. I know you each will give this world something it has never seen before, and I cannot wait to stand by your side, learn from you, and hug you.

NOTES

BEGINNING

3   **In turn, Chodorow writes** Nancy Chodorow, *The Reproduction of Mothering: Psychoanalysis and the Sociology of Gender* 1 (Berkeley: University of California Press, 1999).

3   **As Melissa Febos writes** Melissa Febos, *Girlhood* (New York: Bloomsbury, 2021).

5   **This ghost, however** Virginia Woolf, "Professions for Women," *The Death of the Moth and Other Essays* (New York: Harcourt Brace & Co., 1942), 235–42.

6   **Motherhood was triggering** Lyz Lenz, *Belabored: A Vindication of the Rights of Pregnant Women* (New York: Bold Type Books, 2020), 132.

7   *Roe v. Wade* **has been** Moira Donegan, "Republicans Won't Stop Until Abortion Is Banned across America. And It Could Be," *Guardian*, September 15, 2022.

7   **They are coming** *New York Times* Staff, "Tracking the States Where Abortion Is Now Banned," interactive graph and update; last accessed October 8, 2022, https://www.nytimes.com/interactive /2022/us/abortion-laws-roe-v-wade.html.

7   **Lenz wrote in 2020** Lenz, *Belabored*, 132.

8   **We don't only normalize** Chelsea Conaboy, "Maternal Instinct Is a Myth That Men Created," *New York Times*, op-ed, August 26, 2022, https://www.nytimes.com/2022/08/26/opinion/sunday/maternal -instinct-myth.html.

8   **These beliefs are regularly** Conaboy, "Maternal Instinct Is a Myth That Men Created."

8   **The unreasonable expectations** Silvia Federici, "Wages Against Housework (1975)," *Revolution at Point Zero: Housework, Repro-duction, and Feminist Struggle* (Oakland, CA: PM Press, 2020), 18, available online at http://www.churchland.org.za/wp-content/uploads/2013/08/Federici-Silvia-Revolution-Point-Zero-Housework-Reproduction-and-Feminist-Struggle.pdf.

8   **Women are expected** Federici, "Wages against Housework," 12.

9   **Rather these attacks** Jenny Brown, *Birth Strike: The Hidden Fight over Women's Work* (Oakland, CA: PM Press, 2019), 1.

9   **As philosopher Kate Manne** Regan Penaluna, "Kate Manne: The Shock Collar That Is Misogyny," *Guernica*, February 7, 2018, https://www.guernicamag.com/kate-manne-why-misogyny-isnt-really-about-hating-women.

10   **Often this coercive** Kate Manne, *Down Girl: The Logic of Misogyny* (London: Oxford University Press, 2018), xxi.

10   **#MeToo eventually** Moira Donegan, "There's an Antifeminist Backlash Silencing Women—More and More Literally," *Guardian*, July 7, 2022, https://www.theguardian.com/commentisfree/2022/jul/07/theres-an-antifeminist-backlash-silencing-women-more-and-more-literally.

10   **They saw the collars** Sabrina Tavernise et al., "Why American Women Everywhere Are Delaying Motherhood," *New York Times*, June 16, 2021, updated September 30, 2021, https://www.nytimes.com/2021/06/16/us/declining-birthrate-motherhood.html.

10   **Journalists declared** Sam Sanders, "Less Sex, Fewer Babies: Blame the Internet and Career Priorities," *All Things Considered*, NPR, August 6, 2019, transcript, https://www.npr.org/2019/08/06/747571497/less-sex-fewer-babies-blame-the-internet-and-career-priorities.

11   **Women in the United States** Brown, *Birth Strike*, 143.

11   **Jenny Brown writes** Brown, *Birth Strike*. Year to year, since 2007, the birth rate has occasionally ticked upward, but since then it has "generally been in a free fall." See Dana Goldstein and Daniel Victor, "U.S. Birthrate Ticks Up 1 Percent, Halting a Steady Decline," *New York Times*, May 24, 2022, https://www.nytimes.com/2022/05/24/us/birth-rate-increase.html.

14   **As many as six** Time's Up Foundation, "Black Survivors and Sexual Trauma," May 20, 2020, https://timesupfoundation.org/black-survivors-and-sexual-trauma.

14   **Transgender people** Williams Institute, UCLA School of Law, "Transgender People over Four Times More Likely Than Cisgender People to Be Victims of Violent Crime," press release, March 23, 2021, https://williamsinstitute.law.ucla.edu/press/ncvs-trans-press-release.

14   **We have become** Carrie Gillespie et al., *Equity in Child Care Is Everyone's Business*, Education Trust and US Chamber of Commerce Foundation, February 22, 2022.

14   **Between February 2020** Claire Ewing-Nelson, "All of the Jobs Lost in December Were Women's Jobs," fact sheet, National Women's Law Center, January 2021, https://nwlc.org/wp-content/uploads /2021/01/December-Jobs-Day.pdf.

14   **Claims that motherhood** Pooja Lakshmin, "How Society Has Turned Its Back on Mothers," *New York Times*, February 4, 2021, https://www.nytimes.com/2021/02/04/parenting/working-mom -burnout-coronavirus.html.

16   **As Koa Beck writes** Koa Beck, *White Feminism: From the Suffragettes to Influencers and Who They Leave Behind* (New York: Atria Books, 2021), 68.

17   **In parenting** Alice Notley, "Women and Poetry," *Coming After: Essays on Poetry* (Ann Arbor: University of Michigan, 2005).

PAIN

21   **The appointment was at** Yoselin Person, "High Maternal Mortality Rate in Erie County among Black and Brown Women," ABC Buffalo, April 29, 2022, https://www.wkbw.com/news/local-news /high-maternal-mortality-rate-in-erie-county-among-black-and -brown-women.

25   **Feminist author and activist** Susan Brownmiller, *Against Our Will: Men, Women and Rape* (New York: Fawcett, 1975), 315–25.

25   **Deutsch also argued** Helene Deutsch, quoted in Brownmiller, *Against Our Will*, 316.

25   **Brownmiller writes that** Brownmiller, *Against Our* Will, 316.

26   **Leslie Jamison writes** Leslie Jamison, "Grand Unified Theory of Female Pain," *VQR Online*, April 2014, https://www.vqronline.org /essays-articles/2014/04/grand-unified-theory-female-pain.

27   **I read Dick-Read's** O. Moscucci, "Holistic Obstetrics: The Origins of 'Natural Childbirth' in Britain," *Postgraduate Medical Journal* 2003: 79:168–73.

27   **Dick-Read, a general** Grantly Dick-Read, *The Natural Childbirth Primer* (New York: Harper & Row, 1955), 15–16.

27   **He referred to "the big** Dick-Read, *The Natural Childbirth Primer*.

27   **And elsewhere he referred** Moscucci, "Holistic Obstetrics."

27   **Drawing on Darwinism** In the West, obstetrics has incorporated racist theories of pain, strongly influenced by experiments that an

American gynecologist, J. Marion Sims, conducted from 1845 to 1849 without anesthesia on Black women who were slaves. See L. L. Wall, "The Medical Ethics of Dr. J. Marion Sims: A Fresh Look at the Historical Record," *Journal of Medical Ethics* 32, no. 6 (2006): 346–50, doi:10.1136/jme.2005.012559. Black women's pain also remains systematically undertreated in America today, and Black women die in childbirth almost three times as often as white women. See "Black Americans Are Systematically Under-Treated for Pain. Why?," University of Virginia, Frank Batten School of Leadership and Public Policy, June 30, 2020, https://batten.virginia.edu/about /news/black-americans-are-systematically-under-treated-pain-why; Donna L. Hoyert, "Maternal Mortality Rates in the United States, 2020," National Center for Health Statistics, Centers for Disease Control, February 23, 2022, https://stacks.cdc.gov/view/cdc/113967.

27   **Woman fails when** Moscucci, "Holistic Obstetrics."

29   **A *Glamour* article** Whitney Perry, "This Nike Maternity Ad Featuring Pregnant and Breastfeeding Athletes Is So Empowering," *Glamour*, March 14, 2021, https://www.glamour.com/story/this -nike-maternity-ad-featuring-pregnant-and-breastfeeding -athletes-is-so-empowering.

29   **No one wants to hear** Jessica Valenti, *Sex Object: A Memoir* (New York: Dey Street, 2016), 15.

30   **Despite all this mystery** Tina Donvito, "Science Pinpoints When Your Labor Will Start," *Parents*, December 16, 2018, https://www .parents.com/pregnancy/giving-birth/labor-and-delivery/science -pinpoints-when-your-labor-will-start.

31   **The medical model** H. M. Callaghan, "Health Beliefs and Childbirth: Is It an Illness or a Normal Life Event?" *Australian College of Midwives Incorporated Journal* 6, no. 4 (1993): 13–17, https://doi .org/10.1016/s1031-170x(05)80137-0.

31   **In *Illness as Metaphor*** Susan Sontag, *Illness as Metaphor* (1978; New York: Farrar, Straus and Giroux, 2013).

31   **But Sontag observes** Sontag, *Illness as Metaphor*.

31   **By the 1920s** Judith Walzer Leavitt, *Brought to Bed: Childbearing in America, 1750–1950* (New York: Oxford University Press, 1986), 61–62.

31   **Scopolamine—which** Íñigo Domínguez, "Burundanga: The Stealth Drug That Cancels the Victim's Willpower," *El Pais*, July 25, 2016, https://english.elpais.com/elpais/2016/07/25/inenglish/1469445136 _776085.html.

31 **These birthing bodies** Jessica Pollesche, "Twilight Sleep," *The Embryo Project Encyclopedia*, May 16, 2018, https://embryo.asu.edu /pages/twilight-sleep.

31 **In a 1958 exposé** Henci Goer, "Cruelty in Maternity Wards: Fifty Years Later," *Journal of Perinatal Education* 19, no. 3 (2010): 33–42.

32 **Despite these alarming** Marguerite Tracy and Constance Leupp, "Painless Childbirth," *McClure's Magazine* 43 (1914): 37–51.

32 **Women traced** Leavitt, *Brought to Bed*.

32 **Pauline Manford remarks** Edith Wharton, *Twilight Sleep* (New York: D. Appleton & Co., 1927).

33 **Like Mrs. Manford's** Wharton, *Twilight Sleep*, 18.

37 **Rich wrote, "childbirth** Adrienne Rich, "The Theft of Childbirth," *New York Review of Books*, October 2, 1975, https://www.nybooks .com/articles/1975/10/02/the-theft-of-childbirth.

39 **In a text I studied** Julia Kristeva, "Stabat Mater," trans. Arthur Goldhammer, *Poetics Today* 6, no. 1–2, *The Female Body in Western Culture: Semiotic Perspective* (1985): 133–52.

PLEASURE

41 **The void you discover** Marguerite Duras, "Alcohol," *Practicalities* (New York: Grove, 1987), 15–19.

42 **Alcohol was an** Duras, "Alcohol."

44 **I used terms** Katherine Angel, *Tomorrow Sex Will Be Good Again: Women and Desire in the Age of Consent* (Brooklyn, NY: Verso, 2022), 17.

44 **Like many men** Angel, *Tomorrow Sex Will Be Good Again*, 18.

48 **The journalist Poppy Harlow** Amanda Arnold, "Survivor of Highly Publicized Rape Case Has Died by Suicide," *The Cut*, August 5, 2020, https://www.thecut.com/2020/08/daisy-coleman-of -maryville-rape-case-has-died-by-suicide.html.

48 **Like Mays and Richmond** Arnold, "Survivor of Highly Publicized Rape Case Has Died by Suicide."

49 **Gay notes** Roxane Gay, "The Way We Talk about Sexual Assault Is Broken," *Salon*, October 17, 2013, https://www.salon.com/2013 /10/17/the_way_we_talk_about_sexual_assault_is_broken.

52 **The phrase, sexual** Chanel Miller, *Know My Name: A Memoir* (New York: Penguin, 2020), 262.

52 **Sometimes I'm too** Miller, *Know My Name*, 262.

55 **Fight the urge** Matt Villano, "A Dad's Guide to Sex after Baby," *Parents*, May 17, 2022, https://www.parents.com/parenting

/relationships/sex-and-marriage-after-baby/a-dads-guide-to-sex
-after-pregnancy-and.

55   **As Adrienne Rich** Adrienne Rich, *Of Woman Born: Motherhood as Experience and Institution* (1976; New York: W. W. Norton, 1986), 264, 183.

55   **Silvia Federici writes** Silvia Federici, "Why Sexuality Is Work (1975)," *Revolution at Point Zero: Housework, Reproduction, and Feminist Struggle* (Oakland: PM Press, 2020), 19–23.

55   **Hormones also dip** Chelsea Conaboy, *Mother Brain: How Neuroscience Is Rewriting the Story of Parenthood* (New York: Holt, 2022).

59   **I am a reflection** Audre Lorde, *Zami: A New Spelling of My Name: A Biomythography* (Berkeley: Crossing Press, 1982).

59   **Lorde views** Audre Lorde, "Uses of the Erotic," *Uses of the Erotic: The Erotic as Power* (Berkeley: University of California Press, 1978).

59   **It's potent medicine** Angela Garbes, "The More I Learn about Breast Milk, the More Amazed I Am," *The Stranger*, August 26, 2015, https://www.thestranger.com/features/2015/08/26/22755273 /the-more-i-learn-about-breast-milk-the-more-amazed-i-am.

60   **Heaven forbid** Kate Manne, *Entitled: How Male Privilege Hurts Women* (New York: Crown, 2021), 111.

60   **And as with most expectations** B. "We Need the PUMP ACT to Protect Nursing Workers Like Me," ACLU, August 3, 2022, https://www.aclu.org/news/womens-rights/we-need-the-pump -act-to-protect-nursing-workers-like-me.

61   **Before the affair** Maggie Nelson, *The Argonauts* (Minneapolis: Graywolf, 2015), 44.

61   **My relationship with** Nelson, *The Argonauts*.

62   **As the child grows** Melanie Klein, "The Early Stages of the Oedipus Complex (1928)," in *Female Sexuality: The Early Psychoanalytic Controversies*, ed. R. Grigg, Dominique Hecq, and Craig Smith (London: Routledge, 1999).

WORK

66   **Drawing on the work** Darcy Lockman, *All the Rage: Mothers, Fathers, and the Myth of Equal Partnership* (New York: Harper, 2019), 178.

66   **Midcentury Americans** Rebecca Jo Plant, *Mom: The Transformation of Motherhood in Modern America* (Chicago: University of Chicago Press, 2010), 32–39.

69   **One 2019 article** Heather Marcoux, "The 2010s: The Decade That Made Childcare Unaffordable," *Motherly*, December 17, 2019,

https://www.mother.ly/life/the-decade-that-made-childcare
-unaffordable.

71   **In truth, for many women** Kim Brooks, *Small Animals: Parenthood in the Age of Fear* (New York: Flatiron Books, 2018), 49–54.

72   **Not only is consistent** Maya Dusenbery, "How America's Lack of Paid Maternity Leave Worsens Inequality," *Pacific Standard*, updated June 14, 2017, https://psmag.com/economics/cmon-america.

72   **But I lived in America** Brooks, *Small Animals*, 49–50.

72   **They never consider** Jessica Valenti, "The Life Abortion Gave Me," *All in Her Head* (newsletter), Substack, September 1, 2021.

73   **As Goldstein put it** Katherine Goldstein, "Stop Saying Women 'Dropped Out' of the Workforce. We Were Pushed," *Romper*, November 10, 2020, https://www.romper.com/life/stop-saying -women-dropped-out-of-the-workforce-we-were-pushed.

73   **Unequal access to childcare** Anne Helen Petersen, "One Weird Trick to Fix Our Broken Child Care System," *Vox*, April 2, 2021, https://www.vox.com/the-goods/22360152/child-care-free-public -funding.

73   **Over 90 percent** Kate Manne, *Entitled: How Male Privilege Hurts Women* (New York: Crown, 2021), 128.

73   **The pay for those** Marcy Whitebook, Caitlin McLean, Lea J. E. Austin, and Bethany Edwards, *Early Childhood Workforce Index 2018* (Berkeley: University of California, Berkeley, Center for the Study of Child Care Employment, 2018), https://cscce.berkeley .edu/wp-content/uploads/2022/04/Early-Childhood-Workforce -Index-2018.pdf.

73   **And due to a high demand** Petersen, "One Weird Trick to Fix Our Broken Child Care System."

74   **As Jenny Brown writes** Jenny Brown, *Birth Strike: The Hidden Fight over Women's Work* (Oakland, CA: PM Press, 2019), 1.

74   **And this only made me** Judith Warner, *Perfect Madness: Motherhood in the Age of Anxiety* (New York: Riverhead, 2006), 9.

76   **In her essay** Marguerite Duras, "House and Home," *Practicalities* (New York: Grove, 1987).

77   **In antiquity, however** Giorgio Agamben, *Homo Sacer: Sovereign Power and Bare Life*, trans. Daniel Heller-Roazen (Stanford, CA: Stanford University Press, 1998), 2.

77   **In the Middle Ages** Constance Classen, *The Deepest Sense: A Cultural History of Touch* (Urbana: University of Illinois Press, 2012), 20–21.

77   **As sociologist Kathryn Jezer-Morton** Kathryn Jezer-Morton, "Is 'Cozy Season' a Cry for Help?" *Mothers under the Influence* (newsletter), Substack, November 10, 2021, https://mothersunder theinfluence.substack.com/p/is-cozy-season-a-cry-for-help?

78   **For many women** Adrienne Rich, *Of Woman Born: Motherhood as Experience and Institution* (1976; New York: W. W. Norton, 1986), 264.

78   **I sometimes thought** Mierle Laderman Ukeles, "Manifesto! Maintenance Art—Proposal for an Exhibition, 'Care,'" https://queen smuseum.org/wp-content/uploads/2016/04/Ukeles-Manifesto -for-Maintenance-Art-1969.pdf, 2.

80   **Arendt noted that** Hannah Arendt, *The Human Condition* (1958; Chicago: University of Chicago Press, 1998), 86.

80   **Ancient political philosophers** Arendt, *The Human Condition*, 87.

81   **As a mother I guessed** Duras, "House and Home," 55.

82   **This gets capitalism** Silvia Federici, "Why Sexuality Is Work (1975)," *Revolution at Point Zero: Housework, Reproduction, and Feminist Struggle* (Oakland, CA: PM Press, 2020), 13.

83   **Lower taxes mean** Kristen R. Ghodsee, *Why Women Have Better Sex under Socialism* (New York: Bold Type, 2018), 3.

84   **Unemployment and poverty** Kristen R. Ghodsee and Gus Wezerek, "Women's Unpaid Labor Is Worth $10,900,000,000,000," *New York Times*, March 5, 2020, https://www.nytimes.com/interactive/2020 /03/04/opinion/women-unpaid-labor.html.

84   **Capitalism "created** Silvia Federici, "Wages against Housework (1975)," *Revolution at Point Zero: Housework, Reproduction, and Feminist Struggle* (Oakland, CA: PM Press, 2020), 3.

84   **Women found themselves** Silvia Federici, *Caliban and the Witch: Women, the Body and Primitive Accumulation* (Brooklyn, NY: Autonomedia, 2004), 74.

84   **The "unity of production** Federici, *Caliban and the Witch*.

84   **No longer "the village** Federici, *Caliban and the Witch*, 200, 73.

84   **Unruly women** Federici, *Caliban and the Witch*, 165–66.

85   **Those attitudes** Rich, *Of Woman Born: Motherhood as Experience and Institution* (1976; New York: W. W. Norton, 1986), 112.

85   **In her cultural history** Classen, *The Deepest Sense*, 71–77.

85   **Martin Luther thought** Classen, *The Deepest Sense*, 77.

85   **Without her even trying** Classen, *The Deepest Sense*, 75–76.

85   **As Rich notes** Rich, *Of Woman Born*, 54.

86   **Women in the US** Cameron Macdonald, quoted in Lockman, *All the Rage*, 178.

86   But why, Rose asks Jacqueline Rose, *Mothers: An Essay on Love and Cruelty* (New York: Farrar, Straus and Giroux, 2018), 17.

86   Feminist sociologist Angela McRobbie McRobbie quoted in Rose, *Mothers*, 17–18.

86   Such a conflation Rebecca Traister, "Can Modern Women 'Have It All'?" *Salon*, June 21, 2012, https://www.salon.com/2012/06/21 /can_modern_women_have_it_all.

87   While I was struggling Koa Beck, *White Feminism: From the Suffragettes to Influencers and Who They Leave Behind* (New York: Atria Books, 2021), 104.

87   But as Anne-Marie Slaughter wrote Anne-Marie Slaughter, "Why Women Still Can't Have It All," *Atlantic*, July–August 2012, quoted in Traister, "Can Modern Women 'Have It All'?"

87   Feminism was not Jessica Valenti, quoted in Traister, "Can Modern Women 'Have It All'?"

88   Women have participated Federici, "Wages against Housework (1975)," 5.

88   Put in her place Federici, *Caliban and the Witch*, 102–3.

88   Housewives went to work Nicole Cox and Silvia Federici, *Counter-Planning from the Kitchen; Wages for Housework: A Perspective on Capital and the Left* (New York: New York Wages for Housework Committee and Falling Wall Press, 1975), 29.

88   Whereas white feminists bell hooks, "Revolutionary Parenting," excerpt from *Feminist Theory: From Margin to Center* (New York: Routledge, 1984), archived at Caring Labor: An Archive, https:// caringlabor.wordpress.com/2010/07/27/bell-hooks-revolutionary -parenting, accessed October 8, 2022.

89   Valerie Solanas began Valerie Solanas, *SCUM Manifesto* (Oakland: AK Press, 1996), 1.

91   But I loved other things Ukeles, "Manifesto! Maintenance Art," 3.

BODY

92   Hannah's touch began Marguerite Duras, "House and Home," *Practicalities* (New York: Grove, 1987).

92   In her book Chelsea Conaboy, *Mother Brain: How Neuroscience Is Rewriting the Story of Parenthood* (New York: Holt, 2022).

95   Even if it were possible Paul Michael Garrett, "Bowlby, Attachment and the Potency of a 'Received Idea,'" *British Journal of Social Work*, July 5, 2022, https://doi.org/10.1093/bjsw/bcac091.

95   This is true of almost Danielle Carr, "Don't Be So Attached to Attachment Theory," *Gawker*, January 25, 2022.

96 **The whole thing** Carr, "Don't Be So Attached to Attachment Theory."

96 **Of course some differences** Regan Penaluna, "Kate Manne: The Shock Collar That Is Misogyny," *Guernica*, February 7, 2018, https://www.guernicamag.com/kate-manne-why-misogyny-isnt -really-about-hating-women.

97 **The Searses encouraged** Bill Sears, "Attachment Parenting Babies," Ask Dr. Sears (website), https://www.askdrsears.com/topics /parenting/attachment-parenting/attachment-parenting-babies, accessed October 8, 2022.

98 **Motherhood became a religion** Judith Warner, *Perfect Madness: Motherhood in the Age of Anxiety* (New York: Riverhead, 2006), 197.

98 **On top of all the sources** Kim Brooks, *Small Animals: Parenthood in the Age of Fear* (New York: Flatiron Books, 2018).

102 **Most of our sexual encounters** Silvia Federici, "Why Sexuality Is Work (1975)," *Revolution at Point Zero: Housework, Reproduction, and Feminist Struggle* (Oakland: PM Press, 2020), 93.

103 **One 2016 article** Yael Breimer, "Getting in Touch with the 'Touched Out' Feeling," La Leche League, March 31, 2016, https:// lllusa.org/getting-in-touch-with-the-touched-out-feeling-2.

104 **The La Leche League article** Breimer, "Getting in Touch with the 'Touched Out' Feeling."

105 **By 2022, when Winter** Jessica Winter, "The Harsh Realm of 'Gentle Parenting,'" *New Yorker*, March 23, 2022, https://www.newyorker. com/books/under-review/the-harsh-realm-of-gentle-parenting.

105 **Everyday moms and parenting** Caitlin Beale, "Are You Touched Out, Mama? A Psychologist Shares the Signs," *Motherly*, February 8, 2002, https://www.mother.ly/life/touched-out-expert-signs; Erica Djossa, Instagram post, https://www.instagram.com/p/CX61 m7WFjxa, accessed December 6, 2022; Kristen Hollowood, TikTok post, https://www.tiktok.com/@mindfullymendedmama/video /7108832926946790702?, accessed December 14, 2022.

105 **His cries were so piercing** Becca Maberly, Instagram caption, November 10, 2020, https://www.instagram.com/p/CHZybDglGro.

105 **All day my body belongs** Amanda Montei, "How American Moms Got 'Touched Out,'" *Slate*, July 14, 2022, https://slate.com/human -interest/2022/07/touched-out-science-psychology-moms.html.

106 **The article accepted** Elizabeth Bernstein, "Feeling Too Schlubby for Sex? It's Not Just You." *Wall Street Journal*, October 19, 2021, https://www.wsj.com/articles/less-sex-covid-19-pandemic-stress -feeling-schlubby-to-blame-11634641390.

107 **Despite the clearly complex** Rachel Paula Abrahamson, "Being 'Touched Out' Is a Thing: How Parents Can Cope During Quarantine," *Today* (online magazine), April 20, 2020, https://www.today .com/parents/moms-are-touched-out-kids-during-coronavirus -quarantine-t179277.

108 **The duty to please** Silvia Federici, "Why Sexuality Is Work (1975)," *Revolution at Point Zero: Housework, Reproduction, and Feminist Struggle* (Oakland: PM Press, 2020).

109 **Mothers especially felt** Anne Helen Petersen, *Can't Even: How Millennials Became the Burnout Generation* (Boston: Mariner Books, 2020), 209.

109 **As Dr. Pooja Lakshmin, a board** Pooja Lakshmin, "How Society Has Turned Its Back on Mothers," *New York Times*, February 4, 2021, https://www.nytimes.com/2021/02/04/parenting/working -mom-burnout-coronavirus.html.

110 **In his best-selling 1964** Philip Wylie, *Generation of Vipers* (1942; 2nd ed., Champaign, IL: Dalkey Archive Press, 1996). See also Peter L. Winkler, "The Man Who Hated Moms," *Los Angeles Review of Books*, August 13, 2021.

111 **His writing was also** See especially "Common Women," in Wylie, *Generation of Vipers.*

111 **Bettelheim's "refrigerator** See Bruno Bettelheim, "Joey, a 'Mechanical Boy,'" *Scientific American* 200, no. 3 (March 1959): 115–27, https://cpb-us-e1.wpmucdn.com/blogs.uoregon.edu/dist/d /16656/files/2018/11/Bettelheim-Joey-A-Mechanical-Boy -1ao74zg.pdf.

114 **It is composed of art** Adrienne Rich, *Of Woman Born: Motherhood as Experience and Institution* (1976; New York: W. W. Norton, 1986), 275.

115 **According to the Motherhood** "Get Involved in Maternal Mental Health Month," Motherhood Center of New York, April 17, 2019, https://www.themotherhoodcenter.com/blogindex/2019/4/17 /pdzne5vkewgcamzdok6uy29z7651j5.

116 **This rate is higher** Tula Karras, "PMADs—Such as PPD and Anxiety—in African American Moms," Seleni, https://www.seleni .org/advice-support/2018/3/16/pmads-such-as-ppd-and-anxiety -in-african-american-moms, accessed October 10, 2022.

116 **Studies show that** E. P. Dib, F. H. P. Padovani, and G. B. Perosa, "Mother-Child Interaction: Implications of Chronic Maternal Anxiety and Depression," *Psicologia: Reflexão e Crítica* 32, no. 10 (April 11, 2019), https://doi.org/10.1186/s41155-019-0123-6.

116 **Depressed mothers** Irene Mantis, Marisa Mercuri, Dale M. Stack, and Tiffany M. Field, "Depressed and Non-Depressed Mothers' Touching During Social Interactions with Their Infants," *Developmental Cognitive Neuroscience* 35 (2019): 57–65, https://doi.org/10.1016/j.dcn.2018.01.005.

116 **Touch is an essential** A. J. Bremner and C. Spence, "The Development of Tactile Perception," *Advances in Child Development and Behavior* 52 (2017): 227–68, doi:10.1016/bs.acdb.2016.12.002.

116 **Infants' awareness** Sari Goldstein Ferber, Ruth Feldman, and Imad R. Makhoul, "The Development of Maternal Touch across the First Year of Life," *Early Human Development* 84, no. 6 (2008): 363–70, https://doi.org/10.1016/j.earlhumdev.2007.09.019.

116 **Rather than follow** Edward H. Hagen, "The Functions of Postpartum Depression," *Evolution and Human Behavior* 20, no. 5 (1999): 325–59, https://doi.org/10.1016/S1090-5138(99)00016-1.

117 **She became** Adrienne Rich, *Of Woman Born: Motherhood as Experience and Institution* (New York: W. W. Norton, 1976), 38.

117 **Again, clinical studies** Jonathan Levy, Karen Yirmiya, Abraham Goldstein, and Ruth Feldman, "Chronic Trauma Impairs the Neural Basis of Empathy in Mothers: Relations to Parenting and Children's Empathic Abilities," *Developmental Cognitive Neuroscience* 38 (2019), https://doi.org/10.1016/j.dcn.2019.100658.

118 **Federici supposes** Nicole Cox and Silvia Federici, *Counter-Planning from the Kitchen; Wages for Housework: A Perspective on Capital and the Left* (New York: New York Wages for Housework Committee and Falling Wall Press, 1975), 9.

118 **Instead of recognizing** Rich, *Of Woman Born*, 262–63.

118 **Angry parenting** Rich, *Of Woman Born*, 67.

119 **As Audre Lorde writes** Audre Lorde, "The Uses of Anger: Women Responding to Racism," keynote presentation, National Women's Studies Association Conference, Storrs, CT, June 1981, https://www.blackpast.org/african-american-history/speeches-african-american-history/1981-audre-lorde-uses-anger-women-responding-racism.

119 **As Minna Dubin, author** Minna Dubin, "'I Am Going to Physically Explode': Mom Rage in a Pandemic," *New York Times*, July 6, 2020, https://www.nytimes.com/2020/07/06/parenting/mom-rage-pandemic.html.

120 **To do so she must step** Marianne Hirsch, *The Mother/Daughter Plot: Narrative, Psychoanalysis, Feminism* (Bloomington: Indiana University Press, 1989), 170.

120 **Two jobs have only** Cox and Federici, *Counter-Planning from the Kitchen*, 5.

120 **We are seen as nagging** Federici, "Wages against Housework," 12.

121 **What Adrienne Rich had written** Rich, *Of Woman Born*.

REFUSAL

123 **These "complaint genres"** Lauren Berlant, *The Female Complaint: The Unfinished Business of Sentimentality in American Culture* (Durham, NC: Duke University Press, 2008).

129 **Usually, in film and TV** Katherine Angel, *Tomorrow Sex Will Be Good Again: Women and Desire in the Age of Consent* (Brooklyn, NY: Verso, 2022), 56.

130 **There are obvious** Kristen R. Ghodsee, *Why Women Have Better Sex under Socialism* (New York: Bold Type, 2018), 115.

130 **When we talk about sex** Ghodsee, *Why Women Have Better Sex under Socialism*.

130 **Research on female** L. de Oliveira and J. Carvalho, "Women's Sexual Health During the Pandemic of COVID-19: Declines in Sexual Function and Sexual Pleasure," *Current Sexual Health Reports* 13, no. 3 (2021): 76–88, https://doi.org/10.1007/s11930-021 -00309-4.

130 **Sexual rights and other** Michel Foucault, *The History of Sexuality, Volume 1*, trans. Robert Hurley (New York: Pantheon, 1978).

132 **Kate Manne argues** Kate Manne, *Entitled: How Male Privilege Hurts Women* (New York: Crown, 2021), 70–71.

133 **And so a woman's own** Angel, *Tomorrow Sex Will Be Good Again*, 56.

133 **Federici notes that** Silvia Federici, "Why Sexuality Is Work (1975)," *Revolution at Point Zero: Housework, Reproduction, and Feminist Struggle* (Oakland: PM Press, 2020).

134 **Women often end up** Pauline Harmange, *I Hate Men*, trans. Natasha Lehrer (London: Fourth Estate, 2021), 21.

134 **The radical feminist writer** Lauren Oyler, "The Radical Style of Andrea Dworkin," *New Yorker*, March 25, 2019, https://www.new yorker.com/magazine/2019/04/01/the-radical-style-of-andrea -dworkin.

135 **Dworkin has been misquoted** Catharine A. MacKinnon, "Who Was Afraid of Andrea Dworkin?" *New York Times*, April 16, 2005, https://www.nytimes.com/2005/04/16/opinion/who-was-afraid -of-andrea-dworkin.html.

135 **Nothing is one's own** Andrea Dworkin, *Intercourse* (New York: Basic Books, 1987), 61.

135 **Angela Garbes writes** Angela Garbes, *Essential Labor: Mothering as Social Change* (New York: Harper Wave, 2022), 208.

136 **In heterosexual relationships** Lisa Taddeo, "My Husband and I Don't Speak the Same Love Language," *New York Times*, February 11, 2022, https://www.nytimes.com/2022/02/11/opinion/my -husband-and-i-dont-speak-the-same-love-language.html.

137 **Taddeo writes. "About the years** Taddeo, "My Husband and I Don't Speak the Same Love Language."

138 **In truth, love is** bell hooks, *All About Love: New Visions* (New York: William Morrow, 2000), 183.

138 **Our culture may make** hooks, *All About Love*, 178.

139 **I had already spent** hooks, *All About Love*, 221.

144 **All that time they spend** Harmange, *I Hate Men*, 5.

144 **And, for that matter** Harmange, *I Hate Men*, 25.

CONSENT

152 **The loss of innocence** Andrea Dworkin, *Intercourse* (New York: Basic Books, 1987), 14.

152 **Dworkin, frequently criticized** Dworkin, *Intercourse*, 175.

153 **But she also would have noted** Dworkin, *Intercourse*, 175, 61.

157 **As they grow older** Kate Manne, *Down Girl: The Logic of Misogyny* (London: Oxford University Press, 2018), 293.

157 **Later, he killed a man** Nicky Woolf, "Chilling Report Details How Elliot Rodger Executed Murderous Rampage," *Guardian*, February 20, 2015, https://www.theguardian.com/us-news/2015/feb/20/mass -shooter-elliot-rodger-isla-vista-killings-report; Martin Pengelly, "California Killings: UK-Born Elliot Rodger Blamed for Deaths," *Guardian*, May 25, 2014, https://www.theguardian.com/world /2014/may/25/elliot-rodger-suspect-california-mass-murder -shooting-stabbing.

157 **Some commentators claimed** Kate Manne, *Entitled: How Male Privilege Hurts Women* (New York: Crown, 2021), 42.

157 **Amia Srinivasan argues** Amia Srinivasan, *The Right to Sex: Feminism in the Twenty-First Century* (New York: Farrar, Straus and Giroux, 2021), 75.

157 **These were the rules of Elliot** Chanel Miller, *Know My Name: A Memoir* (New York: Penguin, 2020), 257. Italics in original.

157 **Rodger's case has been** See especially Manne, *Entitled*, and Srinivasan, *The Right to Sex*.

158 **The incel movement, however** Dworkin, *Intercourse*, 175.

159 **The same was often true** Melissa Febos, *Girlhood* (New York: Bloomsbury, 2021), 241.

159 **Women know that their sexual** Katherine Angel, *Tomorrow Sex Will Be Good Again: Women and Desire in the Age of Consent* (Brooklyn, NY: Verso, 2022), 5.

160 **"Once a woman is thought** Angel, *Tomorrow Sex Will Be Good Again*, 4.

161 **Girls and women often** Manne, *Down Girl*, 293–94.

161 **She references a line** Manne, *Down Girl*, 293–94.

161 **David, reflecting** Manne, *Entitled*, 70–71.

161 **It also illustrates** Manne, *Down Girl*, 294.

162 **They worry about repercussions** Manne, *Entitled*, 73.

162 **This disconnect made girlhood** Febos, *Girlhood*, 241.

163 **As the prominent feminist** Willis, "Lust Horizons," *No More Nice Girls*, quoted in Srinivasan, *The Right to Sex*, 83.

164 **For years, I fostered** Roxane Gay, ed., *Not That Bad: Dispatches from Rape Culture* (New York: Harper, 2018), x–xii.

164 **I began thinking more** Gay, *Not That Bad*, xi.

165 **As Gay writes** Gay, *Not That Bad*, x.

166 **My sister turned me** For more on sportscasting and Gerber's nonprofit, Resources for Infant Educarers, see the website Magda Gerber Legacy, https://www.magdagerber.org.

167 **About what Ashley Simpo called** Ashley Simpo, "The Rough Rough Road to Gentle Parenting," *Gloria*, accessed December 6, 2022, https://www.hellogloria.com/essays/gentle-parenting.

171 **Sometimes, it turned into** Angel, *Tomorrow Sex Will Be Good Again*, 38–40.

172 **In 2022, Senator Ron Johnson** Ron Johnson, "The Left Wants the Government to Run the Family. I Believe the Parents Do," Twitter, January 26, 2022, https://twitter.com/RonJohnsonWI/status /1486392666829078534.

172 **Choice and agency** Susan Bordo, *Unbearable Weight: Feminism, Western Culture, and the Body* (Berkeley: University of California Press, 1993), 88.

172 **As Silvia Federici writes** Nicole Cox and Silvia Federici, *Counter-Planning from the Kitchen; Wages for Housework: A Perspective on Capital and the Left* (New York: New York Wages for Housework Committee and Falling Wall Press, 1975), 7.

172 **When a woman does** Bordo, *Unbearable Weight*, 79, 94.

172 **Even though informed** Bordo, *Unbearable Weight*, 75.

172 **One American Civil Liberties Union summary** American Civil Liberties Union, "Coercive and Punitive Governmental Responses to Women's Conduct During Pregnancy," ACLU website, https://www.aclu.org/other/coercive-and-punitive-governmental-responses-womens-conduct-during-pregnancy, accessed October 9, 2022.

173 **At the time of writing** For a summary of states' responses to the Supreme Court's *Dobbs. v. Jackson* ruling and links to stories, see Jessica Valenti, "Abortion, Every Day (7.21.22)," *All in Her Head* (newsletter), July 21, 2022, https://jessica.substack.com/p/abortion-every-day-72122#details.

173 **But even before that ruling** Advancing New Standards in Reproductive Health, "The Turnaway Study," University of California, San Francisco, https://www.ansirh.org/research/ ongoing/turnaway-study, accessed October 18, 2022.

173 **Pregnancy was also already** Jason Williams, "Our System Criminalizes Black Pregnancy. As a District Attorney, I Refuse to Prosecute These Cases," *Time*, May 21, 2021, https://time.com/6049587/pregnancy-criminalization.

173 **In such cases the historical effacement** Bordo, *Unbearable Weight*, 76.

175 **Valenti writes, "This is closer** Jessica Valenti, *Sex Object: A Memoir* (New York: Dey Street, 2016), 12.

178 **Because the home** Adrienne Rich, *Of Woman Born: Motherhood as Experience and Institution* (1976; New York: W. W. Norton, 1986), 64.

178 **"To hold power over** Rich, *Of Woman Born*, 65.

178 **As hooks writes, love** hooks, *All About Love*, 30.

179 **"In the move from powerlessness** Rich, *Of Woman Born*, 64–66.

BEGINNING AGAIN

182 **The anthropologist Dana Raphael called** Dana Raphael, *Being Female: Reproduction, Power, and Change* (Paris: Mouton, 1975).

183 **Nor is the physical** Dr. Aurélie Athan, personal communication, email, July 10, 2022.

183 **As the blogger and author** Rebecca Woolf, "How Do I Rediscover My Sexuality When I'm Completely Touched Out?" *Romper*, June 29, 2022, https://www.romper.com/life/how-to-reclaim-your-sexuality-as-a-mom.

188 **As journalist Katherine Goldstein, creator** Katherine Goldstein, quoted in Amanda Montei, "The Problem with 'Mom Boss' Culture," *Vox*, April 8, 2021, https://www.vox.com/the-goods/22368693/mom-boss-capitalism-scary-mommy.

188 **And as Klein writes** Naomi Klein, *The Shock Doctrine: The Rise of Disaster Capitalism* (New York: Picador, 2007), 580.

189 **In aspirations to** Silvia Federici, "Precarious Labor: A Feminist Viewpoint," lecture, Bluestockings Radical Bookstore, New York, October 28, 2006, https://libcom.org/article/precarious-labor -feminist-viewpoint, accessed December 15, 2022.

189 **But by the mid-2010s** Valenti, *Sex Object*, 4.

189 **But over time, as Federici** Silvia Federici, "Wages against Housework," *Revolution at Point Zero: Housework, Reproduction, and Feminist Struggle* (Oakland, CA: PM Press, 2020), 15–16.

190 **As she points out** Silvia Federici, "Putting Feminism Back on Its Feet," *Revolution at Point Zero: Housework, Reproduction, and Feminist Struggle* (Oakland, CA: PM Press, 2020), 50–58.

191 **The project was in some ways** Mierle Laderman Ukeles, "Manifesto! Maintenance Art—Proposal for an Exhibition, 'Care,'" https:// queensmuseum.org/wp-content/uploads/2016/04/Ukeles -Manifesto-for-Maintenance-Art-1969.pdf, 1.

192 **For Fraser, however, the most** Nancy Fraser, "After the Family Wage: A Postindustrial Thought Experiment," *Fortunes of Feminism: From State-Managed Capitalism to Neoliberal Crisis* (Brooklyn, NY: Verso Books, 2020), 111–35.

192 **After all, as Fraser points out** Fraser, "After the Family Wage," 135.

193 **And everyone needs access** Fraser, "After the Family Wage," 135.

193 **Recognizing the work** Federici, "Putting Feminism Back On Its Feet," 53.

193 **Reducing or reorganizing** Federici, "The Restructuring of Housework and Reproduction," *Revolution at Point Zero: Housework, Reproduction, and Feminist Struggle* (Oakland, CA: PM Press, 2020).

193 **In the future society** Federici, "The Restructuring of Housework and Reproduction."

193 **As Federici points out** Federici, "The Restructuring of Housework and Reproduction."

194 **In her book *Silences*** Tillie Olsen, *Silences* (1978; New York: Feminist Press at the City University of New York, 2003).

195 **At its best, one of the most** Federici, "Putting Feminism Back on Its Feet," 56.

195 **Kelly writes that *Post-Partum Document*** Mary Kelly, *Post-Partum Document* (London: Routledge & Kegan Paul, 1983).

196 **As Maso writes** Carole Maso, *The Room Lit by Roses: A Journey of Pregnancy and Birth* (Berkeley, CA: Counterpoint, 2000), 2.

196 **There is evidence that** Chelsea Conaboy, *Mother Brain: How Neuroscience Is Rewriting the Story of Parenthood* (New York: Holt, 2022).

198 **In *Regarding the Pain of Others*** Susan Sontag, *Regarding the Pain of Others* (New York: Penguin, 2003), 40.

200 **In *Essential Labor*, Angela Garbes writes** Angela Garbes, *Essential Labor: Mothering as Social Change* (New York: HarperCollins, 2022).

200 **After all, in the earliest human** Rich, *Of Woman Born*, 96–99.

200 **As Federici writes, the women's** Federici, "Putting Feminism Back on Its Feet," 58.

202 **As Jean Piaget noted** Jean Piaget, *The Origins of Intelligence in Children*, trans. Margaret Cook (New York: International University Press, 1952).

202 **What children create** See *Piaget—Stage 2—Preoperational—Lack of Conservation*, https://www.youtube.com/watch?v=GLj0IZFLKvg.

INDEX

abortion(s): family history of, 155–56, 174; rights to have, 7, 8, 9, 72, 173

abstinence, 150

academia, and motherhood, 81

Acconci, Vito, 53

ADHD (attention deficit hyperactivity disorder), 105

adjustment disorder, 140–41

affirmations, for childbirth, 34–35, 56

Affordable Care Act, 22

Against Our Will (Brownmiller), 25

alcohol: and being overwhelmed, 112–14; and lack of fulfillment, 122–23, 141; and memory loss, 44, 47–48; and sexual refusal, 131–32, 147–48; and sexual violence, 41–49

Alley, Kirstie, 19–20

American Civil Liberties Union, 172–73

Angel, Katherine: on consent, 43, 44–45, 160; on desire, 129, 159; on pleasure, 133

"Angel in the House" (Woolf), 5, 194

anger: at children, 119–20; male *vs.* female expression of, 119–20; at men, 137, 141, 144; at refusal, 144–45; at sexual assault, 52

anxiety: of child, 168, 191, 197; parental, 74, 98, 125, 126; and perinatal mood and anxiety disorder, 116–17; during pregnancy, 140–41; and pressure to perform, 110, 112

"anxious" personality, 95, 96

AP (Attachment Parenting), 94, 97, 103, 104

appearance, comments about, 2–3

Arendt, Hannah, 57, 80, 199

art, taught by early childhood educators, 200–202

art institutions, reliance on hidden labor by, 191

Athan, Aurélie, 183

Attachment Parenting (AP), 94–97, 103, 104

attachment theory, 94–97, 104

attention deficit hyperactivity disorder (ADHD), 105

autism, 111

autonomy: and breastfeeding, 60, 62; childbirth and, 21, 38–39; of children, 170–71; communal care systems and, 15;